ML
1711.8
.N3
R5
1989
3

$29.95

Riis, Thomas
   Laurence.

Just before jazz.

DATE			

JUST
BEFORE
JAZZ

Smithsonian Institution Press

Washington and London

JUST BEFORE JAZZ

Black Musical
Theater
in New York,
1890–1915

Thomas L. Riis

Library of Congress Cataloging-in-Publication Data
Riis, Thomas Laurence.
    Just before jazz.
    Bibliography: p.
    1. Musical revue, comedy, etc.—New York (N.Y.)
2. Afro-Americans—New York (N.Y.)—Music—History and
criticism. 3. Afro-American musicians—New York (N.Y.)
I. Title.
ML1711.8.N3R5   1989   782.81'0899607307471   88–600332
ISBN 0-87474–788–0 (alk. paper)
British Library Cataloging-in-Publication data are available.

Editor: Judy Sacks
Designer: Janice Wheeler

∞ The paper used in this publication meets the minimum requirements of the
American National Standard for Permanence of Paper for Printed Library
Materials Z39.48-1984.

To my parents, Ruth and Larry Riis, for their understanding and unfailing love, and to Ira and Joe for performing all the offices of friendship longer than I could have wished

Contents

List of
Illustrations

List of
Musical Examples

List of
Original Sheet Music
Facsimiles

Preface

Several years ago I chanced to pick up a copy of Eileen Southern's *Readings in Black American Music* and casually turned to an article about the black composer-conductor Will Marion Cook (1869–1944).[1] Cook, I discovered, had studied violin in Europe with Brahms's friend Joseph Joachim. After returning to America, he associated with the Bohemian composer Dvořák during the latter's American sojourn. Cook composed successful musical comedies; he even took his shows and his own orchestra to Europe. Elsewhere I learned that such contrasting personalities as jazz titan Duke Ellington and the eminent Swiss conductor Ernst Ansermet had showered praise on Cook's musicianship: his orchestra, Ansermet reported in 1919, played with "astonishing perfection."[2] As an ambitious graduate student in music history I had heard of Ellington and Ansermet, Joachim and Dvořák, but who was Will Marion Cook? His name had never appeared in any music text of which I knew. Thus began a long journey which has led to this book.

When I began to hunt for more detailed information on Cook, I real-

ized why I had never before encountered his name. Only sparse dictionary entries of questionable accuracy and a few articles (but no books)
existed about him—or his background or his milieu. At first I determined
to correct the historical omission of Cook's name, but soon I came to see
that earlier writers had committed an even bigger oversight, of which
Cook's life and work were only a part: the exclusion of the majority of
black musical theater history, especially the period from the Civil War to
the 1920s.

Cook's generation—black men and women who grew to maturity at the
end of the nineteenth century—were a uniquely optimistic group. They
were the first blacks born free after the Civil War in an America that, with
the Emancipation Proclamation and the postwar constitutional amend-
ments, finally seemed favorably disposed to them. A sense of exuberance
and possibility is fairly palpable in the writings of blacks of the period.[3]
The prevailing assumption was that white Americans, previously skeptical
about the fitness of blacks for civilization, had realized the cruelty and
injustice of slavery and would now witness the rise of a new people. All
folk of good will would foster the increase of black economic prosperity
and cultural advancement. So the argument went. The backlash of Reconstruction manifested through the mechanisms of Jim Crow, lynch law-
lessness, political double-dealing and vigilante terror had not taken its full
toll, and, having internalized the assumptions of progress, young blacks in
the 1880s did in fact make great strides in business, law, commerce, and
the arts.

Reconstruction has long fascinated political and social historians, but
the cultural achievements of blacks at the end of the nineteenth century
have generally been neglected in favor of the group that succeeded
them—the "New Negro" generation of the 1920s, a period often characterized as the Harlem Renaissance. The men and women of the Harlem
Renaissance are undeniably magnetic, and the neglect of the cultural
realm of the earlier period may be linked to the nature of black (as well as
white) entertainment at the time, filled as it was with humor, songs and
attitudes widely felt nowadays to be dated if not irrelevant and trivial if
not racist. But black musical theater from 1890 to 1915, though built on
conventions unfamiliar to modern theatergoers, was not insignificant,
either in itself or in the larger picture of the development of American
musical theater.

When both theatrical and musical histories of the turn of the century are compared (a relatively rare exercise), the coincident emergence of black music, especially ragtime, as a favorite form of popular music and "musical comedy" as a distinctively American theatrical form stand out in bold relief. But there is more than coincidence in this pairing. Singers in musicals of the period frequently introduced new songs into their shows—often arbitrarily and without respect to the dramatic niceties—and this custom created not only a link but a symbiotic relationship between show composers and musical comedy singers attempting to build careers.

Repressive legislation in the South and the wide advertisement of economic opportunities in the North had resulted in an unprecedented northward migration of blacks. New York in particular, with its established black communities, served as an urban magnet. The expansion and increased prosperity of black New York's middle class created a milieu in which theater could flourish. Black performers staged some thirty shows in the period from 1890 to 1915 in black New York neighborhoods and on Broadway, shows filled with thoroughly syncopated songs written by black composers. A talented coterie spurred by optimism and solid training began to gain a sizable audience in the 1890s.

The quarter century encompassed by the dates 1890–1915 represents an era in which several important musical and theatrical motifs sprang up and flourished. 1890 saw the beginning of black burlesque in the Creole Show. This touring spectacle ran for several years and used the talents of many of the leading showmen and composers whose careers would blossom in the following two decades. It may justly be termed a seminal show. By 1915 a surprisingly large number of the leaders from the 1890s were either retired or dead, and the prohibitive costs and persistent discrimination encountered by road companies had decisively influenced producers to create black shows for Harlem rather than for Broadway. Furthermore, ragtime music was clearly in decline by 1915, international touring was curtailed because of the war in Europe, and jazz elements were not yet completely assimilated into New York theater music.[4]

Nothing said so far should be taken to denigrate the importance or influence of composers on Tin Pan Alley and Broadway who were not privileged to be involved with the black shows. But while there are many books about minstrel shows and operettas, about Victor Herbert and

George M. Cohan, there are none (or very few) about Will Marion Cook, Ernest Hogan, and J. Rosamond Johnson. Although I will comment about the contribution of whites from time to time, my focus here is on the unturned stones of history. Why were so many shows with all-black casts produced in the decade from 1898 to 1908? Of what did the shows consist? How, if at all, did these shows differ from other musical comedies of their time? How did audiences and critics respond to them? How do their songs compare with other popular music of the same period?

Fortunately, some of these questions can be addressed. Sheet music from the period is relatively well-preserved, some black newspapers survive, and personal papers and the memories of a few long-lived veterans can still be consulted. Programs, playbills, and librettos have been uncovered. A sufficient amount of material is concentrated in New York archives to make it possible to sketch a general picture of theatrical activity in the United States as a whole. The complete story of American musical theater, even of black musical theater, cannot be told by looking at New York alone, but New York saw first and saw more completely what the rest of the country would see only in part. New York not only had the most theaters and the largest number of people employed as actors of any city at the turn of the century, it was also the starting and ending point for many touring shows. Its critics were the most experienced and discriminating, its standards the most exacting. New York was not the sole Northern city to benefit from the great northward influx of black Americans in the late nineteenth and early twentieth centuries, but as the home of theaters and of a theatrical tradition for blacks dating at least to the 1820s, it held the most promise for growth in that tradition.[5]

The object of this study, then, is to piece together a musical story—not to relate a cultural history (as has been done recently and excellently by Jervis Anderson in *This Was Harlem*)[6] but to give an account of the shows and the songs that constitute the specific contribution of black entertainers and musicians. Because dozens of individual writers, players, and composers were involved in the shows mentioned in these pages, it is obvious that the last word will not be said here. Nevertheless, a synthesis of some of the data together with a musical analysis is long overdue.

Acknowledgments

When this book was still a dissertation, many important contributions were made to it by Richard Crawford, Eileen Southern, Dena Epstein, William Bolcom, Harold Cruse, Lawrence Gushee, Judith Becker, Marva Carter, John Graziano, Mercer Cook, Jewel Cobb, Francis "Doll" Thomas, Mildred Johnson Edwards, and James Dapogny. The suggestions and critiques of Richard Crawford, Larry Stempel, Judith McCulloh, and Martin Williams have been essential to its transformation from thesis to book.

The staff members of several archives and libraries have provided sources and services cheerfully and efficiently: Wayne Shirley at the Library of Congress, Music Division; Faith Coleman at the Museum of the City of New York; Tom Camden and his associates at the Hargrett Rare Book and Manuscript Library of the University of Georgia Libraries; Deborrah Richardson, Esme Bhan, and Marguerite Battle Bracey at the Moorland-Spingarn Research Center, Howard University; Steven Jones at the Beinecke Rare Book and Manuscript Library, Yale University;

xxiv —·❧· *Acknowledgments*

Maurice Wheeler, curator of the Azalia Hackley Collection at the Detroit Public Library; and the staffs of the William L. Clements Library at the University of Michigan, the Schomburg Center for Research in Black Culture, and the Theater and Music Collections of the New York Public Library at Lincoln Center.

For permission to publish part of a letter in the James Weldon Johnson collection, I gratefully acknowledge the Collection of American Literature, Beinecke Rare Book and Manuscript Library, Yale University.

Rolf Wulfsberg at A-R Editions has been of special assistance in preparing the in-text musical examples, the cost of which has been graciously underwritten by the University of Georgia.

Caroline Newman and Judy Sacks of the Smithsonian Institution Press staff have made many invaluable suggestions in the editing and shaping process. Without their contributions this book would be much weaker than it is.

The dedicatees have been a constant inspiration, even when they were not present in person, and a host of other friends have supported all of my best efforts and warned me about pitfalls to avoid.

1

The Performers,
The City,
The Music

Tableau from *The Southerners* (1904), a rare example of onstage integration at the turn of the century, with black, white, and blackface performers. Photograph by Byron, the Byron Collection, Museum of the City of New York.

1
Black Song and Dance in the Nineteenth Century

Black entertainers emerged in America virtually simultaneously with the arrival of black people on the continent. In mimed song that preserved traditional African stories, in dancing and patting patterns that reflected pervasive drum and language intonations, in weeping chants that expressed the crushing burden of slavery and separation, black people— Africans who were not yet Afro-Americans—made a profound impression on their masters and one another.

Records of slave dancing and singing, the masterful playing of the banjo and other instruments in the eighteenth and nineteenth centuries point to the persistence of African customs and the roots of Afro-American culture.[1] Believing in the old gods and practicing the old rituals also must have sustained a large number of the new arrivals. Religion provides explanations for trouble and chaos and a means to cope with the world; therefore, prayer and chants and rites directed against the white slavers could have relieved the emotionally overburdened slaves. All ritual has a theatrical component, and to the extent that African rituals were transferred to American shores along with African instruments, musical sounds, and concepts of mimetic storytelling, we can presume the beginnings of a musical theater of sorts.

In the nineteenth century, blackface minstrelsy arose—the first original form of American musical theater not imitative of traditional storytelling, formal ritual, or the European stage. Minstrel shows consisted of a series of activities, not primarily telling a story but involving such actions as jokes, riddles, and songs, performed by men wearing blackface makeup. The sequence of events became regularized fairly quickly in a now-familiar three-part structure: "first part," olio, and afterpiece.[2] Events were not related to one another like the acts or scenes of a play; they simply occurred in a predictable but unrigid series. The entertainment was fast-paced and varied, and the gestures of the actors were broad, designed to appeal to a wide audience.

Significant to the rapid spread of minstrelsy in the 1840s was its appeal to an essentially illiterate society and its use of devices associated with orally based entertainments: concrete, earthy, and episodic skits and songs, rather than literarily abstract and complex plays.[3] Minstrelsy's highly animated and additive rather than dramatic format aided its acceptance by numerous groups of Americans, even literate individuals, such as Abraham Lincoln, who were not ashamed of rough humor or backwoods fun. Black show people began to form touring minstrel companies in the 1850s. Four short-lived troupes appeared in the late 1850s, and a dozen more are recorded in the 1860s. The most important of these early companies was the Brooker and Clayton Georgia Minstrels, which toured to great acclaim in the Northeast for many years.[4]

The songs of minstrelsy, as they have come to us in sheet music form, can be linked to an oral/aural performance tradition as well. In actual performance, melodies notated with a few simple chords often were treated heterophonically and accompanied by banjos, fiddles, and bones, an approach comparable to other nonnotated traditions of music making.[5] Kathryn Reed-Maxfield has distinguished among groups of early minstrel songs by examining performance traditions they seem to reflect: either oral improvisation or more formal rendition, by solo voice and piano accompaniment, in a parlor setting. This distinction in song style is further clarified by information about the songs' composers. Pieces from the oral tradition often had anonymous composers, and the song arrangers whose names are known often were promoters who chiefly were performers and wished to stress their identity as such. In the identifiable parlor pieces the named composers were more deft at handling notated musical material (that is, writing "correct" chord progressions and more operatic melodies) and often had composed in areas outside of minstrelsy. Some individuals, such as Stephen Foster (1826–1864), successfully bridged the gap by writing songs that used elements from both parlor and theater styles.[6]

The historical development of black musical styles, considered apart from their theatrical function, is difficult to trace. Trying to imagine sounds heard long ago, with only verbal descriptions to go on, obviously presents problems. We can be sure, however, that where black performers and composers were active a strand of authenticity resided. The vigorous, unsentimental tunes of 1840s minstrelsy, only rarely identified with known black composers, present persistent syncopations, asymmetrical note groups, and the call-and-response pattern. These features all point to the retention of African elements, although the evidence for direct African provenance is slim. The first undeniably black idiom to reach the American concert stage, the spirituals of the Fisk University students in the 1870s, like many minstrel songs, probably grew out of extemporaneous practice, the blend of the home-grown, family traditions of the original participants. Informal and unnotated musical practices of choral performance surely influenced the concert stage performance of the spirituals. Of course, any association of the spirituals with the theater would have been offensive to the Fisk students, who were religiously trained by white Protestant ministers. But within the decade in which the Fisk Singers began performing, harmonized spirituals were used on the stage in productions of *Uncle Tom's Cabin* as well as in minstrelsy.[7]

The white promulgators of blackface minstrelsy have been accused of creating inaccurate portrayals of black life and therefore fixing biased attitudes about black people in the public mind, but many early blackface minstrels took pains to demonstrate that their acts were based on real life. One of the forbidding problems in the analysis of minstrelsy has been the difficulty of reconciling its patently degrading and grotesque caricatures with the fact that large numbers of black people not only participated in but flocked to see the minstrel shows. How to explain this seeming contradiction? Rather than assuming that minstrelsy's inherent racism and nefarious character tell the whole story of its impact, we might profitably consider the near indispensability of exaggeration and grotesque elements in oral-culture entertainments.

Oral cultures conceive of the world in fundamentally different ways than do literate or print-based cultures. Comically absurd portrayals of blacks originally were perceived in a context very different from the modern one, in a time when oral and literate world views (not incidentally linked to social and economic class) were in genuine conflict. The famous Astor Place Opera House riot of 1849 in New York, probably the most violent upheaval in America directly related to the theater, pitted the fans of populist American actor Edwin Forrest (1806–1872) against the intellectual, cultivated elite that championed the British actor Charles Macready (1793–1873). Public statements made by the principals about the manners and politics of Americans precipitated the actual street fighting, during which the police killed thirty-one people, but close to the heart of the matter was the question of stage style and presentation. An orally based, animated, gestural style like Forrest's, which encouraged audience participation, was significantly opposed to the more high-minded, text-conscious style of Macready, which demanded an attentive if not immobile audience, preferably well-dressed. It was the partisans of Forrest who would carry the day for minstrelsy.[8]

The presence on the minstrel stage of African and Afro-American instruments—drums and banjos—and of strong black characters drawn from American folklore and songs—John Henry and his kin—confirms a unique black influence, in comparison with other ethnic groups, on the development of minstrelsy. The irony of a turnabout in which blacks themselves "blacked up" to become minstrels is no more significant than the performers' clever exploitation of the emerging sensibilities of some white audiences perhaps more inclined to view slavery as a great moral wrong, stereotyping as inoffensive in itself, and blackness as a "problem" rather than as a stigma. Placing oppressor and oppressed face to face in a public but formally controlled relationship within the theater might have had any number of effects. Afro-American tricksters, used to wearing the mask for white slaveowners, could show the white minstrel audiences what they wanted them to see. As Robert Toll has reported, the truly repugnant caricatures inherited from white minstrels were tempered in the black skits. Some of the old images of the plantation were maintained, but within a nostalgic framework of black family unity. Mention of white masters was limited; the themes of antislavery, freedom, Emancipation Day, and religion were underlined.[9] Considering that the black troupes also played to black audiences with tremendous success, the magnetic attraction of orally based stage performance must have struck a familiar note far too strong to resist even if it indulged in stereotypes that later, literate generations, with only a script to go on and not a visual or auditory memory, would find offensive. Indeed, minstrelsy's appearance in Africa in the late nineteenth century suggests how adaptable the style was.[10] Even the erudite James Monroe Trotter (1842–1892), voicing the sensitivities of the literate black middle class in the late nineteenth century, granted "two sides to the minstrel question" and felt that the Georgia Minstrels had "presented so much that was really charming in a musical way as to almost compensate the sensitive auditor for what he was ready to confess he suffered while witnessing that part of the performance devoted to caricature."[11]

For Trotter and others, the text—the professional and plastic transformation by black performers—was compelling and worthwhile; the context—the appearance of conformity to degraded stereotypical tableaux and acts—was repulsive. Both remain so today. Ralph Ellison sheds new light on Trotter's discomfort, writing a century later: "Americans live in a constant state of debate and contention. And we do so no matter what kinds of narrative, oral or written, are made in the reconstruction of our common experience."[12] The roles played and the masks worn in minstrelsy were shared superficially by both black and white entertainers, but they were used for quite different purposes. Ellison's distinction between archetypes—"embodiments of abiding patterns of human existence"—and stereotypes—"malicious reductions of human complexity"—should be kept in mind here.[13] But separating the image from the reality has never been easy for Americans confronted by the stresses of an interracial, multicultural society.

In addition to the products of minstrelsy, plays with racial or slave themes pervaded the nineteenth century. In 1856, for example, *Darling*

Nelly Gray, which dealt with the plight of slaves, was successfully given in the North. Possibly the oldest play written by a black American was Henry Brown's *Drama of King Shotoway,* produced in 1823. William Wells Brown (1814–1884) wrote *Escape, or A Leap for Freedom,* one of the oldest extant published dramas by an American black, in 1858. Especially popular subjects for a number of these works written after the war were the sentimentalized Old South and the "tragic mulatto" stereotype, in which apparently Caucasian characters are revealed to have Negro blood, and tragic consequences ensue. The most successful of all were the many dramatizations of Harriet Beecher Stowe's *Uncle Tom's Cabin* (1852), arguably the most influential novel in American history. By December 1852, nine separate stagings of the work were playing in New York. Blacks rarely were seen in the early productions, but their roles as singers, banjo players, and supernumeraries gradually increased in importance in the 1870s. By the end of the century, black musicians constituted a major attraction in "new" versions of this thoroughly familiar play.[14]

One direction taken by popular urban theater during the reign of minstrelsy is mirrored in the shows of Harrigan and Hart, which focused on a mixture of city characters (mostly Irish, German, and black) engaged in comic situations but eschewed both the exaggerated caricatures of minstrelsy and the mawkishness of the sentimental melodramas also popular at the time. Edward "Ned" Harrigan (1845–1911) created his Irish hero, Dan Mulligan, who served as the focus for a long series of successful shows with songs inserted, beginning with *The Mulligan Guard* in 1873. His partner, Tony Hart (1855–1891), concentrated on dialect and "wench" (comic female) roles. The Mulligan shows parodied the various neighborhood paramilitary organizations that arose in New York following the Civil War and contained relatively well-rounded, believable characters. They enjoyed a decade of popularity before the team separated.

Harrigan and Hart broke new ground in terms of accurate ethnic portrayal, but the musical language of the songs in their shows was conservative. David Braham (1838–1905), the British-born composer who created the shows' music, was an adept worker of basic material (two- and four-measure phrases, triadic melodies, and harmonies primarily of the tonic, dominant, and subdominant). He is credited with contributing significantly to the popularity of Harrigan's plays.[15]

The relationship of music to drama in the pre-1890s musical was relatively simple: Songs were added to a show wherever directors or leading actors and actresses deemed them appropriate. The process of interpolation (discussed further in Chapter 4) was universally recognized and practiced, even when one composer wrote most of the music for the show. This freewheeling attitude was prevalent at least until the turn of the century.

Blacks became involved in producing original dramas with music when the Hyers Sisters "combination"—that is, a touring company combining different kinds of acts—announced its intention to stage plays in 1876. The troupe arose from the efforts of two singing sisters under the management of their father, Sam Hyers. Anna Madah and Emma Louise Hyers, who had won acclaim in their native California and during extensive concertizing, mounted no less than a half-dozen shows (and possibly more) during the late 1870s and 1880s. Their plays, such as *Out of the Wilderness* by Joseph Bradford (1843–1886) and *Colored Aristocracy* by novelist Pauline Hopkins (1859–1930), emphasized racial themes.[16] Show business chronicler Tom Fletcher appeared with the sisters in shows named *Out of Bondage, The Underground Railroad* (also by Hopkins), and *Princess Orelia of Madagascar* in 1877. The *San Francisco Pacific Appeal* referred to *Urlina, the African Princess* (might Urlina be Orelia?) "written especially for them" in April 1879, and in 1886 the *Cleveland Gazette* noted that "a dramatic company of color," including the Hyers Sisters, Wallace King (1840–1903), who toured with the sisters, and Sam Lucas (1840–1916), probably the most famous of the nineteenth-century black minstrel men, would present *Out of Bondage* and *Hotel de Afric (sic)*.[17]

The relationship these shows bore to minstrelsy, especially the sentimental afterpieces, is clear from a rare preserved program of *Out of Bondage*. Nine characters are listed, and three acts are described:

Act I.   Uncle Eph's Cabin, down South before the War. The Possum Supper, Jubilee Songs, Dances and Choruses

Act II.   During the War "De Yankees are comin' fifty million strong! all ten feet or more high!" Farewell Plantation Breakdown by the Company

The Inimitable Big-Mouthed Comedian, Fred Lyons

The Funniest Man on Earth, in his specialties

Act III.   Up North, 5 years after. Readings from the Poets, by Miss
Mary Reynolds. Meeting of Uncle Eph and Aunt Naomi in the
Children's happy home. Grand Finale:
"Ah, Those Golden Slippers"[18]

Unlike minstrel shows, *Out of Bondage* follows a logical structure. But
the themes of emancipation ("De Yankees are comin'"), communal activities ("The Possum Supper") and family unity ("Uncle Eph and Naomi
in the Children's happy home"), presented within a tripartite frame,
together with olio-style specialties (Fred Lyons's comedy and Miss Reynolds's poetry), were typical of the minstrel show. Musically the show
included jubilee songs (spirituals), dances, and the finale, "Ah, Those
Golden Slippers," one of the most popular songs by black composer
James Bland (1854–1911).

Another song in *Out of Bondage*, "Good-By, Old Cabin Home," was
composed by a white Bostonian, C. A. White (1829–1892) and dedicated
to Emma Hyers.[19] It features solos for the characters Kaloolah (Emma
Hyers) and Henry (Fred Lyons, later Sam Lucas) and provides enough
information to reconstruct the dramatic scene. The cover illustration depicts two middle-aged blacks realistically drawn (not caricatured, as was
often the case), wistfully gazing on their cabin. The sixteen-measure musical introduction is captioned "Echoes from the Plantation" and is a
jaunty triadic melody. Kaloolah then sings:

O golly, ain't I happy!
De Yankee's day hab come;
I hear de shout of freedom,
I hear dar fife and drum;
Dar's gwine to be a smash-up
Dis chile is gettin' shy,
She'll leab de old plantation,
Old cabin home, good-by.

The refrain echoes "Good-by, good-by. . . ." Even though the leave-
taking results from the long-awaited emancipation, it is tinged with sad-
ness and nostalgia—earmarks of the nineteenth-century sentimental
song. After Henry's verse and refrain, another tune, "You Can't Lose

Me," follows (Example 1.1). Perhaps this snappy, Irish-sounding melody accompanied a dance. The final sixteen measures is a four-part choral reprise of the refrain. Two performance options are suggested: "CHO-RUS. To be sung after last verse as an invisible chorus, or as a Duet while leaving the stage." Presumably this number occurred somewhere in the second act (Facsimile 1.1).

The Hyers Sisters traveled with their own shows at least until the mid-1880s and were still appearing on stage in the 1890s.[20] The *Colored American Magazine* noted in November 1901 that, although Emma Louise Hyers had died, Anna Madah was traveling with one of John Isham's shows.[21] Ike Simond, in his *Old Slack's Reminiscence and Pocket History of the Colored Profession From 1865–1891,* called the Hyers Sisters' Combination "the greatest of all colored efforts; as I have seen all the colored shows in the country, I must say this one was a great go."[22]

An influx of foreign operettas in the 1870s and 1880s brought new ideas to American creators of plays with music. Composers and writers, seeing sophisticated European products, realized that more extensive musical-dramatic integration within popular theater pieces not only was possible but also had box-office appeal. American composers such as John Hill Hewitt (1801–1890) and Julius Eichberg (1824–1893) imitated the European operetta, and even Harrigan and Hart expanded old one-act farces to three acts, perhaps attempting to equal the scope of the ambitious imports.

Another theatrical genre that influenced the direction of black theater was the spectacle or extravaganza, a play in which all plot and character development was subordinated to the presentation of movement and tableaux—elaborate costumes, complex and marvelous scenic effects, group dancing, and mime. These shows did not emphasize music, which

Example 1.1. C. A. White, "Good-By, Old Cabin Home" (Boston: White, Smith and Co. [1880]), final dance

was rarely mentioned in reviews and functioned mainly to accompany stage movements and dramatic gestures. Little is known of the composers who wrote for these entertainments.[23]

Extravaganzas typically contained at least one "transformation scene," in which characters and scenes were instantaneously metamorphosed by means of an array of lighting techniques, elaborate mechanical devices, and optically deceptive sets. In a matter of seconds oceans became deserts, castles forests, people animals, and so on. *The Black Crook* (1867), which involved no Afro-American characters, was a famous and expensive example of this sort of show, although its longevity and its numerous revivals have led some historians to overestimate the importance of the extravaganza in general.[24]

An indispensable ingredient in many extravaganzas was the burlesque. The word and genre originally referred to a comic spoof or parody of a familiar, serious work, but the prominence of bare-legged women in Laura Keene's burlesques of the 1860s gave it the more modern connotation of striptease. The Creole Burlesque Show was born in 1890, the brainchild of theater entrepreneur Sam T. Jack and minstrel man Sam Lucas. It used the format of a minstrel show, but for the first time with black women in the front semicircle and the famous male impersonator, Florence Hines, as the interlocutor (the endmen and orchestra members were male). The show's novelty and presumably the beauty of the females in it made it a long-running success.[25] Popular cakewalks and songs from the traditional minstrel repertory probably constituted the musical part of the program. The publishers Brooks and Denton advertised the songs "Colored Aristocracy," "Fly, Fly, Fly," "Dem Golden Clouds," and "Move Up, Johnson," all by Bob Cole (1869–1911), as "introduced by Sam Jack's Creoles." The first number probably deals with social climbing in the black community, a fairly typical theme. The last three, judging from the titles, are ersatz spirituals—optimistic, admonitory, or otherworldly dialect songs written by both whites and blacks, songs that Charles Hamm has dubbed "minstrel-spirituals."[26] "Move Up, Johnson," for which the sheet music exists, is replete with homilies. A lapsed sinner given to overeating and shooting craps is told, "While the sun is shining you had better make some hay," "don't tarry on the way," "you can get there [heaven?] if you try," "when your troubles are all over you'll be rolling in the clover." The chorus includes several musical features typical of this type of song (Facsimile 1.2): octaves and broken chords in a repeated quarter-note bass pattern, a dotted-eighth- and sixteenth-note usage in the right hand harmonically consonant with the vocal melody, and an occasional isolated syncopation (m. 3) supporting the word accent.

The Creoles were first advertised in the *Haverhill* (MA) *Evening Gazette* of August 4, 1890: "The pearly gates have swung ajar. Sam T. Jack's Creole Burlesque Co. 50 Artists 50. 20 Egyptian Beauties 20. 30 Creole Queens 30. The Charmers of the Nile and the Enchantresses of the Mississippi. In the Grandest Entertainment Under the Canopy of Heaven. Silk, Satin, Glitter, and Gold. . . ." This hybrid of minstrelsy and burlesque, presented in Haverhill for "one night only," moved to the Howard Theatre in Boston later in the month and opened at Proctor's Novelty Theatre in Brooklyn on August 25 "to a packed house." *The Dramatic Mirror* reported ". . . crowded houses every night during the week. All in all it is an A-1 company. The DeWolf sisters in duets and Jackson and Jones as clowns were particularly good. Mr. and Mrs. Sam Lucas did a good act, including a solo on the cornet by Mrs. Lucas, and duets, vocal and on the zither and guitar [sic]."[27] The show played successfully in at least seven other New York theaters throughout the next five or six seasons and toured the East, Midwest, and Canada with a changing cast that always numbered between fifteen and thirty. These tours can be traced through the pages of the *Dramatic Mirror,* which provided complete lists of the personnel in the Creole Show annually from 1891 to 1896.

Another category of entertainment directly linked to the black musical shows of the 1890s was the revue, a topical variety show in which a group of performers work in several different sketches and roles. The revue was introduced by George Lederer (1861–1938) to the American public in *The Passing Show* in 1894.[28] Its creators called it "a topical extravaganza," but its principal novelty consisted of including a medley of operatic arias at the beginning of the third act. The variety shows of the Black Patti Troubadours and John Isham (1866–?), the two largest nonminstrel black companies of the time, immediately adopted this innovation but promoted the operatic medley to the grand finale in order to feature the outstanding vocal talents of Sissieretta Jones (1869–1933) and Mamie Flowers.

The fusion of apparently diverse elements, ranging from acrobats to blackface comics to opera singers, coincided with an improvement in quality among variety acts fostered by Tony Pastor (1833–1908) and B. F. Keith (1846–1914) in the early 1880s, as well as an increase in the number of vaudeville acts available. Small acts and big shows, vaudevilles and musical comedies routinely exchanged material in the 1890s. All theater people paid attention to the latest novelties, and the borrowings between black shows and white shows went both ways.

As early as the 1870s black showmen were writing their own songs in what Charles Hamm describes as the "postwar minstrel song" style common to white composers such as C. A. White and Will S. Hays (1837–1907).[29] Sam Lucas, James Bland, and Gussie Davis (1863–1899) wrote lyrical songs and ballads that were among the most popular of their time and were used in the historical plays of the Hyers Sisters, as well as in minstrelsy. In the early 1890s, writers of syncopated coon songs frequently were black. Coon song lyrics, filled with images of black chicken stealers, watermelon eaters, and razor toters, often are not pleasant to contemplate, but their importance in the black shows cannot be overlooked. Ragtime songs and piano tunes, defined by their persistent syncopations and quick duple time, shook all of Broadway in the late 1890s, with black songwriters leading the way.

Many black or black-derived stage shows of the nineteenth century featured dance—especially vigorous and inventive dance. As Paul Oliver has noted, "Before much serious attention was paid to the songs of black Americans, their dances were the subject of white interest and mimicry." The black song-and-dance entertainer served an important social function in slavery days, but dancing was favored among free blacks in the North as well. No less a visitor to America than Charles Dickens penned a now-famous description of black dancing in a basement dance hall in the Five Points district of New York, a notoriously wild neighborhood in the 1840s. The dazzling steps of one dancer in particular included the "single shuffle, double shuffle, cut and cross cut . . . spinning about on his toes and heels like nothing but the man's fingers on the tambourine." Fast steps and wild upper body movement seem to have been the ingredients of what later was termed eccentric dancing, but counterclockwise circles for group steps, rapid hip movements, and violent shoulder and arm gestures were all features of the "infinite plasticity," to use Stanley Crouch's phrase, in popular dances after the turn of the century, and they derived from Afro-American styles and ultimately from West African practice.[30]

Dancing provided amusement as well as release, and certainly for slave masters dancing was the perfect slave entertainment. Audiences could construe the dancing of blacks as indicating their contentment (even if the dance mocked white movement); it was devoid of direct message, not apparently disruptive of the social order, yet it was technically impressive and sensually stimulating. It said, "I am thrilling, I am competent, watch me!" Descended from traditional African customs and rituals, yet allowing invention and improvisation upon steps learned from other sources, dance spoke of both the past and the present in ever-changing ways. With so many uses and so much potential to generate excitement, it is no wonder that dance became a prominent feature of black musical theater.

2
Traveling Shows

During the decade in which the Creole Burlesquers were making a name for themselves and the Harrigan-Hart shows were waning in popularity, a series of economic events occurred that was to have a forceful impact on determining the future of American musical theater. The Panic of 1893, a depression that lasted for four years, roused theatrical owners and agents to attempt to achieve some new, more efficient booking arrangements. The predominance of resident stock companies and visiting artists in the early nineteenth-century American theater had given way after the Civil War to the popularity of traveling companies. Booking separate acts and traveling shows nationwide had grown increasingly more difficult as America had expanded westward. Individual theater owners traditionally had lined up the star performers, and the performers themselves had acted as or provided their own advance men to negotiate with the owners. But with large combinations, the situation became more complex. Booking agencies were needed, and gradually group agreements were made among theater managers in the same regions to avoid duplicate bookings and empty houses. Circuits of theaters with a single owner emerged and prospered. Under one owner, scheduling was more convenient for managers. Acts and companies could move from one theater to another along the same train line without long, unpaid breaks between shows.[1]

Haphazard engagement of acts was alleviated even further when six men—Charles Frohman, Al Hayman, Marc Klaw, and Abraham Erlanger of New York, and J. Frederick Zimmerman and Samuel Nixon of Philadelphia—joined forces to form what became known as the Trust or Syndicate. During the Panic, when many managers faced financial ruin, these men had the foresight and fortune to acquire the controlling interest in a large number of theaters throughout the country; by uniting and operating out of one centralized office they were able to control the number, kind, and length of theatrical bookings to be offered all over the country. By 1896 they controlled over five hundred theaters in all regions of America.[2]

Slipshod practices were reformed and inefficient management was ousted, but fears of censorship and the Trust's unscrupulous methods alarmed Broadway. The press began referring to "these men of ignorance and greed who have established a virtual monopoly." Gerald Bordman observes that "for better or worse this group completely changed producing and booking practices in the decades that followed. One of the initial coups was to effectively end the reign of the actor-manager, although, in fairness to the Trust, many a performer was undoubtedly thankful to be relieved of responsibility for his own ledgers."[3]

The Trust dealt mainly with straight dramas and well-known stars. Variety shows, musical productions, and less grandiose shows generally toured on a circuit of so-called popular-price theaters. In this arena a monopolistic arrangement similar to that of the Trust was brought about by the firm of Stair and Havlin, which controlled over 150 theaters around 1900.

For black performers, who because of overwhelming economic prejudice had little chance of ever becoming independent manager-owners under the old system, syndicates provided some advantages. The rising popularity of black acts, especially dance teams, coupled with the big managers' economic motivations, ensured that blacks would be represented on the circuits as long as the vogue for black entertainment continued. Independent black theater ownership increased precipitously in the first decade of the twentieth century, owing to growing segregation in white theaters and Southern black entrepreneurship, and in the 1910s the first black syndicates were formed. By no means ideal, this situation was as beneficial as could be expected for nonunionized black show people.[4]

In the 1890s black performers gained ensemble experience in a large variety of activities connected with traveling shows. Medicine shows, gillies and carnivals, though often modest and crude affairs, helped to train performers for the vaudeville and musical comedy stage. Medicine shows required two or three performers to draw attention to the "doctor" selling his merchandise. A larger cast with perhaps fifty people, touring in painted trucks called *gillies,* attracted both black and white patrons in many small Southern towns. Marshall and Jean Stearns characterize the gilly show

> as a combination of medicine show salesmanship and minstrel show formulas. . . . The program consisted of three parts: first, the comedian and his straight man in front of the curtain cracking jokes—working in local topics, if possible—punctuated with bursts of eccentric dancing; then a series of specialties by members of the company, singing, talking, dancing, with a few "blackouts" i.e., pantomimed jokes; and finally, the afterpiece, sometimes called "Eph and Dinah."[5]

The afterpiece included music, usually nostalgic songs like "Old Black Joe" or "Old Folks at Home," and a dance finale. The plantation characters, Eph and Dinah, date back at least to the 1870s, when they were used in the Hyers Sisters' shows and listed as characters in minstrel afterpieces. A skit called "Uncle Eph's Christmas," reportedly written around 1900 by Will Marion Cook and Paul Laurence Dunbar, shows that these stock figures were retained into the twentieth century.[6]

Performers acquired little money or status from medicine shows and gillies. Working conditions were poor. Crowds sometimes were hostile. But those players who learned their lessons and chose to stay in show business moved up to larger tent shows and minstrelsy.

As the number of experienced black musicians and actors increased, entrepreneurs recognized that substantial profit might be made in sponsoring all-black casts in traveling shows differing from the usual minstrel

John Isham, ca. 1898, associated with Sam T. Jack's
Creole Burlesque Company and leader of two traveling
companies, the Octoroons and Oriental America. Billy
Rose Theatre Collection, the New York Public Library
at Lincoln Center, Astor, Lenox and Tilden Foundations.

arrangement. While these shows made no unique impact in New York,
they provided training for dozens of show people who later appeared in
the big New York shows. Sam T. Jack had already led the way with his
Creole Burlesque Company of 1890. Jack's advance man, John W. Isham,
took the idea a step further. While preserving the overall three-part
shape of the minstrel show, he eliminated the minstrel semicircle, the
formal introductions of an interlocutor, and the farcical or punning wit of
the endmen. Isham's new format amounted to a series of songs, dances,
and specialty acts either preceding or following a thinly plotted playlet,
and the finale was a military drill and dance for the entire company.[7] To
appear with his Octoroon Company, Isham recruited Mamie Flowers,
advertised in 1895 as "the only rival of the Black Patti," a reference to

Sissieretta Jones (1869–1933), the best-known black soprano of the day.
Fred J. Piper, a comedian who previously had appeared with the Creole
Show, also was featured. The *Dramatic Mirror* in June 1895 advertised
the Octoroons as a troupe of nearly fifty people "in a Gorgeous Spectacular Opera Comique."[8] A review of September 21, 1895, confirms that
Isham accomplished at least a highly varied and satisfactory production
and that Mamie Flowers was a draw:

> Isham's Octoroons opened last evening with a good programme
> which included everything in the amusement line from grand opera to
> song and dance. . . . Madame Flowers, "the Bronze Melba," headed
> the bill. Her high-class solos were well-received. . . . The rest of the
> company included Fred J. Piper, tenor, Mattie Wilkes, soprano, the
> Hyers Sisters, Mr. and Mrs. Tom McIntosh, Tom Browne, the mimic
> and the Mallory Brothers.[9]

Although "grand opera" was mentioned, it is not clear that Isham included a solo-and-chorus operatic medley along the lines of Lederer's
Passing Show (1894) until the following season. Both Isham and Lederer
may have gotten the idea for such an addition from Sam T. Jack, who
before his time with the Creole Show had served as one of Lederer's
managers.[10]

The outline of a musical play mounted by the Octoroon Company in
1896, called a "mirthful and melodious farce in ONE ACT," bears the
title "John W. Isham's Octoroons at the Blackville Derby." A cast of nine
characters is listed, and ten numbers are followed by the indication
"song," "music and business," or "dance." The final number reads "'Thirty Minutes Around the Operas' such as Pinafore, Robin Hood, Tar and
Tartar, etc., and wind up with our popular favorite, 'A Trip to Coney
Island.' (They sing for thirty minutes selections from operas and 'A Trip to
Coney Island' is concluded.)"[11]

Freeman writer Richard W. Thompson greeted Isham's ambitious undertaking as a forerunner of a great revival in the black performing arts:
"This preliminary schooling in light comedy, inducing the habit of character study, will eventually make the Negro a factor in all forms of drama,
romantic society and sensational Opera companies, grand and comic, will
come in their season, and time will yet produce the modern successor to

the toga so grandly worn by Ira Aldridge."[12] As if to confirm Thompson's prediction, Isham launched a second company for the 1896–97 season in a show called *Oriental America* (it featured a quartet of "Japanese girls" and a march of "Oriental huzzars"). For this show Isham secured a large chorus and a number of first-class solo singers to present his operatic finale, excerpts from *Faust, Rigoletto, Il Trovatore,* and *Carmen,* which replaced the normal military drill-cakewalk.[13] A script of "Oriental America at Mrs. Waldorf's Fifth Anniversary" outlines what may have preceded the operatic finale. A series of fourteen unnamed songs, dances, and specialties connecting a story set in a "handsome" Florida hotel concludes with a Flower Ballet, "which will be given with the charming floral accompaniment, 'Nature's Repose' (ballet with own vocal music— trees, shrubs and flowers are lightened [*sic*] up with original electrical effect)."[14] Isham brought the *Oriental America* company to Great Britain in 1897, reporting to the *Freeman* that everywhere the company had "met with the heartiest welcome,"[15] and during the following year he consolidated the two groups.

In 1899 a lengthier program for the combined companies began with "a musical farce," which was followed by "vaudeville specialties" as a middle section and a "chorus-march finale." Once again the show's colorful accoutrements proved attractive; one writer declared that Isham presented "the American theatergoer with some of the grandest costumes, scenery and electrical effects the world has ever known."[16] The show clearly was rooted within the genre of spectacle. Despite good reviews and continual claims of success, however, Isham was unable to sustain the considerable expense of touring with such a large company. He declared bankruptcy in 1899 and retired from the business in 1900.[17]

Another important organizer of black talent, and one with the additional gift of persuading moneyed men to back his ideas, was Billy McClain (1866–1950). McClain, born in Indianapolis, worked from an early age to build his expertise in musical and theatrical activities as a cornetist, trombonist, trapeze artist, and endman. During the 1880s he appeared with the Sells Brothers and Forepaugh's Circus as well as several minstrel troupes. Around 1900 one unidentified reporter wrote of McClain, "this young actor-manager . . . is to the theatrical world what Fred Douglass was and Booker T. Washington is, to the educational phase of the negro race of today."[18] Throughout the 1890s McClain worked consistently to gather together black performers in large shows. He assisted in the production of Whalen and Martell's *South Before the War* (1893); *Suwanee River*, under the management of Davis and Keough; *Darkest America* (1897), under Al G. Field; and his biggest effort, *Black America*, sponsored by Nate Salisbury, whose previous ventures had included Buffalo Bill Cody's Wild West Show.[19]

Black America comprised over five hundred people and was produced outdoors in Ambrose Park in Brooklyn during the summer of 1895. In all of his shows McClain sought a variety of talent, employing a large number of singers in so-called jubilee choirs and dancers and supernumeraries in huge plantation tableaux. In addition, *Black America* featured sixty-three vocal quartets, men from the U.S. Ninth Cavalry performing regular army maneuvers, boxing exhibitions and footraces, and numerous other singers and dancers. Among the especially skilled performers were Charles Johnson, the famed cakewalking partner of Dora Dean; May Bohee, who with her brothers taught the banjo to the Prince of Wales; the comedian Billy Farrell; and McClain's singing wife, Cordelia. The plantation atmosphere was executed in impressive detail, with log cabins built in the park, poultry and livestock, and even genuine cotton plants to add a finishing touch. A *New York Times* review was most complimentary:

> "Black America" was opened yesterday afternoon at Ambrose Park, South Brooklyn, with a large attendance and an attractive programme. The evening performance was also well attended.
>
> The show is a unique one. It is a new departure in the field of amusement, and it undoubtedly will be a great success. The management has secured the best negro voices that could be found in the South for the singing, the best dancers obtainable, and those who best represent the Southern days before the war.
>
> "Black America" is as instructive as it is entertaining. It depicts the old slave life, and the bright side of the slave's existence. The old negro melodies are sung by large choruses of natural voices in the same manner that they have always been sung below Mason and Dixon's line. The peculiarities of the Southern blacks are exemplified, and their traits are all shown. The entertainment is a delightful one, as it brings before the spectators the peculiarities of the Southern negro in a manner that most Northern persons have never been able to observe. . . .

The cabins scattered over the grounds are exact reproductions of the old slave cabins in the South, and the work in the cotton fields that they perform is as it was when the negroes were chattels and not free men. The songs that are sung and the superstitious rites and incantations of the Voodoos have a marked effect upon those who are unfamiliar with them.

The dances are peculiar in their attractiveness. The efforts that the white man has made to reproduce them will be seen to be but a faint imitation of what they really are. The naturalness and spontaneity of action on the part of the negroes will be at once recognized and appreciated. Their dances beggar description, and must be seen to be appreciated. Those who take part in the performance have been selected from all the various sections of the South, and are well qualified to enlighten the Northern white man in relation to a life that will soon be extinct. . . .

There is a harmonious chorus, and fine soloists and part-singers, who sing negro melodies that abound in feeling and stir the listeners as no other songs do. The reader is encouraged to visit the park where the entertainment is given daily.[20]

Falsely bucolic though it may have been, *Black America* was a significant aggregation and display of black talent. Musical plays—that is, plotted, staged, integrated works—probably were not performed, but all the necessary elements were present: singing in chorus, dancing, solo performing, acting in costume, picking in ersatz cotton fields, and chanting "Voodoo rites."

After his gargantuan successes McClain organized a minstrel group to tour Hawaii and Australia, spent time in Australia as a boxing promoter, and later returned to Washington, DC, to attend medical school. His experience with trapeze artists and prizefighters had seemingly encouraged him to think about chiropractic medicine. In his memoirs, veteran showman Tom Fletcher proclaimed McClain an "unsung pioneer" and devoted an entire chapter to his life and contributions.[21]

The most successful touring company of the mid-1890s, whether judged by the fame of its star, the quality of the houses it played, or its sheer longevity, undoubtedly was Black Patti's Troubadours. The troupe, led by Matilda Sissieretta Joyner Jones ("the Black Patti") and managed by Rudolf Voelckel and James Nolan, presented a show that varied annually and continued to draw crowds for nearly twenty years.

Jones was one of the most publicized and most talented black performers of the nineteenth-century concert stage; she also was one of many
black classically trained performers whose careers included appearances
with popular music shows.[22] After training in her native Providence and
in New York, she toured for many years as a solo singer, during which
time a New York reviewer coined the sobriquet "the Black Patti" (after
the then-popular Italian soprano, Adelina Patti), which followed her ever
after. Her first appearances earned encouraging but critical reviews. Per-
sisting in her efforts and heeding her critics' advice, she gradually
emerged as an elegant, poised, and powerful singer and was favorably
compared with other prominent singers of the era. As early as 1892 a
Canadian reviewer referred to her as "the unsurpassed songstress." A
New York review testified to her distinction: "the black Patti rendered a
piece by Verdi, called "Sempre libera" . . . and if Madame Jones is not
the equal of Patti, she at least can come nearer than anything the American has heard. . . . Her notes are as clear as a mocking bird and her
enunciation perfect." Another notice commented, "Carnegie Music Hall
presented an animated appearance Monday night, when the brilliant
audience hung with breathless stillness upon the clarion notes of the most
gifted singer the age has produced. . . . It was the first time any company
of colored artists has ever occupied the hall." A Detroit paper declared,
"Her musical voice is of extra-ordinary compass and even power. . . ."[23]
Jones was invited to appear before President Harrison in the White
House in February of 1892, and later in the year she received enthusiastic
bravas for a performance in a "Grand African Jubilee" (a festival of singing
and dancing) in Madison Square Garden.[24]

Perhaps wishing to expand her audience and earnings while drawing
closer to a larger group of black performers, Jones left her solo career in
1896 to form the Black Patti Troubadours. The show began in the minstrel
format and adopted the classical finale of the *Oriental America* show,
calling it an "operatic kaleidoscope," and it included staged scenes from
Lucia, Martha, Il Trovatore, and Sousa's *El Capitan.* The troupe's blend
of minstrelsy, songs, novelties, skits, and operatic excerpts held the stage
for nearly two decades, until 1916. The Troubadours did not attempt to
stage extravaganzas of the McClain sort but offered musical playlets,
sometimes in more than one act. Toward the end of Jones's career, between 1910 and 1914, full-length musical comedies were mounted: *A Trip*

to Africa (1910), *In the Jungles* (1911), *Captain Jaspar* (1912), and *Lucky Sam from Alabam* (1914).

One member of the Black Patti company who was to play a vital role in the future of black musical theater was a young writer and performer named Bob Cole, one of the most versatile and resourceful men in American stage history.[25] Robert Allen Cole was born in Athens, Georgia, on July 1, 1868, the son of former slaves. Apparently he received early musical training in Athens and completed elementary school after his family moved to Atlanta. During his adolescence, Cole moved to Chicago and then to New York and apprenticed in several one- and two-man acts. He signed on with Sam T. Jack's Creoles, probably while still in Chicago in 1891.[26] By 1893 he had published his first songs with Will Rossiter Publishing Company, "Parthenia Took a Likin' To a Coon" and "In Shin Bone Alley." Cole served as comedian and stage manager with the Creoles, where he met Stella Wiley, an attractive young singer with whom he formed a vaudeville act and whom he later married. The team moved to the East, was booked into theaters in New England, and finally reached New York. About 1894 Cole formed the All-Star Stock Company and worked to train a professional group of show people that became the core company of many later shows. Its members included Billy and Willy Farrell, cakewalk dancers; Fred Piper; Mamie Flowers; Mattie Wilkes; Billy Johnson (1858–1916), Cole's songwriting partner; Stella Wiley; and two composer-performers, Gussie Davis and Will Marion Cook. The group worked out of Worth's Museum ("museum" being a nineteenth-century euphemism to avoid the sanctions associated with "theaters") at the corner of Sixth Avenue and Thirteenth Street, a hall formerly used for cheap vaudeville.[27] The shows that John Isham produced in 1895, 1896, and 1897 included members of the All-Star Stock Company. In 1896 Cole joined the newly formed Black Patti Troubadours and wrote a skit for the show called "At Jolly Coon-ey Island."

Cole's songs from the mid-1890s, such as "Mr. Coon, You're All Right in Your Place," "The Czar of the Tenderloin," and "The Wedding of the Chinee and the Coon," contain several themes found in other contemporary coon songs: the high-toned "yaller gal" (mulatto) who won't associate with common folk ("She's educated way up to the key of G"), bullies who rule the neighborhood ("he arrested a cook for beating an egg"), and

Bob Cole and Stella Wiley, ca. 1895, in their vaudeville
duo. Yale Collection of American Literature, Beinecke
Rare Book and Manuscript Library, Yale University.

Oriental ethnic stereotypes, although coon motifs sometimes were ex-
plored in subtle ways. Cole's songs are diatonic and harmonically straightforward, usually in duple time with an occasional syncopation. The most
common rhythmic patterns consist of simple subdivisions of the basic
beats and series of dotted-eighth/sixteenth-note measures. The verses
tend to be longer than the refrains rather than equivalent in length, as
was becoming more and more common in popular song by the 1890s. The
songs differ from other songs of the nineties and from the songs Cole
himself wrote after 1899 in collaboration with James Weldon and J. Rosamond Johnson. Three traits in particular stand out: (1) piano parts that are
active at the ends of phrases (Cole even gives several measures of a verse
to piano alone without singer), (2) the use of the minor or Dorian mode in

the verse, and (3) the literal as opposed to varied repetition of melodic phrases. These traits, used occasionally in conjunction with dramatic dynamic contrast and fermatas, suggest that Cole sought to heighten the contrasts in his songs in nonmelodic ways and recognized how his songs worked on stage. His pieces bristle with puns, humorously disfigured words ("I'm driven to desperism/By her misconstrued behaviorism") combined with musical commonplaces (pentatonic "Chinese" music for Oriental subjects, or slow, "mysterious," minor-mode chords supporting a text about an unknown man in town). One imagines the performer demonstrating his panache by gesturing with hands and face during the piano interludes, when delivering punchlines, or while repeating the final chorus (it is always repeated *forte*). An old girlfriend recalled that Cole resembled Fred Astaire "because of the same general build, same grace, same charm in his dancing on the stage." For Cole's sister, Carriebell Plummer, "he resembled, in features and movements, Leigh Whipper, the original Crab Man of *Porgy*. . . . Today though not as tall as Bob Cole, Sammy Davis, Jr. is the epitome of his stage acting."[28] The directness and wit of his early songs contrast markedly with the suave, cute, but un-"cooney" lyrics and polished, harmonically rich textures of his songs written in the decade following 1899—a change that matched his transformation from a tramp character with a red beard (and no burnt cork) in the 1890s skits to a gentleman in evening clothes in his vaudeville routines with J. Rosamond Johnson.

At the end of the season, unable to come to financial terms with Jones's managers, Cole left the Troubadours, taking with him members Lloyd Gibbs, Tom Brown, Jesse Shipp (1869–1934), Billy Johnson, and Bob Kelly. For demanding more money and better working conditions and carrying off the scripts he had written, Cole was labeled a disturber and was blackballed by Voelckel and Nolan at theaters where they had any influence.[29] Undaunted, Cole proceeded to form his own organization and soon produced *A Trip to Coontown*. This show had a continuous plot and a full cast of characters, and it provided a full evening's entertainment; it thus became the first full-length black musical comedy actually written, performed, and managed by blacks. It sparked many imitators and inaugurated a decade of New York shows patronized and applauded by both black and white audiences.

3
The Scene
and the Players
in New York

New York at the turn of the century was characterized by its citizens and visitors, its boosters and detractors alike, as a city of expansiveness, industry, pleasure, and above all, wealth. It was "a cosmopolis, a world city," as Moses King explained, "the peer of any city, ancient or modern. In great lofty structures; in commercial activity; in financial affairs; in notable scientific achievements; in colossal individual aggrandizements; in mammoth corporate wealth; in maritime commerce; in absolute freedom of her citizens; and in the aggregation of civil, social, philanthropic and religious associations New York stands unsurpassed anywhere on the globe." Theodore Dreiser recalled, "The splendor of the, to me, new dynamic, new-world metropolis! Its romance, its enthusiasm, its illusions, its difficulties! The immense crowds everywhere. . . ." Even its critics were awed. "Remarkable, unspeakable New York!" exclaimed Henry James, who was simultaneously amazed and offended by this "perpendicular" city and its brilliant variety, its "aliens," its wealth, and its prodigality.[1]

New York, a city of inspiring skyscrapers and the newly completed Brooklyn Bridge, of widespread electrification and coal-powered elevated trains, was also frenetic, noisy, and dirty. It was "the shiftless outcome of squalid barbarism and reckless extravagance," scoffed tourist Rudyard Kipling.[2] New York's 1870 population of 1.5 million had nearly doubled by 1900. Manhattan, already a city of enormous ethnic diversity, was getting crowded. In 1900 nearly one-third of the residents of New York were foreign born. Germans constituted the largest ethnic group with over 300,000 people. There were approximately 275,000 Irish, 150,000 Russians, and 145,000 Italians.[3] Of the 60,000 black citizens of New York in 1900, three-quarters of those employed were common laborers or servants, and only about 1,000 people (less than three percent of the total employed) held professional or clerical jobs.[4] The young sociologist W. E. B. DuBois estimated that some 15,000 black people in New York constituted the unemployed, "struggling, unsuccessful sub-stratum . . . 'God's poor, the devil's poor and the poor devils,' and also the vicious and criminal classes."[5] Members of all economic groups were clustered in crowded, poorly ventilated tenements in districts between Twentieth and Fortieth Streets on the West Side, an area frequently referred to as the Tenderloin.[6] The neighborhoods gradually expanded north into the mid-Sixties, a zone which became known as San Juan Hill.

New York's black population, despite its generally low social estate and overcrowded condition, was not entirely isolated from the spirit of verve and optimism of the city as a whole. In his last novel, *The Sport of the Gods*, Paul Laurence Dunbar captures the excited dream of his provincial black heroes when they decide to go to New York: "They had heard of New York as a place vague and far away, a city that, like Heaven, to them had existed by faith alone. All the days of their lives they had heard of it, and it seemed to them the centre of all the glory, all the wealth, and all the freedom of the world. New York. It had an alluring sound. Who would know them there? Who would look down upon them?"[7]

The reality was a mixture of good and bad. Housing and sanitation for the very poor were deplorable, and discrimination and a lack of professional training programs limited blacks' job opportunities, yet a socially active black middle class did thrive. Jacob Riis observed a "neat and orderly" community in Harlem different from the "black and tan slums of the lower city," and there were well-to-do blacks in Brooklyn. A few black entertainers prospered; black sportsmen, particularly jockeys, emerged as heroes of the day; several black businesses thrived, and the number of black professionals gradually increased.[8]

New York also provided commercial entertainment for all of its people. Two dozen first-class theaters existed in 1879, and the number had nearly doubled by 1890. The glamorous Casino Theatre, its novel roof garden a boon on sultry summer nights, opened its doors in 1882, and the Metropolitan Opera House replaced the aging Academy of Music as the locus of cultivated taste in the following year. Broadway, the distinctive main artery of Manhattan, was the center of stage entertainment, although the theater district was located nearer to Union Square than Times Square. New York theaters in 1900 offered entertainments in diverse genres and languages, everything from vaudeville to opera, from Gilbert and Sullivan to Shakespeare.[9]

Segregation was a persistent problem in the large downtown theaters, but Seventh Avenue from the Twenties to the Forties became known as the African Broadway, an area fashionable blacks patronized for shopping and entertainment.[10] The Marshall and Maceo Hotels on West Fifty-third Street between Sixth and Seventh also became social settings, and the Marshall emerged as a site of considerable artistic activity and intellectual discussion. James Weldon Johnson, who achieved renown as a writer and diplomat, and his brother J. Rosamond Johnson moved into the hotel. Bob Cole lived two doors away but came there to work. Bert Williams, a rising young comedian and singer, eventually took up residence there.[11] The Marshall hosted virtually all of the major black entertainers in the decade following 1900. Several white entertainers and socialites visited there as well. James Weldon Johnson observed, "In time, the Marshall came to be one of the sights of New York. But it was more than a 'sight;' its importance as the radiant point of the forces that cleared the way for the Negro on the New York stage cannot be overestimated."[12]

The overriding importance of New York as a center for theater is confirmed by statistics, aside from the many first-person accounts of the period. In 1890, national census figures showed 1,490 "actors and professional showmen" and 1,881 "musicians and teachers of music" among the "colored" population of the United States.[13] Virtually all of the actors were occupied in either minstrelsy or vaudeville, as were many of the musicians. For the city of New York the figures are incomplete; seventy-three black men and women claimed to be employed as musicians or teachers of music; the number of actors and showpeople is not given. However, in 1900 musicians and actors constituted the two largest professional employment categories for blacks nationwide, after clergymen and teachers. In New York (and Chicago as well) musicians and actors outnumbered all other professional groups by a considerable margin (see Figure 1). By 1910 the number of black actors had nearly doubled over the 1890 statistic, perhaps as much because of the large number of traveling musical comedies using New York actors as because of the general increase in population.

The census figures, while providing an index of people who considered themselves "professional" musicians, do not account for all the music making that was going on or all the people involved in it. Black New York enjoyed a rich musical life with dance orchestras led by Miss Hallie Anderson and Mr. Walter Craig, to cite only two well-advertised examples, in the thick of many large social functions. Brass bands, informal

Fig. 1. Blacks employed in "professional service" in New York and Chicago in 1900 (U.S. Census data)

	New York			Chicago		
	Male	*Female*	*Total*	*Male*	*Female*	*Total*
Actors and professional showmen	254	75	329	150	51	201
Musicians and teachers of music	195	73	268	207	49	256
Teachers and professors in colleges, etc.	32	96	128	20	38	58
Clergymen/women	90	6	96	63	6	69
Physicians and surgeons	32	10	42	45	15	60
Artists and teachers of art	22	8	30	7	7	14
Lawyers	26	0	26	46	0	46
Dentists	25	0	25	8	0	8
Electricians	18	0	18	15	0	15
Engineers and surveyors	7	0	7	2	0	2

ensembles, church choirs, and individual amateur performers all were widespread.[14]

Amidst many small schools of music, New York also boasted the National Conservatory of Music, which from its inception in 1885 opened its doors to blacks. Conceived by the idealistic and magnanimous Jeannette Meyers Thurber and incorporated by an act of Congress in 1891, the Conservatory was a bold experiment. Mrs. Thurber obtained the services of a distinguished faculty and an internationally known director, Antonin Dvořák; at the end of its first decade it claimed 57 teachers and 631 pupils.[15] Among the many black musicians who attended the Conservatory were Will Marion Cook and J. Tim Brymn, known for their popular songs; Harry T. Burleigh, singer and art-song composer; and Melville Charlton, composer and organist at St. Philips Episcopal Church and the Temple Emanu-El.[16]

In summary, cosmopolitan New York provided the financial base and the educational apparatus for the creation of black musical comedies, as well as the social networks and diverse audiences that made them viable on the New York stage. By the end of the 1890s several black men and women of talent had congregated in New York, and it is to them that we now turn.

Bob Cole and the Johnson Brothers

Bob Cole was at the right place at the right time. He was working in an environment that had been dominated by the European operetta in the decade following the tremendous success of Gilbert and Sullivan's *H. M. S. Pinafore* (1879). The showy but dramatically unsubstantive extravaganzas temporarily were driven from the boards. At the same time the farce comedy, the direct progenitor of the musical comedy, was attracting more and more viewers. In pieces such as *Patchwork* (1875), *The Brook* (1879), and *Greenroom Fun* (1882), these first modest efforts placed a handful of characters in a familiar scene—at a museum, a street corner, or a country outing, for example—that provided a slim pretext for a string of songs and dances loosely connected by dialogue. The expansion of these sketches to full-evening entertainments turned the corner to musical comedy proper, pieces like *A Trip to Coontown* (1897).

After *A Trip to Coontown* closed, Cole dissolved his partnership with

Billy Johnson because of Johnson's excessive drinking.[17] In the summer of 1899 Cole made the acquaintance in New York of J. Rosamond Johnson, who soon became a close friend and musical collaborator. Rosamond and his brother James Weldon immediately took a liking to Cole. During their first summer in New York, where the Johnsons had come to produce their own musical show, the three published and sold their first group effort; May Irwin paid them fifty dollars for the tune, "Louisiana Lize."[18] The song marked the beginning of the most successful songwriting partnership of the decade. Between 1900 and 1910 Cole and Rosamond John-

May Irwin, ca. 1900, vaudeville singing star who bought the first song written by Bob Cole and the Johnson Brothers in collaboration, "Louisiana Lize." She popularized several other songs by the team as well. Photograph by Sarony, Theatre Collection, Museum of the City of New York.

son, frequently assisted by James Weldon, wrote over 150 songs for more than a dozen shows, including their own shows for all-black casts, *The Shoo-Fly Regiment* (1906) and *The Red Moon* (1908).

Like Cole, Johnson came from a family that encouraged his musical talent. As a boy he took music lessons from his mother and was later sent north to attend the New England Conservatory to study singing, piano, organ, and composition. He pursued his theatrical interest by touring with John Isham's *Oriental America* (1896); after a year on the road he returned to Jacksonville, Florida, his home town, to teach music. He and his brother wrote an operetta, *Toloso,* whose studio presentation was praised by musical leaders in Jacksonville, emboldening the Johnsons to take it to New York. *Toloso* was never produced, although many of its songs later were used in other shows. But together with some letters of introduction, *Toloso* served, in James Weldon Johnson's words, "to introduce us to practically all the important stars and producers of comic operas and musical plays in New York," including Harry B. Smith, Reginald De Koven, Oscar Hammerstein, Williams and Walker, the publisher Witmark, Harry T. Burleigh, Will Marion Cook, Ernest Hogan, the poet Paul Laurence Dunbar, and most importantly, Bob Cole. Rosamond moved to New York permanently in 1900, and the partnership was launched.[19]

Cole and Johnson presented most of their early songs in a vaudeville act in which they appeared in evening clothes. They entered the stage conversing about a party where they were to entertain. Johnson played the Paderewski *Minuet,* sang a German art song, and then both men moved to more modern material, their own original songs. White silk handkerchief in hand, Cole provided soft-shoe dancing "to the choruses played almost pianissimo." The act, described by James Weldon Johnson as "quiet, finished, and artistic to the minutest detail," worked well, and the team played in the top vaudeville houses in the United States as well as the Palace Theatre in London during a 1906 tour. Reportedly, the act was widely imitated.[20]

Publishers and producers pursued Cole and Johnson. They signed a contract with Joseph Stern in 1901, and after a call from Abe Erlanger they agreed to join the production staff of Klaw and Erlanger at the peak of their power. They composed all or nearly all of the music for *The Belle*

Left to right: Robert "Bob" Cole, James Weldon Johnson, and J. Rosamond Johnson, ca. 1906, at the height of their popularity as a composing team. Jewel Cobb.

of Bridgeport (1900), a May Irwin vehicle; *Humpty Dumpty* (1904), a Drury Lane spectacle remade in America for the Christmas season; and *In Newport* (1904), a dramatic flop that closed after a week at the newly opened Liberty Theatre. Many of their most popular tunes, such as "Under the Bamboo Tree," "The Congo Love Song," "The Maiden with the Dreamy Eyes," and "Run, Brudder Possum, Run," were interpolated into *The Little Duchess* (1900), *The Rogers Brothers in Central Park* (1900), *Sally in Our Alley* (1902), *Sleeping Beauty and the Beast* (1902), *A Girl from Dixie* (1903), *Mr. Blackbeard* (1903), *Nancy Brown* (1903), *Mother Goose* (1903), and *An English Daisy* (1904), and probably into other smaller shows for which no credit was given (see Appendix A). In 1905 Cole and Johnson began to plan their own large show, to be called *The Shoo-Fly Regiment*. The time seemed ripe to capitalize on the success of their songs and the popularity of their vaudeville act. Both *The Shoo-Fly Regiment* and *The Red Moon* met with moderate audience and critical favor, but they also cost the stars a considerable amount of money.

In 1910, at the close of the *Red Moon* road tour, Cole and Johnson returned to the vaudeville stage. Cole's collapse in April, 1911, and his subsequent death in a drowning accident (possibly a suicidal response to the onset of tertiary syphilis) marked the end of a phase in the life of J. Rosamond Johnson. It also closed a chapter in the history of black musicals.

Johnson returned to vaudeville but never again took out such a large show on his own. In 1912 he assumed the musical directorship of the Hammerstein Opera House in London. He returned to New York in 1914 and continued to be involved in a wide variety of musical projects: he published and arranged spirituals, headed the Music School Settlement for the Colored People of New York, and continued to act and compose from time to time. He died in 1954.

Ernest Hogan

Another member of the Black Patti Troubadours company who later carved out an independent career and starred in his own shows was Ernest Hogan. Like Cole and Johnson, Hogan was close to the center of the New York musical show activity in the 1890s and early 1900s. He was a protégé of Sam Lucas and Billy McClain, and his younger colleagues remembered him fondly "as the greatest of all colored showmen." Eubie Blake, Flournoy Miller, and Luckey Roberts all agreed that he was a superior performer.[21] In *Black Manhattan*, James Weldon Johnson described him as

> a veteran minstrel and a very funny, natural-blackface comedian. . . .
> Hogan was a notable exception among blackfaced comedians; his comic
> effects did not depend upon the caricature created by the use of cork
> and a mouth exaggerated by paint. His mobile face was capable of
> laughter-provoking expressions that were irresistible, notwithstanding
> the fact that he was a very good looking man. Some critics ranked him
> higher than Bert Williams.[22]

Hogan, born Reuben Crowdus in 1865 in Bowling Green, Kentucky, received his earliest training by acting in summer tent shows and minstrel shows.[23] Little else is known of his early years. He first became prominent as a writer of songs during the 1890s; in 1895 he composed his best-known tune, "All Coons Look Alike to Me." He went to his last years

Ernest Hogan, ca. 1905, multitalented entertainer who
dubbed himself "the unbleached American." Billy
Rose Theatre Collection, the New York Public Library
at Lincoln Center, Astor, Lenox, and Tilden
Foundations.

apologizing for the offense given by the title, although the rest of the
lyrics are quite innocent of racist suggestion. The song succeeded in
fueling a fad for "coon" songs, but Hogan rationalized the negative impact
of his song by insisting that the vogue for such pieces provided money and
jobs for many other composers. He told Tom Fletcher, "With the publication of that song a new musical rhythm was given to the people. Its
popularity grew and sold like wildfire all over the United States and
abroad. . . . That one song opened the way for a lot of colored and white
song writers." Whether or not one takes Hogan's claims at face value, the
coon-song fad was certainly prodigious, producing by one estimate some
600 songs from 1895 to 1900.[24]

Hogan toured with minstrel companies and played successfully in stock on the West Coast. He met Bert Williams and George Walker and helped them find performing opportunities. He returned to the East about 1895 and was eventually hired by the Black Patti Troubadours, remaining with it for two seasons. Will Marion Cook chose Hogan to train and appear with the dancers in his entertainment called *Clorindy, or the Origin of the Cakewalk.* In 1899 Hogan advertised his own forthcoming musical, but it did not materialize; he journeyed to Hawaii, Australia, and New Zealand in May 1899 with a minstrel company he had gathered.[25] By the following summer Hogan was back in the United States and was slated to appear in Will Marion Cook's *Jes Lak White Fo'ks,* a playlet with libretto, lyrics, and music all by Cook. This work, probably no more than forty-five minutes long and with a half-dozen songs, was Cook's least successful show, probably because it lacked catchy lyrics and had a somewhat incoherent plot.[26] Cook never again attempted such a one-man effort, but Hogan, undaunted, joined a traveling company called the Smart Set and then returned to vaudeville. In 1905 Hogan was featured with a group of twenty professional players—mandolinists, guitarists, banjoists, and cellists—calling themselves the Memphis Students (none were students or hailed from Memphis). The ensemble toured Europe successfully as the Tennessee Students—changing its name, according to Tom Fletcher, because the names of American states were more familiar than cities to Europeans—and appeared in Hammerstein's Victoria Theatre, the Olympia in Paris, the Palace in London, and the Schumann Circus in Berlin.

Hogan's own show *Rufus Rastus,* for which he wrote much of the book, music, and lyrics and played the starring role, was produced in 1905. During its sequel in which he also starred, *The Oyster Man,* Hogan contracted tuberculosis. He retired to Lakewood, New Jersey, for a cure but he never recovered, dying on May 20, 1909.[27]

A man in command of both pathos and humor, Hogan was renowned for the versatility of his "natural-blackface act." Although he was one of the few famous performers of this era with little or no formal education, like Billy McClain and George Walker he possessed a business shrewdness and combativeness that enabled him to become "the highest-priced single colored vaudeville performer in the business." He was a compulsive worker, constantly composing, staging, or organizing new acts. His infectious and crusading spirit, talent, and generosity were celebrated by Lester Walton in a *New York Age* obituary:

> That the stage loses one of its greatest colored comedians in the death of Ernest Hogan is admitted by all. But aside from the loss of one whose talents as an actor are well known, the colored members of the theatrical profession also lose one who might be termed in many respects, a "Moses" of the colored theatrical profession. . . .
>
> Just how far the colored theatrical profession, in fact, the entire profession, is set back by the death of Ernest Hogan the writer will not attempt to even surmise; but it has sustained a great loss, for there is no one at this time to take his place.[28]

Will Marion Cook

At the other end of the spectrum from Ernest Hogan in formal education and bearing, yet a person equally involved in the New York scene as well as Hogan's great friend, was the composer and conductor Will Marion Cook. Bob Cole, J. Rosamond Johnson, Williams and Walker, and most other performers of musical theater regarded Cook as a catalytic figure of the era. His training had been extensive, his instruction was inspiring, and his musicianship and conducting skills complemented the stage and business talents of Cole and Hogan. Alain Locke named Cook as one of the most important conductors of the period, and he was consistently cited by his contemporaries as a leader of black musical life.[29] Remarkably, although much of Cook's music is available and biographical material is accessible to scholarly research, scholars generally have overlooked his contribution.[30]

Cook was born on January 27, 1869, in a converted Army barracks behind Howard University in Washington, D.C. He was christened William Mercer Cook, changing his name during his college years. The son of college-educated parents—both Belle Lewis and John Cook had graduated from Oberlin College, and his father was the first dean of the Howard University Law School—Cook probably was expected after college to settle in the large and comparatively wealthy Washington, D.C., black community. But from the beginning Will was a feisty and spirited child, and when his father died from tuberculosis in 1879, Will became difficult. In 1881 he was sent to Chattanooga, Tennessee, where his mother hoped that the masculine and restraining influence of his grandfather William Cook would discourage Will's fighting. It did not. However, in Chattanooga he heard genuine black folk music for the first time and, like many before him, was enthralled.

Encouraged by his grandfather, who played the violin and clarinet, Will began to study violin, and about 1884 his mother sent him to the Oberlin preparatory school as a prelude to his entering Oberlin College. Cook eventually entered the College about 1886; his name is recorded on a few recital programs of that time. He studied violin with Amos Doolittle, who was impressed with the young man's progress. Feeling that a period of European study would improve his chances for a professional career, Doolittle encouraged Cook to audition for the famous German violinist Joachim, who was then teaching at the Hochschule für Musik in Berlin. The major obstacle to a European sojourn was, of course, lack of money. But with the assistance of Frederick Douglass, whose grandson was also an aspiring violinist, a benefit concert was arranged in the First Congregational Church in Washington for the young Cook.[31] He was featured in a recital that included the Mendelssohn Violin Concerto and the Wieniawski *Polonaise,* and the crowd—probably friends and well-wishers—was most generous. Nearly $2,000 was raised, quite enough to allow Cook to set out for Europe.

In his autobiography, Cook reports that despite a shaky audition Joachim recognized some spark of talent and accepted him for study. He remained in Europe for three years studying piano, harmony, counterpoint, and violin. He later continued his study of counterpoint with John White at the National Conservatory in New York. Cook returned to the United States apparently fit for a concert and orchestral career. He met with discrimination and frustration, and finally, during the 1890s, despite years of study Cook, to use James Weldon Johnson's phrase, "threw all these European standards over"[32] and began to pursue a career in popular music. He found his calling in teaching young show performers and stage managing, as well as accompanying at the keyboard and composing. He worked with Bob Cole and the All-Star Stock Company and briefly directed a band in Chicago,[33] but his major entrance into the public arena came with his summer entertainment, *Clorindy, or the Origin of the*

Cakewalk, offered as one of a series of late-evening presentations by Edward Rice on the roof garden stage of the Casino Theatre. The success of *Clorindy* gave Cook some encouragement after months of setbacks. For the next fifteen years he worked at writing music for other all-black shows, as well as an occasional libretto or set of lyrics. He assisted the famous Williams and Walker team on *Abyssinia* (1906), *Bandanna Land* (1907), and their greatest success, *In Dahomey* (1902). He supplied songs to many other shows—May Irwin sang Cook songs in *The Casino Girl* (1900) and *The Wild Rose* (1902); conducted and rehearsed many choral groups; and accompanied his wife, Abbie Mitchell, in solo song recitals. Cook also formed a publishing partnership with R. C. McPherson, the Gotham-Attucks Publishing Company. In 1904 Cook wrote the music for a large show with a racially mixed cast, entitled *The Southerners.* He had no great ability to manage money—his shows, like many others, frequently went into the red—and he possessed an easily ignited temper, but Cook was universally admired for his musicianship. He was involved in rehearsing virtually every large New York black show until 1915. In that year he contracted tuberculosis, the disease that had fatally stricken his father in middle age.[34] His activity declined, of course, but by 1918 he had organized his most successful project since the international tour of *In Dahomey* in 1903, the Southern Syncopated Orchestra, which toured in the United States and Europe until 1920.[35] Cook remained active after 1920 but never was so prominent as he had been in the early years. He continued to perform with Abbie Mitchell and in 1926 collaborated as lyricist with Vincent Youmans for *I'm Comin' Virginia.* He died in New York on July 19, 1944.

Will Marion Cook is perhaps the least recognized among the dominant figures of the era, and in view of his estimable musical accomplishments it is curious that he was so entirely eclipsed long before his death. The answer seems to lie substantially with Cook's personality, specifically his undisguised impatience, his fiery temper, and his occasionally overweening personal vanity. As bitterly as other black public figures may have complained in private about racial discrimination, most managed to achieve stolid and nonthreatening façades that helped them reach their goals in a white society threatened by the prospect of aggressive blacks. Cook developed no such façade. He had received cultured and humane treatment in Europe and refused to tolerate anything less in America. Faced with American prejudice and the normal frustrations and competitions of the professional music world, Cook became ever more suspicious of people's motives and more ill tempered. Cook was not a loner by nature, but he tended to isolate himself, often moving quickly to insult or call into question others' motives. He was bound to run into trouble in a business that relied heavily on personal contacts, friendship, and mutual trust. His experience with his first publisher, Isidore Witmark (as contrasted with Cole and Johnson's long, harmonious relationship with Marks and Stern), says much. Without evidence in hand he accused the publisher of cheating him of royalties for the songs in *Clorindy* after receiving less than he believed he was entitled to; the result was to alienate Witmark permanently.[36] He was not universally popular in his own black world because he assumed a superior mien that many Americans associated with alien European attitudes. Such a posture could work only with equally educated and cultured members of black society. But Cook's refusal to maintain a quiet, dignified, low profile did little to endear him to such high-caste blacks. In short, he catered and kowtowed to no one; hence no one went out of the way to boost him, although his talent was never denied nor credit withheld when credit was due. He succeeded because his talent was unimpeachable, even if he was regarded as eccentric. As the highly diplomatic James Weldon Johnson put it in a confidential letter, "he has many of those personal peculiarities and eccentricities which we, no doubt, ought to expect and excuse in original geniuses."[37] To Cook's credit he consistently encouraged young talent, and Eva Jessye (the choral director of Virgil Thomson's *Four Saints in Three Acts* and Gershwin's *Porgy and Bess*) and Duke Ellington, among others, fondly remembered their instruction in his company.[38]

Williams and Walker

The most famous black comedy team at the beginning of the twentieth century was that of Bert Williams and George Walker. In their heyday, from 1898 to 1908, and for years after, they were the standard against which other comedy acts were compared, and they inspired many imitators. Their success lay close to the heart of black musical theater because they sang and danced as well as acted and joked. Many full-length musical comedies were built around Williams and Walker by the talented team of Alex Rogers as lyricist, Jesse Shipp as stage director, and Will Marion Cook as composer.

Williams was born in Nassau, the West Indies, in November of 1874.[39] His family moved to Riverside, California, in 1885. Williams graduated from Riverside High School and briefly attended Stanford University. In order to raise money for college he tried his luck as an entertainer but never returned to school after the first year. Working in San Francisco in 1893 he met George Walker, a native of Lawrence, Kansas, who had worked his way west with a medicine show. The pair decided to join forces, with Walker doing the comedy and Williams acting as straight man and ballad singer. At that time they worked in street clothes without blackface makeup.[40] They remained in California for over two years and then gradually worked their way east, changed their act somewhat, and made the acquaintance of show producer Thomas Canary, who offered them work in a New York show. The team appeared in Victor Herbert's short-lived *Gold Bug* (1896), which led to a contract to play at Koster and Bial's Music Hall. Williams and Walker developed a popular cakewalk act, capitalizing on the great dance fad of the time, which garnered them sustained runs at the best New York halls. The cakewalk, a duple-time dance with simple syncopations, had appeared in the Harrigan and Hart shows, and it may have been performed in public even earlier. Billy McClain, for example, claimed that he had been "the first to put a cakewalk on stage, with the Hyers Sisters [in the 1870s?]. Then I called it a 'walk around.'" The roots of the cakewalk go back to plantation life, when slave couples competed for a cake or other prizes by performing high-stepping dances. But this dance was not to achieve widespread popularity until the early 1890s, when the dance team of Charles Johnson and Dora Dean thrilled audiences coast to coast and introduced it on Broadway in 1895 (or so Johnson claimed)—three years before Williams and Walker appeared at Koster and Bial's Music Hall with their version of the dance.[41]

In the autumn of 1898 Williams and Walker were invited to assume Ernest Hogan's starring role in the Eastern tour of Cook's *Clorindy*. The cast was expanded to include some sixty people, and the entire presentation was billed as the Senegambian Carnival.[42] The show failed and folded quickly, but the team's fortunes improved under the management of Hurtig and Seamon with a variety show entitled *A Lucky Coon* and more ambitious undertakings that included fuller plots, such as *The Policy Players* (1899), *The Sons of Ham* (1900), and *In Dahomey* (1902), their greatest success. Other later productions included *Abyssinia* (1906) and *Bandanna Land* (1907). Walker fell ill during the tour of *Bandanna Land* and left show business. Williams continued without him in *Mr. Lode of*

Egbert Austin "Bert" Williams, who achieved fame as a cakewalk dancer, then as the comic star of his own shows with partner George Walker, and finally as the only black comic in the Ziegfeld Follies. He was universally hailed as an outstanding entertainer. Schomburg Center for Research in Black Culture, the New York Public Library, Astor, Lenox, and Tilden Foundations.

Koal (1909) and then signed to appear with Florenz Ziegfeld's *Follies of 1910*, the only black member of the cast. Walker's death in 1911 ended any speculation about a revived partnership. Williams remained with the *Follies* until 1919, appeared with Eddie Cantor in *Broadway Brevities* in 1920, and opened in his last show, a Shubert production called *Under the Bamboo Tree*, in 1922. While on tour he contracted a cold that developed into pneumonia and, probably because he insisted on staying with the show rather than taking a proper rest, he collapsed onstage. He returned to New York by train and died on March 4, 1922.[43]

Williams was the most famous black performer, perhaps even the most famous black person after Booker T. Washington, of his day. His comic timing and mimic artistry were widely admired, and the accolades before and after his death consistently resorted to superlatives. It is only fair to note, however, that his fame was guaranteed partly because he elected to appear as the only black star in an all-white revue, a decision for which he received a certain amount of criticism in the black community. He was indisputably a superior performer, but blacks who knew the entire picture of black theater did not always place his talents above those of Ernest Hogan, the minstrel comedian Billy Kersands, or Bob Cole. George Walker's contributions to the musical comedies they did together should also not be underestimated. Walker was the idea man of the team. He devised the plots, and it was his scenic conceptions that were realized (in the case of *Abyssinia* quite extravagantly) onstage.[44] Williams and Walker truly were a team. Following Walker's death and the mixed success of *Mr. Lode of Koal*, Williams was forced to find a new direction, and Ziegfeld provided the best opportunity.

The shows of Williams and Walker, Cole and Johnson, and Hogan constitute the principal, although not the only, contributions to black American musical theater from 1898 to 1911. They were created in an urban environment that had supported a variety of earlier forms of entertainment catering to diverse audiences: minstrel shows, extravaganzas, farce comedies, and operettas. Shows multiplied rapidly, stimulated by a large pool of young black talent that found receptive managers like William McConnell and John Isham and strong leaders like Bob Cole and George Walker. Onstage, however, it was finally the music that put the shows over. The successive vogues for music related to blacks—jubilee songs, coon songs, cakewalks, and ragtime—fueled the success of black stage entertainments. Conservatory-trained composers Will Marion Cook and J. Rosamond Johnson picked up where the earlier minstrel and rag composers had left off. Moreover, from the 1890s on, the growing industry of Tin Pan Alley imitated and reproduced black-composed music in ever-increasing quantity. Given the critical role of music in black shows, it is necessary to examine a little more closely the repertoire of stage songs before considering the individual shows in which they appeared.

4

The Music in the Shows

The object of musical shows of the late nineteenth century was to entertain and soothe the "tired businessman," as writers of the day put it, not
necessarily to present a gripping or even an entirely coherent dramatic
work. The music that black composers (and many white composers) created to achieve this purpose in musical comedies generally consisted of an
overture, between ten and twenty songs, and a few dance numbers.
Programs show that music occasionally was played between the acts as
well, a common feature of many dramatic vehicles in more than one act.
The single song was the most important musical unit; composers usually
conceived of their shows as a series of songs, comic scenes, and tableaux
rather than as unified musical works in which songs bore a structural
relationship to one another. Songs were linked to the play insofar as they
appropriately matched the personas of the characters performing them,
but songs were not required to move the action forward. Moreover, many
songs were included in shows simply because the singer or the audience
happened to like them.

Popular songs had taken on a comparatively fixed and clear structure by the late 1890s. Form and melody in the songs were intimately connected, and the melodic organization determined the form of the individual piece. While the meanings of specific words were sometimes highlighted by accent or depicted by other details in the music, such emphases occurred within the regular poetic structure and seldom disrupt the four-measure phrase. Songs were not shaped to make dramatic statements; they were simply songs, lyrical outpourings in standardized forms, albeit with exceptions from time to time.

Among the three hundred-odd titles located for the shows considered here, about half of which have been collected, analyzed, and compared with a larger body of popular songs, the principal topics of the songs' lyrics are: the "coon" stereotype; romantic love; humorous love and the battle of the sexes; miscellaneous humorous subjects, including ethnic stereotypes and nonsense songs; evocations of nostalgia and the Old South ("good old" days and places); and the pathetic but often amusing sufferer of unremitting bad luck—a "Jonah man," to adopt the title of one such song as a rubric for all. All but the last of these topics was common in the larger repertory of American popular song. The Jonah-man song was the special forte of the influential performer Bert Williams; he wrote several, and other composers wrote songs in imitation of his style.

Lyrics

The use of language and tone varies with the different topics. Simple narrative lyrics with a specific complaint are used, for example, in Cole and Johnson's song for *Humpty Dumpty* (1904), "Man, Man, Man":

> Man! Man! Man! Man!
> He's been a bunch of trouble since the world began
> Man! Man! Man! Man!
> What's his use tell if you can?
> How does he figure in the universal plan?
> Take a look and when his performance you scan,
> You'll find that he is rated in the class of "Also ran";
> So what's the use of man?

Romantic verse tinged with dialect, sometimes tender, sometimes commonplace, appears in the Avery and Hart lyrics for "Down Among the Sugar Cane," sung in *Bandanna Land:*

Can't you see the night am falling?
Whippoorwill am singing low?
Don't you hear the crickets calling?
Calling you and me to go?
Susie don't keep me waiting;
If you do 'twill cause me pain.
The moon am shining and my heart am pining,
Meet me down among the sugar cane.

Crude punning appears in Bob Cole's song from *A Trip to Coontown*, "In Dahomey":

The rules of draw poker were written, you know,
In Dahomey
By an old drunken king called "chicken foot Joe"
In Dahomey
The king had three wives who made his life serene,
The king got drunk clubb'd his wives blue, black
    and green
And since then a king always beats three queens
In Dahomey, In Dahomey.

Roughly one-third of the songs are in dialect or slang suggesting dialect, but its use does not always coincide with the "coon" stereotype lyrics, which comprise only about one-fifth of the total number of songs. Paul Laurence Dunbar's lyrics for Will Marion Cook's songs in *Clorindy* have many earmarks of coon songs: chicken mania, fancy dressing, and generally raucous behavior:

Who dat say chicken in dis crowd?
Speak de word agin' and speak it loud
Blame de lan' let white folk rule it,
I'se a lookin' fuh a pullet
Who dat say chicken in dis crowd?

or

Behold the hottest coon,
Your eyes e'er lit on,
Velvet ain't good enough,

For him to sit on,
When he goes to town,
Folks yell like sixty,
Behold the hottest coon in Dixie.

The determining theme in many coon songs was a virulent, psychological one: all white things and persons were seen as good and all black ones as bad. That "coons" themselves should assert these sentiments of their own inferiority was a most sinister message, even if the singer was not actually a black person. But coon songs were not always pro-white formula pieces. Many contained topical humor that obliquely commented on the state of racial affairs. In "4–11–44," ostensibly about gambling, Bob Cole's lyrics speak to legitimate fears about street violence, express skepticism about the creation of a black police force, and joke about "coons" too hard to see in the dark:

Dey's gwine to be colored policemen, all over dey say
If dey do, it'll be [the] leading topic of de day,
I'd like to see colored people rise up to de mark,
But I'd rather not see a coon on de street or in a park,
For its hard enough to find a white policeman after dark.

Paul Oliver has pointed out that chicken songs easily could be used symbolically and should not be dismissed as mindless, stereotypical mimicry:

Though the "chicken" hunting and stealing subject of a song could be taken at face value, it was relatively easy for a singer to sing "I got chickens on my mind" with an ogling eye to any young women in the audience. To a predominately white crowd he could "play nigger" and satisfy their delight in the chicken stealing black simpleton; to a black audience he could lay more emphasis on harassment by the police or the successful duping of white people.[1]

"When the Chickens Go To Sleep," another song by Bob Cole, is easily interpretable in this context:

While the passengers are sleeping see a pullman porter creeping
When the chickens go to sleep

Ev'ry night he makes his ramble and beneath each pillow scramble
When the chickens go to sleep
A passenger meditating in his birth [*sic*] for sleep awaiting
A porter's hand slipped beneath his pillow shroud
The passenger rose kneeling grabb'd the porter and said "you're
  stealing"
But the porter said, "You mustn't snore so loud."
Chorus: When the chickens go to sleep
    Close their eyes in slumber deep
    Be careful 'bout de lock on your hen house door
    When the chickens go to sleep.

The broad lampooning style that found everything racial to be funny
typifies the 1890s coon song. Most of the vicious and violent elements
were discarded during the next decade, reflecting the largely successful
crusade by black lyricists, composers, and critics to mitigate the most
inflammatory aspects of an all-too-common song type.[2] Racial typing,
such as the use of dialect and the blanket attribution of certain traits to a
group, was not always seen as negative. It was rather the exaggeration,
caricature, and specific words like *nigger* and *coon*, that most offended.
The Williams and Walker songs before 1900, written by Williams and
Walker and R. C. McPherson (a.k.a. Cecil Mack), contain a large dose of
coon lyrics. In *In Dahomey* (1902), *Abyssinia* (1905), and especially
Bandanna Land (1907) and *Mr. Lode of Koal* (1909) the lyrics were more
sentimental and the humor less racially focused.

Of course, some of the writers of lyrics for show songs were not poets
with aspirations beyond the commercial. They sought out formulas that
were successful and that would sell to the expanding market of sheet-
music buyers. They composed "new" songs with the most current conventions in mind. Love songs and humorous songs were produced constantly, corresponding with the demand for and popularity of such songs.
That black writers retained the coon stereotype is not surprising, since
this kind of song was a successful commercial vehicle.

An exception among lyricists both in motivation and in poetic gifts was
Paul Laurence Dunbar, a writer esteemed among both whites and blacks
of his time and a sensitive imagist of many facets of black life. He had
been a bright and popular youth and had edited the school newspaper in a
white high school. As he grew older, he wrote constantly while support-

ing himself as an elevator operator and later as a library assistant at the Library of Congress. His first book of poetry, *Oak and Ivy* (1893), published at his own expense, received favorable notice from William Dean Howells; the critical acclaim that followed brought him into the public eye. He wrote several more books of poetry, some in dialect and some not, as well as four novels. He died of tuberculosis in 1906 at the age of only thirty-four.[3]

Dunbar, while a good writer, was not the first black dialect poet, and by choosing to work in that medium he took on a ready-made set of restrictions. James Weldon Johnson, a friend of Dunbar's, remarked, "Not even he had been able to discard those stereotyped properties of minstrel-stage dialect: the watermelon and the possum." Dunbar himself was conscious of the limitations of the use of dialect and complained to Johnson in 1901, "You know, of course, that I didn't start as a dialect poet. I simply came to the conclusion that I could write it as well, if not better, than anyone else I knew of, and that by doing it I should gain a hearing. I gained a hearing, and now they don't want me to write anything but dialect."[4]

The lyrics of Bob Cole and the Johnson brothers after 1900 are even further removed than Dunbar's from the coon style. By emphasizing fun and love rather than racial self-hate, tension, rowdiness, buffoonery, or violence, Cole and the Johnsons created songs for any genteel, middle-class parlor—black or white. Some songs, such as "The Congo Love Song" or "Sugar Babe," got away from coon images entirely, though retaining dialect and some references to Africa:

> As long as the Congo flows to the sea,
> As long as the leaf grows on the bamboo tree
> My love and devotion will be deep as the ocean;
> Won't you take a notion to love-a but me?

> Sugar Babe, you sho' is sweet,
> Yes, sweeter dan de pie called "minces meat";
> Apple dumplin' Angel cake
> I'm gwinter give 'em all up, love, jes' for your sake;

As one biographer of James Weldon Johnson has pointed out, "Johnson sought an empathy with their predominantly white listeners by emphasizing experiences and emotions common to the human race, and not those supposedly limited to blacks. Johnson's lyrics were not especially original, but it was innovative to imply that both whites and blacks experience the same romantic emotions the same way."[5] The observations apply to the words of Cole at this period and later as well. The direct, simple, and universal sentiments of the lyrics account in some measure for the sustained popularity of the Cole and Johnson Brothers team.

Many lyricists of the other black shows in the decade from 1900 to 1910 followed Cole and Johnson's lead. Lester Walton's lyrics for *Rufus Rastus* (1905) and Henry Creamer's for *The Oyster Man* (1907), for example, are unmarked by caricature of black life, although "Contribution Box" in the latter show makes a black preacher the butt of a prank, a satirical element not unknown to minstrelsy. In W. D. Hall's lyrics for two songs in *Rufus Rastus*, chickens, razors, and watermelons still are present. After 1900 Walton, Creamer, and Alex Rogers (1876–1930), the lyricist for the later Williams and Walker shows, relied heavily on more generally humorous, sentimental, or Jonah-man lyrics.

Tunes

Melodically, the show tunes show a symmetry and regularity of phrase structure and a diatonic idiom. Melodies tend to be constructed in four- and eight-measure phrases, and they favor stepwise motion. They keep to the middle range of the voice and are primarily syllabic and declamatory, allowing for clear pronunciation of the words. The parlando style of most melodies is neither marked by accents nor fragmented by rests. The chromatic vocabulary consists mainly of unaccented upper and lower neighbor notes. Syncopated motives often contain such inflections. Notes sharped or flatted to preserve a real melodic sequence in adjacent phrases or motives and occasionally notes sharped to serve as leading tones in modulatory gestures also appear. Except for an infrequent use of the pentatonic mode or gapped scale to support an oriental or jungle motif, exotic scales do not appear.

All of the songs begin with a piano introduction. Most continue with a verse comprising two or three stanzas of text, each followed by a chorus or refrain of equal length. A significant majority of the songs retain a thirty-two-measure verse (eight-plus-eight-plus-eight-plus-eight) and a thirty-two-measure refrain, although irregularities of length occur more often in the verse than in the refrain. Occasional extensions of one, two, or four measures occur at cadences. Unlike minstrel show songs, seldom is a concluding dance refrain marked in the music. Perhaps it was assumed less often that singers were "song-and-dance" men, as had generally been the case with minstrel and vaudeville entertainers of earlier years.

Certain types of musical organization seem to have been preferred for the verse portions of the songs. Approximately half of the songs in the sample analyzed begin with a four-measure phrase repeated exactly or only slightly varied, followed by a contrasting block of four or eight measures (AABC). AABA and ABAC patterns (normally in eight-plus-eight-plus-eight-plus-eight groupings) account for another quarter of the total, the remainder being through-composed, narrative-style verses or slightly more varied, extended, or truncated combinations of the basic forms.

In the refrains the ABA'C form is most common, followed by the ABAB pattern. Refrains typically do not have the same form as their accompanying verse, nor do they often present the same melodic material as their verse. The shorter the refrain, the more likely it is to be through-composed, and shorter refrains almost always accompany songs of a comparatively early date. In nineteenth-century popular song, verses often were longer than their twentieth-century counterparts; their tune was more important than that of the refrain. As Charles Hamm has suggested, this is not the case with the popular songs of the 1890s and later, in which the refrain is remembered as the real tune of the song. Modern renditions of such tunes often dispense with verses.[6] In five of the eight songs examined in *A Trip to Coontown*, the earliest of the large black shows, the verse is longer than the chorus. In no other show does the verse outlast the chorus in even half of the songs.

The songs show a preference for keys with few accidentals, over half the songs being in G, F, or C. Flat keys dominate the tonalities, with E♭, B♭, and A♭ following next in order of popularity. In the absence of a significant number of performing parts, it is impossible to know if the written keys of the songs were in fact the keys in which they were performed. Virtually all of the songs are written in major keys and use mainly triadic harmonies built on the first, fourth, and fifth scale degrees. Sections in the minor mode and occasional harmonic digressions of three or four measures occur in middle-refrain phrases and verses, especially in Jonah-man songs. Chromatic passing chords—characteristic barbershop harmonies—can be found in several tunes.

Stock harmonic figures, such as drone fifths and ostinati, support Indian and African references. Exotic harmonic devices like polytonality are not found, and complex counterpoint is not a significant feature.

Nine-tenths of the songs are in some duple or quadruple meter exclusively. In about one song in ten, the meter changes at the beginning of the refrain. The three-quarter-time waltz, a tremendously popular dance in the nineteenth century, appears only infrequently in these stage works, although popular acclaim of *The Merry Widow* (1907), with its famous waltz, doubtless led to the unrecorded interpolation of waltzes into several shows. The "Merry Widow Waltz" itself appeared in at least one Williams and Walker vehicle, *Bandanna Land*. In February 1908 the *New York Times* reported: "the 'Merry Widow' waltz, of course, was not forgotten, but was done with dash and spirit."[7] Apparently its inclusion was not considered odd or inappropriate.

Syncopation was a topic of interest for many contemporary critics writing about the black shows, and indeed the wide use of syncopated tunes is a distinguishing feature of several black shows. As Charles Hamm and others have pointed out, syncopation is an idea in need of clarification in discussions of coon and ragtime songs. In addition, it is not always clear that writers about the black shows had a specific idea about what they meant by syncopation, either. An occasional simple syncopation, a short–long–short series (♪ ♩ ♪) occurs in many tunes that are not strictly derived from black sources. For purposes of this discussion, *submetric syncopation* refers to a syncopated treble melody set against an unsyncopated bass, with no bass note simultaneously struck at the time of the offbeat accent in the treble (see Example 4.1).

Edward Berlin also has attempted to clarify the idea of syncopation in ragtime. He observes that early rags heavily favored "untied syncopations" (𝄴 ♫ ♩ ♫) which generally occurred on the first beat of a measure.[8] Syncopation of some kind occurs in about half of the songs under consideration, but only in the works of Will Marion Cook do the number of regularly submetric, syncopated melodies outnumber those that are not syncopated. Ernest Hogan employed simple syncopations and a few submetric syncopations, but the device is by no means pervasive in his songs. Bert Williams embraced easily swaying rhythms that complemented his texts, and syncopation is seldom found in his songs unless the word accent suggests it. There is no continuous and little

Example 4.1. Simple and submetric syncopation

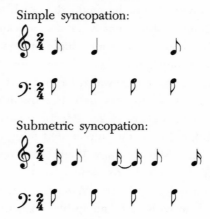

Simple syncopation:

Submetric syncopation:

submetric syncopation in Cole's songs in *A Trip to Coontown*, and Cole and the Johnson brothers' later use of the submetric style is not as frequent as Cook's, although several instances occur in conjunction with the kind of chromatic half-step motion illustrated in Examples 4.2, 4.3, and 4.4. The musical novelty of the black show songs, the trait that caused listeners to sit up and take notice, was this combination of syncopation with melodic chromaticism. These syncopated, chromatic tunes deviated significantly from most popular music at the turn of the century and from show music in particular.

The foregoing discussion of tune structure and style assumes a close relationship between songs as they were printed and songs as they were performed. This might not have been the case for nineteenth-century minstrel pieces, as has already been mentioned, and it is well to keep a caution in mind for later repertories even where a composer is clearly identified on the page. The extant sound recordings of Bert Williams, the only black singer and composer of the period to have recorded several

Example 4.2. Bob Cole and J. Rosamond Johnson, "There's Always Something Wrong" (New York: Jos. W. Stern & Co., 1907), verse, mm. 1–4

I've _____ found out _____ dat dere ain't an - y use to wor - ry, __

Example 4.3. Chas. A. Hunter, Bob Cole, and James Reese Europe, "Ada, My Sweet Potater" (New York: Jos. W. Stern & Co., 1908), chorus, mm. 1–4

A - da, _____ sweet - er dan a sweet po - ta - ter _____

_ Dat ev - er grow'd _____ up - on _____ a de vine

songs onto wax, suggest an inexact correspondence at best between printed and sung versions of his tunes.[9] Although his name appears on the cover, he may have had little or nothing to do with notating his own songs, or may have simply viewed the printed notes as rough approximations—an attitude entirely consistent with that of performers in many other musical traditions. A rare recording of a Williams and Walker duet, "My Little Zulu Babe" from *The Sons of Ham* (1900), features wailing by Williams (Zulu cries? horses neighing?) and a growling male chorus as background to Walker's more or less faithful rendition of the printed tune. These tantalizing fragments suggest the existence of an oral style about whose details we can only speculate.

Ernest Hogan and Bert Williams, songwriters less trained as musicians than as stage performers, seem to have been primarily concerned with communicating the humor of their lyrics to the audience. Their printed songs' focus on declamation rather than harmonic or rhythmic novelty (some highly striking chords and piano accompaniments notwithstanding)

Example 4.4. Cecil Mack and Will Marion Cook, "Brown-Skin Baby Mine" (London: Keith, Prowse & Co., 1903), chorus, mm. 1–8

She ain't no vi - o - let, _____ She ain't no red, red rose _____ An tho' the

li - ly _____ of de _____ val-ley's sweet, _ She's sweet-er _____ yet I _____ knows,

underlines this concern. In contrast, Will Marion Cook—a trained conservatory musician—employed syncopation consistently in vocal lines and heightened its impact with his harmonic skill and ear for musical variety. Indeed, Cook's harmony is especially remarkable, and his skill is uniquely impressive. Secondary dominants, subtle modal gestures intended to obscure key identification, chromatic alterations, and augmented sixth chords are well-integrated into his style. He often used nonharmonic tones and shifting harmonizations of repeated melodic motives.[10] He neither avoided dialect nor sought to expand the basic eight-plus-eight-plus-eight-plus-eight measures into new forms in most of his songs. However, in his connecting together of his songs and in his choral writing Cook had a knack for climactic effect akin to that found in the operetta finales of the time. Rosamond Johnson, the best pianist of the

Example 4.5. Bob Cole and J. Rosamond Johnson, "Pathway of Love" (New York: Jos. W. Stern & Co., 1908), mm. 28–35

group and the arranger of most of the songs in the Cole and Johnson brothers' collaboration, also speaks a sophisticated harmonic language and varies his forms more often than the others, although his rhythmic settings are rarely as striking or as markedly syncopated as Cook's. The general style of several of Johnson's songs suggests the cultivated flow and the high-toned romantic sentiments of some operetta tunes. Charles Hamm has observed that the songs of Reginald De Koven and Victor Herbert epitomize this style, and Hamm's description of De Koven's "O Promise Me" (1889) could serve equally well for "The Big Red Shawl" or "The Pathway of Love" in *The Red Moon* (see Example 4.5): "The vocal line rises to small climaxes in each phrase with the final large climax—the point to which the entire song has been moving—reserved for the end of the last phrase, where the singer has a fortissimo high note supported by a thickened accompaniment and a crashing dynamic level."[11] Johnson's songs lack the extended chromaticism of popular art songs like Tosti's "Goodbye" (Example 4.6) or Nevin's "The Rosary,"[12] although, like these favorites, Johnson's piano accompaniments often are challenging and complex.

The songs of Cook, Hogan, Williams, and Johnson share many features

Example 4.6. F. Paolo Tosti, "Goodbye!" (1881), beginning

in common: a preference for major keys, thirty-two-measure diatonic melodies, the symmetrical verse-chorus form, and the general orientation of lyrics towards love, humor, and black life. In these respects they might appear to be indistinguishable from the larger body of American popular songs and not strongly tied to African traditions or other Afro-American forms. However, a sample of about eighty songs by white show composers from 1891 to 1906, collected from sheet-music archives and anthologies, reveals more clearly the correspondences and differences between the two bodies of songs. They are most similar with respect to key distribution, formal patterns (particularly the ABAC refrain), and the use of triadic harmonies. They contrast most strongly with respect to textual themes, meters, and melodic syncopation. The songs by white composers contained few Jonah-man lyrics, included waltzes much more frequently (accounting for a greater number of pieces in three-quarter time), and seldom introduced syncopated, chromatic tunes.

The distinctiveness of the black melodic idiom within an otherwise familiar style explains in part why songs by black composers have been reckoned among the most popular at the turn of the century. Isidore Witmark and Isaac Goldberg include Cook and Dunbar's four hits from *Clorindy*, "Darktown is Out Tonight," "Who Dat Say Chicken in This Crowd," "Jump Back, Honey," and "Hottest Coon in Dixie," in their list of "song successes" out of a total of twenty-two for the year 1898. E. B. Marks published several popular Cole and Johnson numbers, including "My Castle on the River Nile," "Congo Love Song," and "The Maiden with the Dreamy Eyes"; Marks states that he "witnessed and fostered the first mass invasion of the amusement world by colored America." Compiler John Chipman noted seventeen songs that sold over 100,000 copies in 1901, and six of these were written by black composers; of the twenty-four top sellers in 1902, four were written by blacks. Considering that black people numbered roughly ten percent of the American population in 1900, sheet-music sales point to a disproportionately strong impact by black composers. Add to this that all of the songs included in these statistics were sung in musical comedies, and a strong case can be made for crediting black composers with bringing syncopated song to Broadway and thereby injecting a kind of metrical flexibility into our stage music that it has never lost. Songs from the black shows included many of the most popular songs of the era, establishing that black musicians had a substantial role in the creation of what Charles Hamm has called "traditional music" in America—music from the first twenty-five years of Tin Pan Alley.[13]

Cook and Johnson's syncopated melodies captured the hearts of audiences, and the sounds of ragtime can be detected in the black shows, yet the most sophisticated writer of ragtime piano pieces, Scott Joplin (1868–1917), who resided in New York after 1907, never became part of the theatrical life of the city. Joplin's name is conspicuous by its absence from theatrical news throughout the period from 1890 to 1915. Although Joplin spent time performing on the road from 1907 to 1909, when he finally settled down he attempted to transmute his fame as a ragtime composer into that of a successful theatrical one. It never happened. Years of effort put into *Treemonisha,* completed and published at his own expense in 1911, finally ended in failure. A studio production pitifully achieved in modest circumstances in 1915 was almost completely ignored. Joplin's skill was and remains as an instrumental composer, and the recent revivals of *Treemonisha* notwithstanding, he cannot be assigned a major role in the development of black theater music.

Imitation, Quotation, and Cross-Fertilization

No style or genre in popular music could be isolated from all others, and the amount of borrowing and imitation was considerable. Tunes by Victor Herbert and George M. Cohan, songs from minstrel shows, piano ragtime, and numbers from the English musical stage all were heard by the theatergoing public as well as by young composers hopeful of writing the next hit. These styles influenced black show songs in various ways. Gilbert and Sullivan's popularity encouraged an interest in operetta in the 1880s, and English musicals, such as *A Gaiety Girl* (1894) and *Floradora* (1900), remained popular throughout the 1890s.[14] Rosamond Johnson's indebtedness to operetta already has been suggested.

Some examples of musical imitation were much more apparent. Tune fragments from familiar sources were borrowed so frequently that one can almost speak of "quotation" songs as a musical genre among Tin Pan Alley works.[15] "Yankee Doodle Dandy," by George M. Cohan, which includes parts of "Yankee Doodle," "The Star-Spangled Banner," "Dixie," and

"The Girl I Left Behind Me," and "Alexander's Ragtime Band," by Irving Berlin, containing parts of "Old Folks at Home," are only two of the most famous. The success of Cohan's "You're a Grand Old Flag" in *George Washington, Jr.* (1906) stimulated borrowing of its material; Ernest Hogan's "Cockadoodle Doo" (1906), from *Rufus Rastus*, concludes similarly with a quotation from "Auld Lang Syne." The first few notes of the chorus in "Yankee Doodle Coon" (1907) by Will Vodery, used in *The Oyster Man*, follow the same contour of the refrain of "You're a Grand Old Flag." The lyrics of the refrain are close to those of "Yankee Doodle Dandy":

> There's just one thing in my noodle,
> Get the boodle, get the boodle,
> I am a Yankee Doodle Coon.

"Yankee Doodle Coon" also quotes Foster's "My Old Kentucky Home" as well as "Yankee Doodle." Three Bert Williams songs from *Abyssinia*— "Where My Forefathers Died," "The Tale of the Monkey Maid," and "Rastus Johnson U. S. A."—quote, respectively, "My Old Kentucky Home," Mendelssohn's "Wedding March" from *A Midsummer Night's Dream*, and "The Star-Spangled Banner."

Also common was the use of a melodic formula or motive similar to a current, commercially successful song. Apparently both black and white writers participated in this type of borrowing. David Kempner and Bert Williams's "Late Hours" from *Bandanna Land* and Gus Edwards and Will Cobb's "School Days," both published in 1907, have strikingly similar refrains. One seemingly owes a melodic debt to the other, but it cannot be known with certainty which came first (see Example 4.7).

Widespread text imitation is suggested by a cover advertisement prepared for the Cole and Johnson song "M'aimez Vous?" (1910). The publisher, Joseph Stern, declares:

> Cole and Johnson claim and it is a well-known fact they have originated every vogue or cycle in the evolution of ragtime.
> When they wrote "The Maiden with the Dreamy Eyes" for Anna Held, the success of this song was followed by thousands of similar "eye" songs. When they wrote "Lazy Moon" for George Primrose and "Nobody's Looking But the Owl and the Moon" for Christie

Example 4.7. David Kempner and Bert Williams, "Late Hours" (New York: Gotham-Attucks Music Co., 1907), chorus, mm. 1–4

McDonald, two melodies destined to live as long as any of Stephen Foster's, they started the countless "moon" songs. When they wrote "Under the Bamboo Tree" for Marie Cahill, they were followed by other composers with myriad "tree" songs. When they wrote "The Congo Love Song," they started a rage for "jungle" songs, and now that they are the first to put out their so-called Franco-American song "M'aimez Vous?" ("Do You Love Me?") we shall no doubt find a host of imitators closely following or trailing after this style of love ditty.[16]

Even recognizing the advertising hyperbole, we can still accept the general comment on me-tooism among popular song composers; it is easy enough to demonstrate. Cole and Johnson themselves borrowed when it suited their purposes. A large number of songs on the lore of American Indians appeared in the 1900 decade, among them Harry Williams and Egbert Van Alstyne's "Navajo" (1903), James T. Brymn's "Rowena" (1904), Thurland Chattaway and Kerry Mills's "Red Wing" (1907). In 1909, Cole and Johnson capitalized on this theme in *The Red Moon*, which took up the adventures of black and Indian characters. Featured songs were entitled "Bleeding Moon" (about an Indian curse), "Big Red Shawl" (an Indian love song), and "Life is a Game of Checkers" (that is, a mixture of red and black).[17]

Outright parody of popular songs can also occasionally be found in the black show songs. Rosamond Johnson wrote "Tell me, Dusky Maiden," calling it a "travesty" on the song "Tell Me, Pretty Maiden" by Leslie

Stuart, which was featured by the Floradora sextet in 1900.[18] Johnson included bits of melody and slightly different words from the original song, in addition to incorporating several other musical quotations: parts of Hogan's "All Coons Look Alike to Me," Williams and Walker's "If You Love Your Baby, Make Them Goo Goo Eyes," and his own "If Dat's Society, Excuse Me." Johnson's tune was included in the Cheever Goodwin-John J. McNally show *Sleeping Beauty and the Beast* in 1901, the year following *Floradora*'s New York opening.

Interpolation

In the 1890s and continuing into the twentieth century, many singers arbitrarily interpolated songs with little or no relation to the plot into a musical show. The practice of interpolation mutually benefited both composers and performers. Established singers gave young writers a hand up, and good songs helped to enhance the career of their singers. The list of songs and shows into which they were interpolated, Appendix A, represents only a small sample collected from reviews and sheet-music covers and unquestionably includes only a fraction of the total number of songs used in this way.

Of white composer Charles Hoyt's highly acclaimed show *A Trip to Chinatown* (1891), Gerald Bordman has observed:

> Another illustration of the era's freewheeling practices occurred when road companies were sent out. While the first of the touring companies was in Milwaukee, Charles K. Harris' "After the Ball" was added and soon became one of the show's musical numbers wherever the show was performed. . . . It was easy to insert and remove songs. For the most part the lead-ins were so generalized that with few exceptions . . . almost any song might have followed. . . . A simulated "coon" song, "Push Dem Clouds Away," is sung after Uncle Ben says, "I want you four young people to get round the piano and sing me my favorite quartette." And even though "The Widow" fits logically into the plot, the song is actually brought up by Wilder's comment, "That's a great song Billy Parker wrote and dedicated to her." In short, there were still some instincts prompting librettists to look at songs as extraneous, something to be kept formally apart.[19]

This state of affairs undoubtedly was true for several of the black shows of this period. One of the stage directions in the first act of *In Dahomey* uses a song simply to allow actors to enter and exit. The character Stamp's exit is followed by the note "(Bus., enter Quartette singing 'Annie Laurie' cross stage exit and let singing die out by degrees)." Another character, Reeder, then comments, looking towards them, "Well, that's a jolly crowd." Obviously, almost any song could fit here. In scene 3 of *Abyssinia* the following dialogue leads to the song "Where My Forefathers Died":

> Elder Fowler: You are suffering from nostalgia.
> Aunt Calley: I ain't sufferin' from nothin', much less the disease you're talkin' about, Elder Fowler.
> Elder Fowler: I mean you're homesick.
> Aunt Calley: Well, why didn't you say that at first? Yes, I'm homesick. I'm just naturally full of memories of the South.[20]

Given the many well-known songs on the Old South/nostalgia theme, a willful singer could regard Aunt Calley's line as an open invitation to perform any number of pieces other than the one indicated in the libretto. Such loose construction lent musical theater a flexibility that furthered the careers of many black songwriters.

Well-known actresses such as May Irwin and Marie Cahill favored the songs of Hogan, Cook, and Cole and Johnson and included them in their shows. Songs that a popular singer plugged in this way often sold better in sheet-music form. E. B. Marks relates in his memoirs his many evenings spent convincing even beer hall singers to include newly published songs in their acts.[21] Apparently the show business mogul Abraham Erlanger first noticed the talents of Cole and the Johnson brothers through the interpolation of the team's song "Run, Brudder Possum, Run" in *The Rogers Brothers in Central Park* (1900), a show composed mostly by others. Erlanger subsequently signed the writers to a highly favorable contract and provided them the experience of composing for several major white Broadway shows.[22] Another frequent interpolation by this team was a series of six songs entitled collectively "The Evolution of Ragtime," composed originally for the purpose of "tracing and illustrating Negro music through its various forms down to the present:" African chant, plantation song, black dance music, minstrel song, instrumental folk music, and ragtime.[23] A descending-second-plus-descending-third motive and the rhythmic idea ♪ ♪♫♫♪ | ♪ ♪ appear in several of the tunes in a variety of guises (see Example 4.8). In addition to this unifying device, several quotations reinforce the generic connections. "Darkies Delight" (No. 4) quotes the Sam Lucas minstrel song "Carve Dat Possum." The sentimental plantation number "Echoes of the Day" (No. 2) quotes Foster's "Old Folks at Home," and "The Spirit of the Banjo" (No.

Example 4.8. Bob Cole, James Weldon Johnson, and J. Rosamond Johnson, "The Evolution of Ragtime" (New York: Jos. W. Stern & Co., 1903), excerpts

No. 1 "Voice of the Savage," introduction

No. 2 "Echoes of the Day," introduction

No. 4 "Darkies Delight," introduction

No. 6 "Sounds of the Times," introduction

5) imitates the banjo strumming with arpeggiated chords in a striking verse that repeats the same phrase at four different pitch levels.

The interpolation of two Cole and Johnson songs into the white show *The Little Duchess* (1900) suggests that their songs appealed to audiences for purely musical reasons; they contained extra touches that went beyond simply providing dialect material. In the first song, "Strolling Along the Beach," the ocean's roar is boldly painted by a piano tremolo in the bass as it moves in fleeting waltz time; in the second, "Sweet Saloma," a variety of changing tempos and expression marks combine with clever doublings of the voice in the middle register of the piano to provide a sonorous, Brahmsian effect.

Ernest Hogan's songs were interpolated into shows as early as 1896, when May Irwin chose to do "All Coons Look Alike to Me" in her vehicle *Courted into Court* (which also included the hit, "Mr. Johnson, Turn Me Loose" by ragtime pianist Ben Harney). Irwin also used Hogan's dance song "La Pas Ma La" in another show, *By the Sad Sea Waves*; set in a lunatic asylum, it also included a medley from *The Mikado* as well as some ragtime numbers.[24] Several songs by Chris Smith, R. C. McPherson, and Will Marion Cook appeared as interpolations in shows of the first decade of the twentieth century.

Singers' interpolation of songs into already complete shows raised the hackles of composers during the first years of the 1900s. In particular, Marie Cahill's addition to *The Wild Rose* (1902) caused the first of many such stirs in her career. As Bordman tells it:

> Over the authors' objections and their threats of suits, George Lederer the producer allowed Marie Cahill, as an "aeronaut's lady friend," to interpolate "Nancy Brown," a song by the young writer, Clifton Crawford. . . . *The Evening Telegraph* recorded "Miss Cahill made the hit of the evening with 'Nancy Brown' song" and the *Herald* counted six encores. Since so many other tunes were incorporated into the show, it is hard to determine why there was so much fuss over this one song in particular. If the whole thing was not a publicity stunt, then Harry B. Smith and Ludwig Englander were the very first artists to tackle the problem head on. Until this time only Victor Herbert, Julian Edwards, Reginald De Koven and, apparently, John Philip Sousa had been forceful or prestigious enough to demand contracts that barred other men's songs from being inserted into their shows.[25]

Cahill, having worked her will in *The Wild Rose*, interpolated Cole and Johnson's "Under the Bamboo Tree" into *Sally in Our Alley* (1902). In her next show, *Nancy Brown*, Cahill retained "Under the Bamboo Tree" and added in another Cole and Johnson number, "The Congo Love Song," reportedly keeping it in for over one hundred performances.[26] "The Hottentot Love Song," an obvious imitation of the Cole and Johnson hit by Benjamin Burt and Silvio Hein, two white composers, was added to Cahill's 1906 show *Marrying Mary*, as was the R. C. McPherson-Chris Smith tune "He's a Cousin of Mine." On at least one occasion the producer as well as the composer of a show was challenged. Virginia Earle threatened to walk out of her 1902 show when the producers balked at her attempt to use Cole and Johnson's "The Maiden with the Dreamy Eyes."[27]

Musically, there is no marked difference between the interpolated songs by black composers and the songs composed specifically for the shows of the 1900s featuring all-black casts. Both groups have the same melodic, rhythmic, and formal features and retain the same predominance of humorous, nostalgic, and romance-related texts. Of course, fewer songs in shows with white casts were about black social aspirations—such as the hit of *Rufus Rastus*, "Say, Wouldn't That Be a Dream"—and there was an overall decrease in the interpolation of coon songs of the 1890s type, which had emphasized farcical and violent caricatures.

Neither relevance to plot nor musical consistency with the rest of the songs in a show seemed to trouble producers or stars if they believed they had a hit tune to present. Nor did the audience seem to mind, either. But the composers of musical comedy often wanted to preserve the integrity of their music. The problem of interpolation, if a problem it was, was eliminated for those performers who wrote and directed their own shows; for them, of course, any addition by the performer would have been sanctioned. This essentially is what took place when Williams and Walker, Cole and Johnson, and Ernest Hogan began starring in shows they had also written.

With adequate and occasionally outstanding training and business support in New York, black musicians produced large numbers of popular songs throughout the decade from 1898 to 1908. Using elements of both novelty and conventionality, they sought to address a general audience and also to include the special new audience of theater-going blacks. They were not radicals or propagandists, but along with most urban Americans they were tired of the clichés of blackface minstrelsy and sought to vary the familiar song formulas. They knew that the best way to get new songs to the public was on the stage, preferably in a hit musical show. However, filling in the other elements—details of dramatic dialogue, stage movement, set building, costumes, and lighting—and covering the attendant costs required organizational and fundraising talents beyond the ability to write songs or to sing and dance in public. Fortunately, Bob Cole, George Walker, and Ernest Hogan, while allied with musical friends, demonstrated those talents. Most of the remainder of this book is devoted to examining the syntheses of music and comedy they created.

2

The Shows and
Their Songs

5

"Musical Interruptions and Occasional Specialties," 1898–1902

A Trip to Coontown

Bob Cole and Billy Johnson developed *A Trip to Coontown* as part of a "declaration of independence" by black actors from the financial domination of the Black Patti Troubadours' white managers. It was written by August 1897 and was given a trial run in South Amboy, New Jersey, on September 27, 1897. This modest venture, with only eighteen in the cast, probably was underwritten out of Cole's pocket and the purses of supportive friends aware of his reputation as a skillful vaudeville entertainer. Details of the show's early history are given in William Foster's theater memoir:

> When "A Trip to Coontown" was ready for the road the [syndicate] managers dealt Cole another blow. They had already passed the word that any performer who signed up with the show would be boycotted for life. Now they informed [individual theater] managers that any house booking "A Trip to Coontown" could not expect any other colored show. This threat closed practically every important theater in

the country to Cole and his followers, and the show was "driven into the woods."

After months of terrific "wild catting" the company finally wandered into Canada and obtained a broken date in Ottawa and another in Toronto. Fortunately the American managers had overlooked the Canadian field when they issued their boycotting and lockout orders. The daily papers of the Dominion raved about the novelty of the show and managers began to bid for bookings. When news of the success of the show drifted back to the States, Klaw and Erlanger defied the lockout order and booked the company into Jacob's Third Avenue Theater during Holy Week, the worst week of the year. Nevertheless, crowds were turned away at every performance.[1]

Lester Walton, theater critic of the *New York Age*, confirms the rocky beginnings of the show and its subsequent success: "The *A Trip to Coontown* company had the distinction of doing something unusual in show business—playing the worst houses in every city its first year and playing the best houses the next," returning as it did to play New York's Casino Roof and the Grand Opera House in 1899 after more touring.[2]

The musical and textual components of *A Trip to Coontown* are highly diverse. The *Dramatic Mirror* reported that "the comedy has a well-defined story," which would have set it apart from many musicals of the day; the charge of dramatic weakness frequently was leveled at musical comedies. Nevertheless, the program for the New York performances refers to "musical interruptions and occasional specialties," and the *Dramatic Mirror* notes that "most of the songs have already become popular and were applauded vigorously," suggesting that the show grew up around the songs and not the other way around. That may not necessarily imply dramatic weakness, but it does indicate that the show's success depended on factors other than the story.

The program for *A Trip to Coontown* at its Third Avenue Theatre opening described the show as "the Roaring, Racy, Rollicking Musical Comedy . . . supported by a select company of Colored Artists," and, while small, the cast was experienced. The *Dramatic Mirror* commented, "The company has not one poor performer among its members. The two stars, of course, carried off the honors. Bob Cole as a tramp was fully as good as any white comedian whose specialty is this style of eccentricity.

Billy Johnson as the bunco steerer acted with spirit and sang well."[3] Cole's comic acting as tramp character Willy Wayside set the tone onstage. Tom Brown, a specialist at impersonation who had appeared in many traveling shows, impressed critics in a detective role that enabled him to assume numerous disguises—as rube, Italian, Oriental, and Jew. Lloyd G. Gibbs was the featured male singer; his billing as the "Black Jean De Reszke," after the European tenor, illustrates the vogue among critics, managers, and even performers for using famous European names as sobriquets for American singers (the "Black Patti," Sissieretta Jones, and "the Bronze Melba," Mamie Flowers, followed a similar practice). The singing of veteran minstrel man Sam Lucas in subsequent seasons became another featured attraction.[4]

New York audiences were large and responsive. A show with an all-black cast was considered a novelty, although, as Gerald Bordman has noted, "it created no stir on Broadway." The company toured for at least three years outside of New York. A Boston review that appeared in February 1900 waxed enthusiastic: "Far and away the most satisfactory extravaganza, white, black, or flushing pink, seen in Boston this season was *A Trip to Coontown.*" The writer continued with a highly detailed and provocative description of some of the action:

> The Africans do not often bring forward the women in the fun-making. But this troupe had Carter and Hillman, the lady in which firm mimicked the typical Bowery girl with gum and a jersey. Her partner sang an irresistible new "tough" ditty with rhymes so strong that he could jerk out every syllable hard and fierce. During this the ferocious pair pursued strong men and police, who fled at their threatened approach.
>
> The Freeman sisters abandoned the grace and joy of their native dancing, and formed a style mixed with the idiotic acrobatic of white dancers and contortionists; thus doth civilization ruin the blithe freedom of them that it absorbs.
>
> The first act ended with the most astonishing demonstration of the facility with which the African face can be made to represent other dark-skinned races. It was an elaborate ballet. Four misses looked and acted more like Japanese girls than most white chorus girls in comic opera. A group of men made perfect Arabs. Three more girls were vivid Egyptians, with sinuous suggestion. Two men represented

> Chinamen. One group was of Spanish girls. All of these were
> remarkable in their way, and interesting food for reflection. The
> costuming was rich and tasteful, and the dancing pretty and vivacious
> in a manner not specially recalling the usual ragtime steps.[5]

The comment on the limited participation of women serves as a reminder that black theatrical entertainment up to this time had consisted almost exclusively of the male-dominated minstrel shows. The vogue for "tough ditties" by female singers was created around 1890 by Ada Lewis in a Harrigan and Hart show, *Reilly and the Four Hundred,* and she had several imitators, black and white, in the following decade. Criticism leveled at the Freeman sisters reveals a recurring concern of white critics that black performers not stray too far from what was perceived as their proper domain, "their native dancing." It is seldom possible to determine whether the critic has expectations other than the buck-and-wing and the cakewalk of minstrelsy, although, interestingly enough, here the white products ("idiotic acrobatic") are judged inferior. The final comment about dancing "in a manner not especially recalling the usual ragtime steps" hints that the other dancers were attempting something more original, or perhaps less familiar, than the normal buck-and-wing. Marshall and Jean Stearns, in *Jazz Dance,* pass on the eyewitness account of Noble Sissle that in *A Trip to Coontown,* "the customary cakewalk was omitted."[6]

The popularity of *A Trip to Coontown* is explained only partly by the merits of the show and the performers; it also coincided with the advent of syncopated and ragtime music—and by association other black acts and music—as popular forms. Ben Harney's piano playing first impressed New York audiences in early 1896; in the summer of 1896 Oscar Hammerstein presented "The Creole Nightingale," singer Rachel Walker, at his new Olympia Roof Garden; and the introduction of ragtime songs by white singers like May Irwin brought ragtime influence to Broadway later that year. Cakewalk finales, long featured in minstrel shows and popular with black companies of the early 1890s, were included in a large white show, *Yankee Doodle Dandy* (1898). Bordman points out that by the fall of 1898, "ragtime was sweeping the musical stage. Every loosely structured musical that could incorporate a ragtime tune did so. Even sedate comic operas were soon to capitulate." The music of *A Trip to Coontown* was slightly syncopated, although it had no separate pieces of piano ragtime. Nevertheless the apparent link between black performers and the new black musical style must have aided Cole and Johnson.[7]

Clorindy, or the Origin of the Cakewalk

In the summer following *A Trip to Coontown*'s first New York appearance, Will Marion Cook's skit *Clorindy, or the Origin of the Cakewalk* scored a triumph in the heart of Broadway. Cook himself described the origin of *Clorindy* and its arrival at the corner of Thirty-ninth Street and Broadway, the Casino Theatre Roof Garden:

> On Monday morning, in answer to my call, every man and woman, every boy and girl I had taught to sing my music was at the Casino Roof. . . .
> Luckily for us, John Braham, the English conductor of the Casino orchestra, was a brick. And still more luckily for us, Ed Rice the manager did not appear at rehearsal that morning until very late. When Braham had finished with the smaller acts, he turned to me questioningly. There I sat, orchestra books in hand. In two minutes I told him how I studied violin under Joachim, a bit of composition under Dvořák, harmony and mighty little counterpoint under John White. I explained that I had some new music, a Negro operetta. Right then he stopped me, turned to his orchestra men and said: "Gentlemen, a new composer!" He held out his hand for my orchestra parts. Again I got his ear and told him that my singers understood my direction, they understood my gestures and that I was afraid. . . . He again turned and announced: "Gentlemen, a new composer and a new conductor."

When the show reached the stage in an 11:15 p.m. performance, Cook described the impressive finale executed by only twenty-six people: "My chorus sang like Russians, dancing meanwhile like Negroes, and cake-walking like angels, black angels! When the last note was sounded, the audience stood and cheered for at least ten minutes."[8]

Clorindy appeared in the heyday of the roof garden phenomenon that had started in the 1880s. In these venues, late-night summer entertainments following main-stage productions presented New Yorkers with the latest theatrical novelties. The Casino Roof, ideally suited for dance and spectacle although acoustically inferior, and hence disadvantageous for shows with much spoken dialogue, proved an excellent host for the forty-five-minute show. Apparently little if any of a libretto allegedly written by Paul Dunbar was used. Despite Cook's reference to his "operetta," the dramatic structure of *Clorindy* was unremarkable.[9]

Critically, the show was a success. White patrons of the Casino Roof hailed the singing and dancing of Ernest Hogan, a figure already popular in vaudeville and now esteemed for this additional triumph. The *New York Times* termed the show's reception "sensational." Edward Rice, who at first had opposed even the idea of a black man conducting his orchestra, immediately moved to include more black material on his various vaudeville bills. James Weldon Johnson said of touring show producer and theatrical experimenter George Lederer that he

> learned new things [from *Clorindy*]. He judged correctly that the practice of the Negro chorus, to dance strenuously and to sing at the same time, if adapted to the white stage would be a profitable novelty; so he departed considerably from the model of the easy leisurely movements of the English light opera chorus. He also judged that the injection of Negro syncopated music would produce a like result. Mr. Lederer was at least the grandfather of the modern American musical play.[10]

If this is true, perhaps Cook deserves to be called the great-grandfather. Oddly enough, Cook's name did not appear in the *Dramatic Mirror* reviews of the show (although Dunbar's did), and his presence aroused few comments except by the theatrical professionals, such as Lederer and Braham, who witnessed the show.

After opening in New York, *Clorindy* played throughout the summer at the Casino, took on Williams and Walker to replace Hogan, and toured briefly and unsuccessfully. The Madison Square Roof Garden and Koster and Bial's Music Hall followed the Casino's example in short order. Koster and Bial's brought in Bob Cole, Billy Johnson, and the Freeman Sisters to do summer-season acts in 1898, and Charles Johnson and Dora Dean presented their cakewalk duet there in the following year.[11]

The Policy Players
Probably as an attempt to capitalize on the novel attractiveness of *A Trip to Coontown* and extend the ideas used in the summer shows, Bert Williams and George Walker embarked on their own all-black cast comedy, *The*

The Casino Theatre, whose Roof Garden was the site of Ernest Hogan and Will Marion Cook's successful late-night show *Clorindy, or the Origin of the Cakewalk* in the summer of 1898. Theatre Collection, Museum of the City of New York.

Policy Players. This "musical farce comedy" opened at the Star Theatre, at the corner of Broadway and 13th Street, on October 16, 1899. Originally called *4–11–44*—a winning lottery combination ("policy playing" today would be called playing the numbers)—the play involved the masquerade of a newly rich gambler, Dusty Cheapman (Williams), as the Ex-President of Haiti attending a party of the black elite, part of a scheme devised by man-about-town Happy Hotstuff (Walker). An elaborate second-act party scene followed for the insertion of comedy business and musical numbers. Williams and Walker were the principal musical and dramatic attractions of the show. Hurtig and Seamon, burlesque-house owners who catered to the black population of New York, produced *The Policy Players*. Williams wrote most of the songs, William Tyers did the published arrangements, George Walker wrote the book, and Jesse Shipp served as stage director.

When the show played at Koster and Bial's in April 1900, it was recognized for the personal vehicle it was. The *New York Times* reported, "The farce-comedy has little to do with policy playing, but serves as an excellent means to present Williams and Walker about whom are surrounded a large company who indulge in solos, duets, acrobatic feats, yarn spinning and negro eccentricities." All parts of the show were considered amusing. One Boston reviewer remarked that the show was "ambitious in a musical way," a perception formed perhaps by the skills of Will Marion Cook, who conducted the orchestra, or the talents of the stars, Williams, Walker, and Aida Overton (1880–1914). Williams's almost spoken singing accompanied by vivid facial expressions and pantomimic skill were "much in demand," and the company provided entertainment that lasted for "more than two hours." The show toured into the summer of 1900, when plans began for their next project, *The Sons of Ham*.[12]

The Sons of Ham

Williams and Walker toured for two seasons in their second large production, and Hurtig and Seamon again sponsored the show. In New York it had two week-long bookings in the Grand Opera House, at Eighth Avenue and Twenty-third Street, and at Hurtig and Seamon's Music Hall. Steve Cassin and Jesse Shipp provided the book, although the scenario apparently changed several times throughout the two-year run. Shipp did the staging.

The production included several vaudeville specialties, notably the celebrated Reese Brothers acrobatic act, a dozen musical numbers, a concluding transformation scene for the first act evocative of an African jungle, and a "cake ballet" (a cakewalk) as a finale. Aida Overton (recently married to George Walker), Alice Mackey, and the all-male Golden Gate Quartet sang; George Catlin did his Chinese imitation; and Williams and Walker stole the show. At least six composers contributed the music: Will Accooe, Tom Lemonier, Joe Jordan, J. Rosamond Johnson, Bert Williams, and J. T. Brymn.[13]

Descriptions, critiques, and reviews of these four early shows reveal several similarities among them. All of the shows focused on a star player or duet, and the principal players were surrounded by a supporting cast of diverse talents: impersonators, dancers, singers. Though sometimes referred to as musical comedies, their plots were of little significance. A

Williams and Walker in front of a painted flat that served as a set for *The Sons of Ham* (1900). Photograph by Byron, the Byron Collection, Museum of the City of New York.

Trip to Coontown was termed an extravaganza, *The Policy Players* a farce-comedy. *The Sons of Ham* was praised for presenting "every phase of vaudeville entertainment." What they were called was evidently less significant than what they were: fast-paced variety shows packed with action, humor, coon songs, and other sorts of syncopated music.

The Songs
Some of the most striking songs in *A Trip To Coontown* are those seemingly linked to somewhat rough music-hall pieces. The bouncy tune and mildly suggestive text of "La Hoola Boola," for instance, obviously inspired the college fight song "Yale Boola" (see Examples 5.1, 5.2):

> A Boston girl will treat you nice if you've money
> Sing a Hoola Boola Hoola Boola Hoo
> And a Philadelphia girl will call you honey

Example 5.1. A. M. Hirsch, "Yale Boola" (New Haven: Chas. H. Loomis, 1901), chorus, mm. 1–8

Example 5.2. Billy Johnson and Bob Cole, "La Hoola Boola" (New York: Howley Haviland and Co., 1897), chorus, mm. 9–16

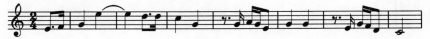

> Sing a Hoola Boola Hoola Boola Hoo
> A girl from Chicago will beseech you
> A girl from Washington will impeach you
> But a New York girl will always want to teach you
> A thing or two 'bout Hoola Boola Hoola Boola.

"In Dahomey," a clever waltz song in five verses (without refrain), jokes about a mythical Dahomey that resembles a one-dimensional racist's view of blacks in America—a view that Cole and Johnson ridicule in this circuitous way. It contains a topical reference to the sultry white Ziegfeld Follies star Anna Held taking pictures of amusing natives, and the lyricists allude to Ernest Hogan's popular song when they slyly declare Dahomey "the only place on earth where all coons look alike."

Bob Cole and Billy Johnson wrote at least one coon song for *A Trip to Coontown* as a vehicle of protest. In "No Coons Allowed" (Facsimile 5.1), the injustice of Jim Crow exclusion is the unambiguous message. The text, about a young man taking his girl out on a date, must have related an all-too-familiar experience:

> He put her in a cab and told the driver
> "To drive us to the swellest place in town
> I'm gwine to buy my gal a fine supper
> So I want the finest place that can be found."
> To a swell restaurant the driver took them
> With his Lulu gal he started in so proud
> But that coon almost went blind
> When he saw a great big sign
> Up o'er the door which read "No coons allowed."

This number has a slightly syncopated chorus typical of the early ragtime song. Another song with only two syncopated measures, "I Wonder What Is That Coon's Game," also appeared in the show. It was popular enough to have been recorded almost thirty years after it was written, and long after the composer's death, as "The Mysterious Coon" by Alec Johnson, a performer whose own identity is somewhat mysterious. [14]

In *Clorindy* all five songs utilize dialect and coon song stereotypes in their lyrics, but Dunbar's poetic lilt and Cook's rhythmic assertiveness convey a gritty vitality. The verse of "Darktown," for example, bubbles with joy:

> Clear de paf! Needn't laf,
> Dat'll be all right!
> White fo'ks yo' Got no sho'!
> Dis huh's Darktown night.

All the songs are pervasively syncopated in their up-tempo choruses and so, as Cook implied, reflect the novel popular music style of that day. The shift from a leisurely $\frac{6}{8}$ meter to a highly syncopated $\frac{2}{4}$ in "Hottest Coon in Dixie" (Facsimile 5.2), for example, must have especially quickened the pulses of listeners, but each song's verse in this show contrasts effectively in mode, meter, tempo, and melodic contour with its chorus.

In *The Policy Players* many of the songs that critics declared to be hits dealt with familiar text themes: Bert Williams sang about fear of ghosts in "Ghost of a Coon," George Walker portrayed the urban dandy in "Broadway Coon," and Aida Overton Walker brassily rendered "I Don't Like No Cheap Man." This last song represents a large family of song texts about money that both black and white lyricists wrote around 1900. Perhaps the widespread use of the topic symbolizes especially clearly the change in popular-music themes from the late nineteenth to the early twentieth century—a trend away from sentimental parlor songs and antebellum "darkey" nostalgia to tougher, cockier material sought by vaudeville and variety shows.

Similar melodic motives composed of rocking half-step and whole-step intervals unite many of the songs in *The Policy Players* (Examples 5.3–5.6). Although the melodic ideas are not highly distinctive (and hardly

Example 5.3. Bert Williams and George Walker, "Why Don't You Get A Lady of Your Own" (New York: Jos. W. Stern & Co., 1898), chorus, mm. 1–4

Why don't you get a la - dy of your own_____

Example 5.4. Bert Williams and George Walker, "I Don't Like No Cheap Man" (New York: Jos. W. Stern & Co., 1897), chorus, mm. 1–4

She said, "I don't like no cheap man Dat spends his mon-ey on de 'stal-ment plan"

Example 5.5. Edward Furber and Bert Williams, "He's Up Against the Real Thing Now" (New York: Jos. W. Stern & Co., 1897), chorus, mm. 9–12

I carv'ed dem in de East, and I shot dem in de West. But I'm

Example 5.6. Bert Williams and George Walker, "The Ghost of a Coon" (New York: Jos. W. Stern & Co., 1900), verse, mm. 9–10

I was strut - ting home dis morn - ing 'bout three bells_____

could be construed as attempts to create a larger structural unity in the show), they nevertheless reveal the stock elements that song composers used to begin, complete, or extend a simple melodic phrase. The middle range and syllabic text presentation common to all these excerpts were well-suited to the delivery of a declamatory text.

As in *A Trip to Coontown*, in *The Sons of Ham* the songwriters addressed the black audience directly. The period was witnessing a massive black migration from the South to the North. When Aida Overton Walker sang her big number, "Miss Hannah from Savannah" by Tom Lemonier and R. C. McPherson, she undoubtedly struck a familiar note. It depicts a proud Southern girl who ventures north with suspicion but uncowed by regional and class distinctions. The verse is a brief narrative:

> Up from the land of the fragrant pine,
> Came a dusky maiden to the Northern clime;
> She told all her friends, Ah's gwine to see
> The diff'rence in the sassiety
> Ah's heard so much 'bout their high-toned ways,
> 'Bout dem actin' more like white folks ev'ry day,
> If dey tries to come it on me too gran'
> Ah'll tell 'em who I am—

The chorus proclaims joyfully, "My name's Miss Hannah from Savannah, Ahm some blueblood ob de land-ah!" The show also contained a non-dialect but still slightly syncopated love song by R. C. McPherson and J. T. Brymn, apparently an interpolation since it was not included on the printed program. "Josephine, My Jo" (Facsimile 5.3) features a chromatic turn that ornaments the melodic descent to each cadence (not yet a cliché of popular music). Williams's song "Fortune Telling Man" takes up an item of black folklore, humorously describing a conjuror. A series of melodic intervals in it convey a whiff of the black spiritual "Who Dat Comin' Ovah Yondah" (Examples 5.7 and 5.8). Resemblances between popular songs and the older traditions were not unusual; at least a few songs show in their melodies clear relationships to specific spirituals.[15] Another song about doctors, but doctors of a less awesome sort than the traditional fortune-telling man, is "Phrenologist Coon," with words by Ernest Hogan and music by Will Accooe. The pun-filled text mocks the pretensions of a quack who says, "By just feelin' in your pocket, I can tell what's in your head." It was sung by Williams, whose familiar droll delivery guaranteed its full satirical effectiveness.

"My Castle on the Nile," one of the Cole and Johnson brothers' all-time hits, was published in 1901 (probably having been composed in 1900 or early 1901) and was interpolated into the "second edition" of *The Sons of Ham.* The song's persona, who warns "dere ain't no use in tryin' to rise up in de social scale 'less you can trace yo' name back to de flood," discovers he has illustrious African ancestors and vows to return to his "castle on the river Nile." The verse is supported musically by the clichés of jungle

Example 5.7. "Who Dat Comin' Ovah Yondah," mm. 1–4

O, _____ who dat a - com - in' o - vah yon - dah

Example 5.8. Bert Williams and George Walker, "Fortune Telling Man" (New York: Jos. W. Stern & Co., 1901), chorus, mm. 1–4

I am dat for - tune tell - ing man

depiction—a minor key, drone fifths, and pulsating eighth-notes. In contrast, the chorus, the most familiar part of the song, uses a compact, mildly syncopated motive placed firmly in G major. The dialect lyrics are buoyant and humorous:

> In my Castle on the river Nile
> I am gwinter live in elegant style
> Inlaid diamonds on de flo'
> A Baboon butler at my do'
> When I wed dat princess Anna Mazoo
> Den my blood will change from red to blue
> Entertaining royalty all the while
> In my Castle on the Nile.

A clever compositional touch, and a characteristic indication of the care J. Rosamond Johnson took in composing, appears in mm. 1, 3, 9, and 11 of the chorus, in which a brief chord progression from "Su! del Nilo al sacro lido," a chorus from Verdi's *Aïda* about the River Nile, is approximately quoted (Examples 5.9 and 5.10). Although it can be argued that this use of a bass descent through the submediant is a perfectly normal way to harmonize the melody of three repeated notes and that no quotation need be assumed, it is also true that Johnson, as an accomplished art-song singer and graduate of the New England Conservatory, was familiar with *Aïda* and may even have had it in mind, since a Conservatory classmate of his, Louise Homer, was preparing at this very time to make her New York Metropolitan debut as Amneris in the opera.[16]

Example 5.9. James Weldon Johnson, Bob Cole, and Rosamond Johnson, "My Castle on the River Nile" (New York: Jos. W. Stern & Co., 1901), chorus, mm. 1–2

Example 5.10. Giuseppe Verdi, *Aida* (1871), "Su! del Nilo al sacro lido," beginning

The shows and songs written from 1898 to 1902 exhibited initiative and energy on the part of their black creators and reflected their growing confidence that moneyed whites would support the talents of black performers. Hurtig and Seamon found it wise to invest in Williams and Walker without insisting on artistic control of the results. Bob Cole and the Johnson brothers were steadily providing successful songs sung by leading singers in major shows.

But musical comedies with all-black casts were more visible to the white public than starring duet acts or composers and lyricists who worked behind the scenes, and so the step up to full-length shows was indeed a significant achievement.

Audiences responded favorably to the black casts, and the shows played to both black and white as well as some integrated houses. One major barrier remained, however: Up to 1902, no identifiably black musical comedy had played on the main stage in any important Broadway house. This changed with Williams and Walker's next and most famous show, *In Dahomey*.

6

On Broadway, 1903–1905

In Dahomey

On February 18, 1903, a major Broadway theater hosted for the first time a full-length black musical comedy. *In Dahomey* opened at the New York Theatre, between Forty-fourth and Forty-fifth Streets on Broadway. A cast of fifty, headed by Williams and Walker, was featured in three continuous acts and with expertly arranged contemporary popular music. *In Dahomey* had toured for seven months before arriving in New York, where it played for fifty-three performances. The show was more dramatically coherent than the earlier vaudeville medley shows, and it carried Williams and Walker to the height of their fame. The Williams-Walker-Shipp-Rogers-Cook coalition that had created *The Policy Players* and *The Sons of Ham* shaped this show as well. Hurtig and Seamon provided $15,000 to mount it and ultimately made a three hundred percent profit on their investment.[1]

In the play, the two leading characters, Rareback Pinkerton (Walker) and Shylock Homestead (Williams), become involved in a scheme to

George Walker, usually photographed in fashionable
dress with hat and cane, in "native" costume for *In
Dahomey.* Yale Collection of American Literature,
Beinecke Rare Book and Manuscript Library, Yale
University.

defraud would-be African colonizers and in particular their rich leader,
Mose Lightfoot (William Barker). When it turns out that the slow-witted
Homestead is actually far wealthier than the old man, his partner manages to extract enough money to put himself into elegant clothes and get
elected governor of Dahomey. After rollicking adventures and uncomfortable setbacks abroad, the pair, with their colonial entourage, decides to
return to America.

A complete piano score—the only one of its kind for an American black
show in this period—was published when *In Dahomey* toured in En-

gland, providing an unusually complete picture of the musical items used in the show, including the climactic choral numbers that repeatedly impressed critics in this and other shows (see Figure 2).

A prologue set in Dahomey "three months before the beginning of the play" features a song by Frank Williams and J. Leubrie Hill entitled "My Dahomian Queen." The chorus melody is built around ascending and descending seventh chords and triads in combination with a few well-placed syncopations—a pleasant and structurally typical tune. A pentatonic melody with a pulsating drone constitutes the music for the "Caboceer's Entrance," the second musical item of the prologue, performed in a scene designed to create the mood for a trip to Africa. A resonant chorale, "Brightest Vision of the Morning," a paean to the caboceers (governors), concludes this section.

The big opening chorus of act I, "Swing Along!" (Facsimile 6.1), is a vigorous number with two basic musical ideas, both syncopated:

The first sixteen measures put the first motive into a familiar four-times-four-measure phrase structure; all four phrases are closely related. They are followed by the second theme in a sixteen-bar refrain that is repeated. Fourteen of the first opening measures return, and a harmonically varied repeat of the second theme follows. Eleven measures of a climactic, rhythmical treatment of the first theme precede a fortissimo conclusion.

The choral effect must have been impressive. Long after *In Dahomey* closed, "Swing Along" was programmed on choral concerts by Cook and others. Dunbar's dialect text added to the urgent impact of the syncopation:

> Swing along chillun, swing along de lane
> Lif yo' head and yo' heels mighty high.
> Swing along chillun, 'taint agoin' to rain
> Sun's as red as de rose in de sky.
>
> Come along Mandy, come along Sue
> White fo'ks a watchin' an' seein' what you do
> White fo'ks jealous when you'se walkin' two by two
> So swing along chillun, swing along chillun, swing along.

Fig. 2. Synopsis of musical material in complete score, Will Marion Cook's *In Dahomey*

Page #	Titles	Lyricists, Composers*
1	Overture	
17	No. 1, Song. "My Dahomian Queen"	
		Words by Frank B. Williams
		Music by J. Leubrie Hill
22	No. 2, Chorus. "Caboceers Entrance"	
	Act I	
29	No. 3, Opening Chorus. "Swing Along"	
37	No. 4, Song. "Molly Green"	
		Words by Will Marion Cook and Cecil Mack
43	No. 5, Song. "On Broadway in Dahomey Bye and Bye"	
		Words by Alex Rogers
		Music by Al. Johns
	Act II	
51	No. 6, Song. "I Wants To Be A Actor Lady"	
		Words by Vincent Bryan
		Music by Harry Von Tilzer
57	No. 7, Song. "Brown-Skin Baby Mine"	
		Words by Cecil Mack and Will Marion Cook
63	No. 8, Song. "Leader of the Colored Aristocracy"	
		Words by James Weldon Johnson
70	No. 9, Solo and Chorus. "Society"	
83	No. 10, Song. "I'm A Jonah Man"	
		[Words and music by] Alex Rogers
89	No. 11, Chorus and Solo. "The Czar"	
100	No. 12, Song. "On Emancipation Day"	
		Words by Paul Laurence Dunbar
110	No. 13, March. "On Emancipation Day"	
116	No. 14, Cakewalk. "Chocolate Drops"	
121	No. 15, Jig.	
126	No. 16, Cakewalk. "Happy Jim"	
		[Music by] James Vaughan

*Unattributed numbers are presumably by Cook.

The sentimental waltz-time ballad popular in the nineteenth century was preserved in *In Dahomey* in "Molly Green." Using neither dialect nor syncopation, Will Marion Cook produced a number very different from the swinging tunes of *Clorindy* or even the other songs of *In Dahomey*.

The concluding tune for act I, with music by Al Johns rather than Cook, was entitled "On Broadway in Dahomey Bye and Bye." This pleasant, humorous number recounts the transformation anticipated when the erstwhile colonizers arrive in Africa ("You'll see on sides of rocks and hills, 'Use Carter's Little Liver Pills' "). It contains no dialect and adds only an occasional syncopation. Both verse and chorus are based on the same quarter-note ascending scale motive (B to A in the key of G).

An extremely jaunty tune, Harry Von Tilzer's "I Wants to Be a Actor Lady," was only one of several numbers interpolated from time to time into performances of the show. Von Tilzer, a well-known white composer, was at the height of his fame as a songwriter for Tin Pan Alley in 1903. Profits from his most famous piece, "A Bird in a Gilded Cage," had enabled him to establish his own publishing house in 1902. He did not usually write for Broadway, but this number showed his understanding of the striking syncopated element in the new black style. Programs from a variety of performances show that no fewer than two dozen songs besides those listed in the English piano score occasionally were included, a remarkably high number even considering that interpolation was commonplace. It appears that the creators were almost continually adapting the show to suit different audiences or perhaps to surprise return customers.[2]

Cook's song "The Little Gypsy Maid" (Facsimile 6.2) had been used in a musical in 1902, when Marie Cahill interpolated it into *The Wild Rose*. With a new text it became "Brown-Skin Baby Mine." Following *In Dahomey* it remained one of Cook's most performed works. A gently swinging piece, it achieves its melodic distinction by a combination of half-step motion and leaps by fourths and sixths within an alternately rising and falling line. It is a sentimental love song in dialect and with more than the normal dose of poetic freshness:

> She ain't no violet,
> She ain't no red, red rose

An tho' the lily of de valley's sweet
She's sweeter yet I knows.
She ain't no tulip rare
Nor mornin' glory fine;
But 'mongst de flowers fair kaint none compare
With brownskin baby mine.

Fig. 3. Structure and table of motives for Will Marion Cook's "Society"

[$\frac{4}{4}$ meter key of a/A]	Intro. (instr.)	Verse (solo)	Refrain (solos + chorus)	Verse (solo)	Refrain (solos + chorus)
(total mm.)	5	16	8	16	8
		A	B	A	B'
	"Recita-tive"		[quasi-recitative]		
			(solo + chorus)	(solo)	(chorus)
	8		5	6	6
			transitional material based on A&B		

[$\frac{3}{4}$ meter key of B♭]	Verse (solo)	Verse (duet)	𝄆 Refrain (duet) 𝄇	Refrain (duet + chorus)	(instr.)
	16	16	16	16	6
	C	C	D	D'	

The lettered motives begin their respective lettered sections above. Each of the motives is distinct from the others, but within each 16 measure group there is a high degree of interval and phrase repetition. B' is partially derived from B through melodic inversion.

"The Leader of the Colored Aristocracy" describes the colonizers' scheme to raise the social-class consciousness of the Dahomians, and analogously "Society" discusses how to achieve a better social position at home. The latter piece is the most extended number of the show, approaching at times operatic dimensions. It is a long sectional piece with several

Example 6.1. Will Marion Cook, "Society" (London: Keith, Prowse & Co., 1903), recitative

changes in tempo, meter, and texture; once again Cook displays his knack for grand choral effect enhanced by harmonic fluidity and melodic variations of repeated tunes. It also contains eight measures of recitative in a melodramatic opera parody. Its complete textural and harmonic dimensions are sketched in Figure 3.

The piece contains two large sections, each with solo verses and choral refrains. These sections are connected by a long transitional section of twenty-six measures featuring both a solo recitative (Example 6.1) and a quasi-recitative by the chorus, together accomplishing the harmonic movement from the opening key of A major to the second key of B♭. The strong preparation of B♭ and the concluding chorus in that key lead to final phrases, marked "much slower" and *molto pesante,* in which the soloist's high B♭ reinforces the grandiose effect (Example 6.2).

Example 6.2. Will Marion Cook, "Society/Love is King" (London: Keith, Prowse & Co., 1903), conclusion

"I'm a Jonah Man," words and music by Alex Rogers (the lyricist for several other Williams and Walker songs), was one of Bert Williams's most popular hits. Harmonically it is among the most novel in the repertory. The verse in the minor mode is rare, although slightly more common in sad songs of this type ("My hard luck started when I was born . . ." the song begins). But the poignantly funny tag line, "They named me after Papa and the same day Papa died," is underlaid with a rich progression that includes a rare and surprising 7–6 suspension (Example 6.3).

The chorus in F major is through-composed, yet each phrase connects well to the following one. Its last phrase contains a repeated melody note with changing chords that gives extra impetus to the final sforzando in the next-to-last measure (Example 6.4).[3]

"The Czar" is an extended sectional piece like "Society," essentially an ABA form of fifty-three, sixty-two, and fifty-three measures, respectively. Again, in "The Czar" Cook shows how to create climactic effects and continuous music from a relatively small amount of basic material (see Figure 4). Section a^t retains the words and rhythm of a but is texturally expanded with the addition of female voices and is harmonically varied leading to a repetition of a in four parts, retaining the melody in the tenor. A five-measure tag, labeled *Maestoso*, concludes both a^2 sections. Both the chorus and verse are syncopated, but the song otherwise is unified with the sevenfold repetition of the refrain text and tune. The

Example 6.3. Alex Rogers, "I'm a Jonah Man" (London: Keith, Prowse & Co., 1903), verse, mm. 13–16

They nam'd me af - ter   Pa - pa and the _ same day Pa - pa   died.

Example 6.4. Alex Rogers, "I'm a Jonah Man" (London: Keith, Prowse & Co., 1903), chorus, mm. 13–16

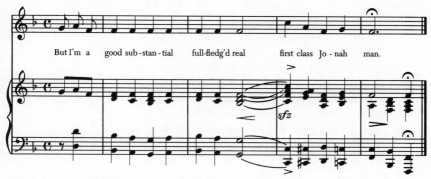

placement of the verse text so clearly in the center of things and the unusual ternary organization distinguish this song from other popular titles in this period.

The dialogue preceding the song refers to a portrait identified as the Czar of Dixie, but the comment about it is tangential and has no special significance in the plot. The Czar is not a character in the show. The song seems dramatically inessential, yet it is one of the longest numbers in the

Fig. 4. Structure and table of motives for Will Marion Cook's "The Czar"

$\frac{2}{4}$ meter	Intro.	Refrain	Refrain	Refrain	
key of D	(instr.)	(male chorus)	(full chorus)	(full chorus)	(chorus)
	8	16	16	16	5
		a	a^t	a^2	extension

"Moderato"	Intro.	Verse		Refrain	Verse	
	(instr.)	(solo)	(instr.)	(solo)	(solo)	(instr.)
	6	16	4	16	16	4
		b		*a*	*b*	

	Refrain	Refrain	Refrain	
	(solo)	(full chorus)	(full chorus)	(chorus)
	16	16	16	5
	a	a^t	a^2	extension

show, and its retention for the English tour suggests that it must have been well received. The gist of the text, stated in the verse, is:

> There's a man who's mighty grand
> Who rules supreme in Dixie Land
> He's the President, the Mayor and the Governor,
> He's the citizen's private counselor,
> You will find if you engage him in a social chat,
> He's a gentleman, a scholar and a diplomat,
> 'Mongst the leaders of the race he is the brightest star,
> And throughout the whole of Dixie he is called the Czar.

In "Emancipation Day" Cook again highlights the energy of Dunbar's text with persistent syncopation, economical motivic construction, and melodic chromaticism. The ragtime tune, the exuberant tempo, and the kick at white folks in the text ("On Emancipation Day all you white fo'ks clear de way") recall Cook's *Clorindy* hit, "Darktown is Out Tonight."

Many of the songs in *In Dahomey* are well integrated into the fabric of the play. The musical numbers sometimes serve to introduce characters—the Caboceers in the Prologue or the Florida "girls" in act II, for example—or situations that call for comment. Dreams of African building projects prompt "On Broadway in Dahomey Bye and Bye"; a reference to a "gentleman down in Cheaterville dat can find royal ancestors for anybody dat got $50.00 to spare for his trouble" leads to "Evah Darkey Is A King." "Society" is an extended conversation in music among three characters, Pansy Lightfoot, Hamilton Lightfoot, and Leather, and the chorus. Part of the Williams and Walker formula was to include at least one example from several familiar perspectives: In *In Dahomey* the Jonahman song was "I'm a Jonah Man," the song knocking the black upper crust was "The Leader of the Colored Aristocracy," the song focusing on race-building optimism was "Emancipation Day," and the love song—for black lovers especially—was "Brown-skin Baby Mine."

In Dahomey's indebtedness to nineteenth-century minstrelsy can be seen in the first act, which begins with a "crowd assembled around a fakir." The stage directions continue: "Applause at rise of curtain. Banjoist, tambo and bones tell one or two jokes, Banjoist acting as interlocutor sings song, then Fakir addresses crowd." Dr. Straight, the

Fakir, then gives a traditional stump speech—a mélange of puns, mal-apropisms, doubletalk, and bombast characteristic of hundreds of min-strel openings.

The *New York Times* praised the show, although the novelty of the production's location in the New York Theatre seems to have impressed the critics most. Williams won praise for "his electric connections with the risibilities of the audience." "The show as a whole," the writer con-cluded, "was well up to the not very exalted average in this kind of show." The reviewer noted, "The book was well above the average, for it was, in its main outlines, an admirably conceived satire on racial foibles that gave scope to no little fun in the picturing of character types."[4] It was ethnic humor in a posh setting, and everybody likes that sort of thing, the critic seems to say. The racially diverse though segregated New York audience reportedly enjoyed the show and gave it many ovations.

In April 1903 the cast boarded the S. S. Urania bound for London and began a run that eventually took them to Buckingham Palace. The show had achieved only modest success at its nightly performances at the Shaftesbury Theatre when a presentation was requested for the birthday party of the young Prince of Wales. The royal family was amused. After such recognition, the attention and attendance of London society were assured.

English audiences, presumably quite familiar with American blackface minstrelsy, nevertheless found the show peculiar in some respects. One critique, entitled "The Strangeness of 'In Dahomey,' " ran:

> From a casual glance at the notices we had vaguely supposed *In Dahomey* to be like any other "musical comedy" save in the complexion of its performers; and it was in an idle kill-time mood we visited the Shaftesbury Theatre. We found something quite unexpected; a new aesthetic "thrill," the fascination of the beautiful-uncanny, and a widening in the world of the horizon of the humorous. Here, indeed, was *aliquid novi ex Africa* [something important and new from Africa]. Since the Japanese performances of *Sada Yacco* we had seen nothing so curiously disquieting as *In Dahomey*. The resultant impression left on our mind was one of strangeness, the strangeness of the colored race blended with the strangeness of certain American things.[5]

The writer enumerated what he viewed as a queer mélange in the play: a prologue with no relation to the plot but showing "the noble savage running wild in the woods"; diverse characters (a policeman, a bootblack, a cook and a postman) with no apparent function; a listless and obsequious chorus; and the "sheer joy" of Williams and Walker. Perhaps the heavy use of American slang contributed to the strangeness and confusion such critics felt. An American in London, S. J. Pryor, warned his readers:

> One great feature of *In Dahomey* the average Englishman must make up his mind to miss. That is the interminable flow of the amazing American language of slang. It is to the exiled American and to the fortunate traveler who had been in America one of the funniest things about the show.
> But it would take a whole page of *The Express* to elucidate the meaning of "a thousand cold" and "the possession of the dough" and "a lead pipe cinch," and the hundreds of other slangy colloquialisms that begem the play.[6]

Despite their puzzlement, the critics seemed to find the show satisfying. They liked Williams especially: "His presentment of a large, foolish, morose and always unlucky negro is something quite new to the English stage, and is excessively amusing, one cannot tell exactly why." The appreciation of Williams in England, despite other misgivings critics may have had about the show, confirms the consistent superiority of his performances and his ability to reach out to audiences of all kinds. Indeed, *Theatre Arts* declared Williams "a vastly funnier man than any white comedian now on the American stage."[7]

In Dahomey at home and abroad was a success. A British critic, writing in May 1903, proved prophetic: "The entertainment at the Shaftesbury is certainly unique, and as it has in many ways real merit as well, it should attain something more than the success of curiosity which one would say is assured."[8] A tour of England and Scotland followed the seven-month London run, and the cast finally returned to the United States in August 1904. A second troupe, with Dan Avery and Charlie Hart in the lead roles, set sail for England soon afterwards. The original cast continued to tour at home, traveling coast to coast in a forty-week trek that ended in June 1905.

SHAFTESBURY THEATRE

SHAFTESBURY AVENUE, W.

Proprietors ... Representatives of the late JOHN LANCASTER
Sole Lessee ... ... Mr. GEO. MUSGROVE

Every Evening at 8.15, Matinee Wednesday and Saturday at 2.15,
Messrs. HURTIG & SEAMON present

WILLIAMS & WALKER

IN THEIR RECENT SUCCESS,

"IN DAHOMEY,"

A Musical Comedy in Two Acts, Preceded by a Prologue, Written and Staged by JESSE A. SHIPP.
Lyrics by PAUL LAWRENCE DUNBAR and ALEX ROGERS. Music Composed by WILL MARION COOK.

PROLOGUE.
TIME—Three months before beginning of Play. PLACE—DAHOMEY.
CHARACTERS.

Je-Je, a caboceer ... ... CHAS. MOORE
Menuki, Messenger of the King ... ... WM. ELKINS
Mose Lightfoot, Agent of Dahomey Colonization Society ... ... WM. BARKER
Soldiers, Natives, etc.

Cast of Characters.
Shylock Homestead, called "Shy" by his friends ... ... BERT A. WILLIAMS
Rareback Pinkerton, "Shy's" personal friend and adviser ... GEO. W. WALKER
Hamilton Lightfoot, president of a colonization Society ... PETE HAMPTON
Dr. Straight (in name only), street fakir ... ... FRED DOUGLAS
Mose Lightfoot, brother of Hamilton, thinks Dahomey a land of great promise ... WM. BARKER
George Reeder, proprietor of an intelligence office ... ... ALEX ROGERS
Henry Stampfield, letter carrier, with an argument against immigration WALTER RICHARDSON
Me Sing, a Chinese cook ... ... GEO. CATLIN
Hustling Charley, promoter of Get-the-Coin Syndicate ... J. A. SHIPP
Leather, a bootblack ... ... RICHARD CONNORS
Officer Still ... ... J. LEUBRIE HILL
White Wash Man ... ... GREEN TAPLEY
Messenger Rush, but not often ... ... THEODORE PANKEY
Pansy, Daughter of Cecilia Lightfoot, in love with Leather ... ABBIE MITCHELL
Cecilia Lightfoot, Hamilton's wife ... ... Mrs. HATTIE McINTOSH
Mrs. Stringer, dealer in forsaken patterns, also editor of fashion-notes in
"Beanville Agitator" ... ... Mrs. LOTTIE WILLIAMS
Rose'ta Lightfoot, a troublesome young thing ... ... AIDA OVERTON WALKER
Colonists, Natives, etc.

SYNOPSIS.
PROLOGUE ... Scene—Garden of the Caboceer (Governor of a | ACT II., Scene 1, Exterior of Lightfoot's House, Gaterville, Flor'da
ACT I., ... Province) | Scene 2 ... Road, one-and-a-half miles from Gaterville
... Public Square, Boston | Scene 3 ... ... Interior of Lightfoot's Home

SPECIAL.—At Finale of last Act will be presented a Grand Spectacular CAKE WALK.

MUSICAL NUMBERS.
PROLOGUE.
Dahomian Queen ... Anna Cook, Morris Smith and Company | "Caboceers Choral" ... ... Company
ACT I.
Overture ... ... | "My Castle on the River Nile" (Interpolated) ...
Opening Chorus ... "Swing Along" ... | Geo. W. Walker and Chorus
"Molile Green" ... ... Henry Troy and Chorus | "Broadway in Dahomey" (Interpolated) ...
| Williams, Walker and Company
Entre Act
ACT II.
"A Actor Lady" ... Ai'a Overton Walker | "The Jonah Man" (Interpolated) ... Bert Williams
"Brown Skin Baby Mine" ... Abbie Mitchell, Richard Cor'nors | "A Rich Coon's Babe" (Interpolated) ... Ai'a Overton Walker
and Chorus | "The Czar" ... ... George Walker, assisted by
Leaders of Coloured Aristocracy" ... | Aida Overton Walker and Company
... Hattie McIntosh and Company | "Emancipation Day" ... Williams, Walker and Company
"Society" ... Pete Hampton, Hattie McIntosh, Lloyd Gibbs, | Emancipation Day March and Cake Walk Finale.
Richard Connors and Company |
(Soprano Solo by Ella Anderson),
The Statue in this scene is done by Mr. Walter Richardson.
The Orchestra under the Direction of the Composer, assisted by Mr. James Vaughan.
Lyrics of "Broadway in Dahomey" "Jonah Man," "Rich Coon's Babe," "The Czar," by ALEX ROGERS. "Dahomian Queen"
written by F. B. WILLIAMS and J. LEUBRIE HILL.

Music published by Messrs. KEITH, Prowse & Co., Ltd., 48, Cheapside, E.C.

Program for *In Dahomey* during its English run at the Shaftesbury Theatre, London 1903. The show's appearance in London led to a royal command performance for the birthday party of the Prince of Wales. Billy Rose Theatre Collection, the New York Public Library at Lincoln Center, Astor, Lenox, and Tilden Foundations.

The Southerners

On May 23, 1904, *The Southerners,* with a book by Will Mercer and Richard Grant and music by Will Marion Cook, appeared at the New York Theatre. Dubbed "a study in black and white," in euphemistic reference to its inclusion of large numbers of black and white performers, the show seems to be a rare example of onstage integration in Broadway musical comedy. It was a potpourri, a return to the revue/variety formula

Black child actors in *The Southerners* (1904). Child acts or "pick" (pickaninny) routines also were popular in black vaudeville. Photograph by Byron, the Byron Collection, Museum of the City of New York.

of previous years. One writer declared, "The piece has the earmarks of a musical comedy, but even that elastic term can scarcely be stretched far enough to take in all the features, specialties, turns and acts that go to make up this typical Lederer summer show . . . and it is just about the sort of thing that seems most in demand in New York during the hot weather." Among its varied acts the show included acrobatic dancing and a number called "The Chipmunk and the Squirrel," featuring a half-dozen black children in "squirrelesque garb."⁹

The show did have a plot that connected its diverse elements. Le Roy Preston (William Gould), after arguing with his sweetheart, Polly Drayton (Elfie Fay), leaves his plantation home to escape his burdensome duties to follow the life of a roving seaman. The plantation slaves, whom Le Roy had wanted to free, are about to fall into the clutches of the dastardly, lecherous "Irish Turk" Brannigan Bey (Junie McCree). In the face of this and other complications, Polly repents of the lovers' quarrel, and in disguise as a naval officer she seeks out Le Roy. Predictably he is reconciled to Polly, returns to the plantation, and quashes Bey's schemes.

With the plantation setting, another inheritance from minstrelsy, the songs deal with familiar Old South topics and have titles like "Darktown Barbecue" and "It's Allus de Same in Dixie." They also contain several artful touches by the composer, such as a striking slide from an F to a G♭7 chord between the verse and the refrain of "Darktown Barbecue" (Example 6.5). The refrain of "Mandy Lou," an uncomplicated love song, includes four grace notes that allow brief vocal slides on the syllable "Lou" (Example 6.6). "As the Sunflower Turns to the Sun" (Example 6.7), another romantic song, employs a similar effect. It may be that Cook was

Example 6.5. Will Marion Cook, "Darktown Barbecue" (New York: John H. Cook Publishing Co., 1904), interlude between verse and chorus, mm. 17–20

Example 6.6. Will Marion Cook and R. C. McPherson, "Mandy Lou" (New York: John H. Cook Publishing Co., 1904), end of verse, beginning of chorus

notating what had already become a standard ornamental procedure. Even greater liberties certainly are evident on later sound recordings of tender, bluesy songs.

One writer referred to Cook's music as "commonplace," while another felt it was the saving grace of the show: "It was the 'black'—rather than the 'white'—half of the musical study that made the great hit last night, in the persons of a most amusing and well drilled troup of colored people. Their songs and dances roused the house from polite applause to genuine enthusiasm, and more than once held the stage against the reentrance of the principals."[10] Cook's tunes did contain elements already well worn in earlier songs from *Clorindy* and *In Dahomey*, but if they sounded commonplace, this should perhaps be taken to indicate how completely popular-music composers had adopted the black syncopated style by this time.

Albert Hart, a white bass, and Abbie Mitchell, Cook's wife, were cited as the outstanding singers in the show. Eddie Leonard, a famous white minstrel dancer, also performed, and the *New York Times* noted that "his stunts of fantastic dancing were acclaimed." The same critic summarized the contrasting elements and finally approved: "There is a large public for this sort of thing, and beyond question it will carry the show well into the summer months. For those who like black and white, this black and white is all right."[11] The show ran for thirty-six performances in New York.

Example 6.7. Richard Grant and Will Marion Cook, "As the Sunflower Turns to the Sun" (New York: John H. Cook Publishing Co., 1904), chorus, mm. 1–4

Abbie Mitchell, ca. 1904, popular soubrette in *In Dahomey, The Southerners,* and other shows composed by her husband, Will Marion Cook. She continued a successful solo career after the demise of the big shows and was the first Clara in Gershwin's *Porgy and Bess* (1935). Billy Rose Theatre Collection, the New York Public Library at Lincoln Center, Astor, Lenox, and Tilden Foundations.

The Early Cole and Johnson Brothers Shows

After their initial good fortunes in songwriting, Bob Cole and the Johnson brothers did not turn immediately to writing music for all-black cast shows but instead were hired by the Klaw-Erlanger organization, the most powerful production company of the day. In composing for Klaw-Erlanger shows, the team wrote songs for white singers in productions aimed at the average white Broadway theatergoer, rather than an exclusively black or even racially mixed audience, as had been the case with Williams and Walker. The songs of *Humpty Dumpty* (1904), the most successful and ambitious of these shows, generally are devoid of dialect and are built on the familiar thirty-two-measure pattern. Syncopation is sparing, but one can find occasional touches of originality and distinctiveness. Critics of the early performances at the newly opened New Amsterdam Theatre, on Forty-second Street, unanimously cited "Mexico," sung by Maud Berri, as the popular song hit of the show (Facsimile 6.3). A repeated dotted-eighth/sixteenth note figure ♩. ♪ ♩ ♪ ♪♪ ♪♪♪♪ and a habañera basso ostinato dominate this impassioned love song about a "dark-eyed beauty from over the Rio Grande." The final choral reprise is marked fortissimo and is transposed a fourth above the principal key of B♭ major. The cumulative effect, allowing the singer to reach g″ several times, partly explains the tremendous success of the song in the show. Its climactic finale courted applause.

Humpty Dumpty was intended as a lavish holiday show (it began as an imported English pantomime) aimed to appeal to children. A saccharine number like "The Pussy and the Bow-wow," with a cute text and simple tune, therefore can be excused as the sort of song one would normally expect to find in such pieces. It sounds as if it were tossed off at one sitting:

> But if I were a little pussy cat,
> And you were a little bow-wow,
> I'm sure we'd join in a social chat
> In fact we'd have quite a pow-wow.
> chorus:
> (he)   I'd bark my love
> (she)   and mine I'd mew
> (both) As all good kitties and doggies do.
>   If I (you) were a little pussy,
>   And you (I) were a little bow-wow.

In such sugary surroundings, a genuinely charming piece like "Sambo and Dinah" stands out (Facsimile 6.4). The title suggests coon clichés, but this guess is not accurate. Even the use of dialect is minimal in this straightforward love lyric. The key, the melodic contours, and the accompaniment patterns all vary subtly among the nine four-measure phrases of the verse. In the second phrase, the sweetness of the progression I–I$^6_5$–IV supports the words "sing sweet songs" as the bass line breaks into smooth quarter-notes interrupting the previous eighth-note broken chords. The unprepared shift to a B♭ triad in m. 17, the flatted third degree of the original key (admittedly a popular Romantic compositional shift), is an enlivening gesture that appears in many Cole and Johnson songs. The ragtime chorus is reminiscent of "Josephine, My Jo" and "Miss Hannah from Savannah" in its quick, agile melodic line.

In a very brief period, fame and financial security came to Cole and the Johnsons as a result of their collaboration with the Klaw-Erlanger organization and Joseph Stern Publishing, and it came at a level unprecedented for black songwriters. Simultaneously Will Marion Cook's songs became staples of an increasing number of black shows. One of these shows, *In Dahomey,* completed a celebrated international tour. The impetus that these events provided to black performers must have been extraordinary, and the years following 1905 saw a playing out of the dreams that proceed from such achievements. George Walker conceived of even grander extravaganzas for himself and his cohorts. Ernest Hogan managed to open his first big show, *Rufus Rastus,* in New York a month before Williams and Walker's Dahomian sequel, *Abyssinia,* in early 1906. And in 1907 Cole and Johnson, with the Williams and Walker models before them, finally attempted their first full-length, black-cast production, *The Shoo-Fly Regiment.* Clearly, the black musical comedy had emerged.

7
Williams and Walker
Set the Pace

Abyssinia

In February 1906 Williams and Walker appeared at the Majestic Theatre in their road-tested production, *Abyssinia*. With many of the same players who had acted in *In Dahomey* and with the financial backing of Melville Raymond of the Klaw-Erlanger staff, the team mounted a spectacle that included brilliant lighting effects, elegant costumes for a cast of one hundred, a market scene "full of picturesque quality and color," a manmade waterfall, and wild animals. The plot told of the misadventures of Rastus Johnson (Walker) and Jasmine Jenkins (Williams), a pair of Kansas rascals, returning to the land of their forefathers, Abyssinia, accompanied by numerous female cousins, a Baptist minister, and an Oriental cook.[1]

Programs and reviews credit Will Marion Cook and Bert Williams with composing the music, but nearly all of the individually published songs list words by Alex Rogers and music by Williams alone. Cook probably contributed the orchestrations and the unpublished choral parts.

Aida Overton Walker and Bert Williams (r.) in a scene from *Abyssinia* (1906). Schomburg Center for Research in Black Culture, the New York Public Library, Astor, Lenox, and Tilden Foundations.

Abyssinia contains songs musically and textually similar to those of other shows, but an unusually large number of songs seem to have been integral to the musical. The Jonah-man persona appears in "Here It Comes Again," and Shangri La is evoked in the ballad "The Island of By and By." "Rastus Johnson, U. S. A.," "It's Hard to Find a King Like Me," and "Jolly Jungle Boys" all introduce the arrival of characters onstage. As was true for the songs in *The Policy Players* and *The Sons of Ham*, in *Abyssinia* Bert Williams was not inclined towards syncopated rhythms. Williams's parlando-rubato style of performance was inimical to the rhythmic strictness required for ragtime or rag-related styles.

Between 1901 and 1922 Williams recorded about eighty songs, mostly with Columbia (a few more than once), generally on discs rather than cylinders. Brian Rust has compiled a five-page list of these songs in his *Complete Entertainment Discography*. Eight songs from the 1919–21 period were reissued in the 1940s, and others in 1981, but only a few of Williams's songs from the pre-Ziegfeld shows have been preserved.[2] "Let

It Alone" (Facsimile 7.1) and "Pretty Desdemona" from *Abyssinia* are two of the few. "Let It Alone" illustrates the flexibility, rhythmic freedom, and variety of tone characteristic of his singing. The modulations of his voice reflecting the earnestness that moved audiences to tears and his flawless comic timing are vividly present. The special popularity of "Let It Alone" is confirmed by a story related by West Coast performer Billy King. Having forgotten his music en route to a show, he had to come up with a substitute song quickly. He chose to convert "Let It Alone" into a jingoistic parody aimed at the Japanese at the time of the Russo-Japanese War (1904), "Let *Us* Alone":

> Let us alone, let us alone
> They use some sense and let us alone.
> When the Star-Spangled Banner is unfurled,
> It's the emblem of the greatest fighting nation in the world.
> So if the Japs don't know, I'll tell them so—
> They can turn around and beat it and LET US ALONE.

King reported that the "audience went into pandemonium, throwing hats, and parading up and down the aisle."[3]

"Pretty Desdemona" on record includes a long, yodeling falsetto descant by Williams with Walker singing the main (printed) melody. The effect is unlike anything on Williams's solo recordings. Singing with Walker demanded of Williams more rhythmic strictness than he usually demonstrated but resulted in much more melodic freedom, approximating a jubilee-style or gospel-style solo. Unfortunately these rare recordings are very noisy and are unavailable commercially. Two songs can't convey the effect of a Williams and Walker show, but they suggest how much an actual performance might have differed from the printed notes.

Unlike *In Dahomey*, *Abyssinia* was not published in complete score. Considering the documented luxuriance of the staging of *Abyssinia*, with more or less the same personnel, it is tempting to assume that the musical score as a whole, particularly the structure of the choral numbers, would have been as impressive as that of *In Dahomey*. The individual song sheets give no hint about the magnitude or even the existence of production numbers like those found in *In Dahomey*, although the critics wrote approvingly of the chorus.

Despite the show's variety and novelty, "far in advance of their last

vehicle," it enjoyed only a brief run in New York of some thirty performances. One Boston reviewer who enjoyed the show saw in the use of
onstage animals "the lineal descendants of the heifer in 'Evangeline'
[1875], and the mule in 'Conrad the Corsair,' and a relative of the various
animals that have crossed the Atlantic from British pantomime. . . .
These comic opera indispensables will continue to be used as long as
theatres stand, and their employment in 'Abyssinia' is simply what white
librettists have done and will continue to do." Other critics commented
on poor enunciation, lapses in intonation of choral singing, and excessive
length.[4] Perhaps the songs, dances, and specialties, though familiar and
enjoyable, were in their cumulative effect finally tiresome, or perhaps the
dancing chorus—the mainstay of *Clorindy* and *In Dahomey*—was not
given enough time onstage. The prospect of paying off expenses through
less luxurious road shows also may have encouraged the team to leave
New York. William Foster notes that four tours of *Abyssinia* were sent out
during one season, but he describes neither the theaters nor the audiences to which these tours played.[5] Chicago critic Sylvester Russell

Bert Williams on a human "camel" and George Walker on a real donkey in a
scene from *Abyssinia* (1906). Schomburg Center for Research in Black Culture,
the New York Public Library, Astor, Lenox, and Tilden Foundations.

reported that "the manager [of the show] lacked integrity and was hostile to the proportions of the organization as a whole and caused the comedy to be chopped up in such a manner that it had to take the road in a condensed form, much to the dissatisfaction of Mr. Walker, who ordered the season closed early."[6]

Bandanna Land

Despite the less than successful tours of *Abyssinia,* the Williams and Walker company envisioned another ambitious undertaking in 1907. A large cast was assembled, and F. Ray Comstock agreed to fund the project; Hurtig and Seamon, the team's former backers, apparently decided that the cost was too high. Once again Williams, Walker, Rogers, Shipp, and Cook formed the creative nucleus of the show. Additional songs by J. Leubrie Hill, Tom Lemonier, R. C. McPherson, and Chris Smith were interpolated. The presentation of a new Williams and Walker show seemed to be emerging as a biennial tradition in New York. *Bandanna Land* reached the Majestic Theatre on February 3, 1908.[7]

The plot involves a minstrel show player, Skunkton Bowser (Williams), who inherits $25,000 and agrees to finance a real estate deal, the sale of land to a railroad. Bowser and his partner, Bud Jenkins (Walker), hatch a scheme to create a park, Bandanna Land, adjacent to the proposed railroad, with the intent of encouraging the railroad owners to pay any price to eliminate their black neighbors. Eventually all works out happily to Bowser's interest. The presence of a minstrel show character, an end-man–interlocutor type dialogue in the script, and a cakewalk finale in the second act caused at least two reviewers to remark on the roots of the show in minstrelsy.[8] *Bandanna Land* once again illustrates the retention of successful minstrel show conventions played in modern circumstances where blacks triumph through luck and pluck.

Cook's music was lauded, although most of the surviving songs were not written by him. What Cook composed and what most impressed the critics, if we can judge from critical comments on the choral singing in other black shows, were the unpublished ensemble numbers specific and integral to the stage presentation. One solo song receiving much critical acclaim was Kempner and Williams's "Late Hours," about a forlorn alcoholic. The grace notes at the beginning of the vocal line in the chorus are perhaps an attempt to suggest inebriated waddling. The wry and gentle "I'd Rather Have Nothing All of the Time, Than Something For a Little While" was Williams's Jonah-man song:

> One wintry day while on my way to pawn my overcoat
> My eagle eye it chanced to spy a brand new dollar note,
> I picked it up and then remarked, "I will not have to freeze,"
> When someone from behind me said, "Return my dollar please."
> And as I gave that green-back back, I murmured, "Goodbye, Bill,"
> The best of friends do separate, this parting grieves but still.[9]

"Fas', Fas' World," also written and performed by Williams, contains the unusually large melodic range of an eleventh and an F minor passage, illustrating Williams's occasional deviation from the major-key cast of this repertory. The text expresses bewilderment at the unrelenting pace of modern society (even in 1908!), and the chorus is indeed "fas'er" than most show tunes, taking only twelve measures rather than the normal sixteen.

The most famous of all Williams's songs, "Nobody," also was sung in *Bandanna Land*. The droll lyric and sighing repetitions of the word *nobody* combined humor and pathos so effectively that subsequently it was difficult for Williams to appear onstage without being requested to do it. The use of triads on the modal-scale degrees in the opening measures lends freshness and an appropriately melancholic tinge to the basic key of C major, and the mildly surprising flatted sixth at the midpoint and conclusion of the verse (Example 7.1) underlines the plaintive humor of the forlorn final word of each half-stanza.[10]

"Just the Same," a Viennese waltz tune by Will Marion Cook, is matched with a world-weary text:

> Same old hug, same old kiss,
> Same old rapture, same old bliss
> Some love's different, some folks claim,
> But if it's love, then it's just the same.

The "same old" rhythm is used repeatedly throughout the refrain
$\frac{3}{4}$ 𝅗𝅥. | 𝅗𝅥. | 𝅗𝅥. ⌣ | 𝅗𝅥 𝄽 and, true to form, a leaping, agogically accented second beat occurs in the first measure of each phrase of the verse.

Example 7.1. Alex Rogers and Bert Williams, "Nobody" (New York: The Attucks Music Publishing Co., 1905), verse, mm. 1–7

George Walker's most famous motto song, written by Rogers and Cook, was "Bon Bon Buddy" (Facsimile 7.2). It contains a narrative verse that leads to a rambunctious refrain proclaiming:

> Bon Bon Buddy the chocolate drop, Dat's me,
> Bon Bon Buddy is all that I want to be
> I've gained my fame but I ain't 'shame'
> I'm satisfied with my nickname,
> Bon Bon Buddy the chocolate drop, Dat's me.

Four beats of rest in the vocal part before the words "Dat's me" presumably allowed a quick dance step and flourish. An unadorned bass line marked *marcato* rhythmically fills this gap, and pictures of Walker captioned "Bon Bon Buddy" often show him poised, hat and cane in hand, ready to execute such a step.

Bandanna Land included many players featured in the earlier Williams and Walker shows. Abbie Mitchell sang "Red Red Rose" (Facsimile 7.3), and Aida Overton Walker sang and danced. Peppered with well-trained, highly experienced veterans, the show was well received by critics and audiences. Some thought it was Williams and Walker's best work to date,

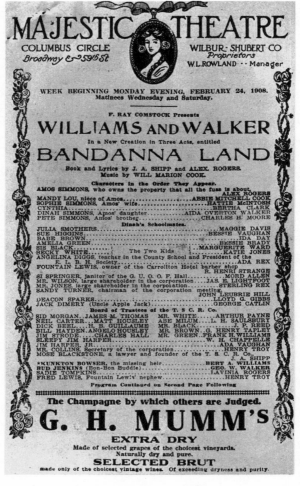

Program for *Bandanna Land* during its New York run at the Majestic Theatre. Theatre Collection, Museum of the City of New York.

and it drew sizable crowds of white customers. The *Dramatic Mirror* recommended it "for wholesome merriment, genuine humor of the cleanest sort [something always scrutinized in black shows] and singing of great volume and sweetness." It noted further, "This colored show stands with the foremost of musical entertainments. . . . With all its savor of a minstrel performance the piece comes close to being opera comique. There is a plot and most of the songs relate to it; the comedy is a natural outcome of the story, and the music, some of it at least, is far above the ordinary."[11] Such praise for the musical and dramatic integration of a show is rare in this period. Unfortunately, no libretto survives, frustrating any attempt to verify the critical plaudits. Within the dramatic frame Williams included not only his most famous song but also his well-known poker game pantomime, in which he created the impression of four individually characterized players playing out an entire game. This routine became a favorite of audiences, remained in Williams's repertory for years after, and was preserved on film.[12]

The show toured widely and successfully. A Cincinnati reviewer wrote in March 1909:

> There is just one thing a fair-minded person can say regarding the
> negroes who participate in Williams and Walker's 'Bandanna Land,'
> and that is, they are natural singers and comedians. The latter might
> suggest to one who had not seen these negroes act, a wild revel of low
> comedy, a cheap exaggeration of effects, a buffoonery of style and all
> the clownishness that goes with outright burlesque; but that is a
> mistake. These negroes have a real sense of comedy. They make their
> points quietly and with restraint. They enjoy it. Every time they speak
> a line, they do it as if it was new and fresh to them. They seem to
> throw themselves into the very heart of it, and instead of striving for
> points, for personal applause, they work to one end, for the thing itself.
> Privately they may be egotistical, jealous of one another and full of
> professional pettiness, but it does not show in the general result, and
> that is what the audience wants. There are some pointers in the way of
> enthusiasm and conscientious work by which their white confreres in
> the profession might profit. And as to singing they are marvels. They
> tackle the big finales with a vim, a discretion, a judgment as to points
> and effects, which is a revelation. Attention was called to this same
> characteristic in these columns last year, but the effect of this aptitude

for large choral numbers is equally noticeable this year. Twelve months of familiarity with the same songs and finales have not seemed to dull either the interest in nor the execution of them. They are sung as if the mixed chorus loved every note, and with a freedom from mechanical results which is refreshing. Someone said during the week, "I would like to be blind-folded and hear that chorus and the chorus in the Savage company sing the first act finale in The Merry Widow, and see which I would like best." It would be hard to decide.[13]

In its second year *Bandanna Land* carried a cast of seventy-five and an orchestra of twenty, and so the size of the company may have contributed to the positive impression of this Cincinnati enthusiast. Nevertheless, the review confirms the raves of the New York critics from the previous year. Among its other accomplishments, the show was the first black production to play for the predominantly white audiences at the Belasco Theatre in Washington, DC. It was also the last joint effort of the famous team. Walker was taken ill in February 1909, and Aida Overton Walker, donning both her husband's costume and his song, "Bon Bon Buddy," replaced him for the remainder of the run. *Bandanna Land* finally closed at the Yorkville Theatre in Brooklyn in April 1909.[14]

Mr. Lode of Koal

Bert Williams set out on the road without his partner in another Shipp-Rogers collaboration, *Mr. Lode of Koal*, in September 1909. Williams, with the assistance of J. Rosamond Johnson as arranger, provided most of the music, and J. Leubrie Hill and Al Johns contributed a few tunes. Stair and Havlin booked the tour.

The political kidnapping of an island ruler named Big Smoke and the installation of Chester Lode (Williams) as his replacement on the island of Koal constitute the motivation for the plot and title. Lode's brief but action-packed reign ends with the unexpected return of Big Smoke and the relegation of Lode to servant status.

Along with the usual hard-luck and Old South/nostalgia numbers, Williams sang about figures of the day such as Booker T. Washington and Jack Johnson, the heavyweight fighter, in "My Ole Man." "Chink, Chink Chinaman" exploits a popular ethnic theme, the problems of the poor "Chineeman," picked on by everyone else, white and black. It is not, of course, genuine Chinese music, but it embodies the surface features of

Example 7.2. Alex Rogers and Bert Williams, "Chink, Chink Chinaman" (Chicago: Will Rossiter, 1909), chorus, mm. 1–4

Chink, chink, chink, chink   Chi - nee man   run   a - way   wi'   loys - ter   can

the American stage Oriental style. Though the pentatonic melody is mitigated by several leading tones, it retains a typical pattern of short, staccato eighth- and sixteenth-notes. The song was performed by George Catlin, one of the stalwart and stable attractions of the Williams and Walker shows (Example 7.2).

In "Mum's the Word, Mr. Moon," Alex Rogers rhymes *moon* and *June* (and later, *June* and *moon* and *tune*). J. Leubrie Hill's melody helps the stilted verse; the final leaping phrase on "mum's the word" gives some dash to the normal formulas (Example 7.3). Hill's syncopated, melodic style has a certain fragmented quality, and each phrase simply follows the previous one rather than growing out of it. He writes neither the tightly constructed tunes of Johnson and Cook nor the extended phrases characteristic of Cole's melodies.

Al Johns wrote the music and Alex Rogers the lyrics for "In Far Off Mandalay," which suggests the dreamy Shangri La with a minor tune in the verse, a drone bass, an abundance of seventh and ninth chords, a larger than usual number of chromatic passing chords, and even an occasional augmented one (Example 7.4).

The critics unanimously agreed that *Mr. Lode of Koal* was a vehicle for Williams and not much more; they liked him but not the show as a whole. One black critic writing for the *Freeman* took Williams himself to task, calling him " a great comedian of only one style of work—as an old-time darkey—with humor divided into three classes: grotesque dancing; an original method of walking; and explosive talking."[15] Some viewers, it

Example 7.3. Alex Rogers and J. Leubrie Hill, "Mum's the Word, Mr. Moon" (Chicago: Will Rossiter, 1909), chorus, mm. 15–18

Mum's the word _ Mis-ter   Moo - n   Mum's the word _ Mis-ter   Moon. _

Example 7.4. Alex Rogers and Al Johns, "In Far Off Mandalay" (Chicago: Will Rossiter, 1909), beginning of chorus

seems, were tiring of the old comical attitudes and the ubiquitous, self-deprecating Jonah-man style.

Although he was usually fulsomely praised for his solo performances at this point in his career, Williams brooded over Walker's illness (apparently syphilis) and doubtless was distraught that Walker was not able to return to the partnership. Mabel Rowland, in her collection of reminiscences of Williams, comments, "he had become so used to the support of his partner . . . that he told newspaper men he felt like a ship without a rudder."[16]

After touring for six months, *Mr. Lode of Koal* ended its run on March 5, 1910, at the Court Street Theatre in Brooklyn. Williams joined Florenz Ziegfeld's Follies of 1910 two months later. Walker died on January 6, 1911.

8

"African Operettas" and Other Star Vehicles, 1906–1911

Rufus Rastus

Ernest Hogan realized a long-cherished dream to mount his own musical comedy when *Rufus Rastus* began touring in late 1905. It opened in New York at the American Theatre, on Forty-second Street, on January 29, 1906. The book was by W. D. Hall; the lyrics by Frank Williams, Lester Walton, Howard Herrick, Arthur Gillespie, and W. D. Hall; and the music by Joe Jordan, Tom Lemonier, Ernest Hogan, and H. Lawrence Freeman. Hurtig and Seamon underwrote the production. The critics recognized *Rufus Rastus* as part of a trend toward the production of more black-cast shows—they grouped it readily with *In Dahomey* and the shows of a relatively new traveling company, the Smart Set—and they wrote approvingly of the results.

The story line, deemed "sufficiently consistent" by the *Dramatic Mirror*,[1] involved the adventures of an actor working off his debts through various jobs, ranging from bootblack in a Florida hotel to doorkeeper at Madison Square Garden. Good fortune finally catches up with him when he locates thousands of dollars in a cereal box. Hogan appeared in many comic guises to accompany his occupational changes. Songs by other performers and specialty acts such as acrobatic displays also were worked in.

A favorite song in the show was "Oh, Say Wouldn't It Be a Dream," a clever, topical, and rousing number (Facsimile 8.1). Its text contains an interesting combination of coon themes and social aspirations, reminiscent of Bob Cole's tunes of ten years earlier:

Ernest Hogan as the title character in his musical comedy, *Rufus Rastus*. Billy Rose Theatre Collection, the New York Public Library at Lincoln Center, Astor, Lenox, and Tilden Foundations.

If I could blow a horn and lead a circus band,
Say wouldn't it be a dream,
If coons could only rule this great United Land,
Say wouldn't it be a dream.
We'd make Bert Williams President and Walker would be Vice,
Joe Walcott for the Senate where he'd cut a lot of ice;
Affairs of State they'd settle with a pair of poker dice;
Oh, say wouldn't it be a dream.

The repeated final line, the same in the verse and the chorus, intensified by optional high notes of the last two measures, invite audience assent and applause. Hogan did not claim any credit for this song—Joe Jordan wrote the music and Earl Jones the lyrics—but it was by all accounts the standout number of the show because of its text and Hogan's delivery. Hogan composed most of the other published songs, collaborating with different lyricists.

Judging only from the scores and not taking into account onstage emendations, Hogan's music is unimpressive. The songs are the standard length, the melodies are not markedly syncopated, and the accompaniments do not employ any harmonic or rhythmic novelties. One critic, while commenting that the "ragtime" music was enjoyed by all, noted the paucity of actual, thoroughgoing syncopation.[2] The songs are typically in common or duple time, and Hogan (or his arranger) seems to have had a decided preference for the key of G major; six of the eleven songs examined are in this tonality. That the show and these songs were successful reaffirms a point already raised with minstrels and the Williams and Walker team: It was most often the personality of a single star performer, combined with the verve and skillful improvisation upon familiar materials by all the supporting players, that gave many black shows their appeal. While this was often true of white shows as well, the meager markings beyond the notes on the Hogan scores serve as a reminder that a great deal of what must have happened onstage was never written down. None of Hogan's later songs achieved the success of "All Coons Look Alike to Me," or even his earlier "La Pas Ma La,"[3] and it is ironic that a man who prided himself on avoiding burnt cork should be remembered principally for his earliest coon songs.

The Oyster Man

In 1907 Hogan followed up on the successful tour of *Rufus Rastus* with a production called *The Oyster Man*, again with himself in the lead role, Rufus Rastus. He wrote or collaborated with Will Vodery on most of the tunes. Henry Creamer and Lester Walton wrote the lyrics, and Hal Reid contributed the story. Flournoy Miller and Aubrey Lyles, two recent graduates from Fisk University, wrote one of their first books for this show. Hurtig and Seamon managed and funded the production. It was an unabashed sequel to *Rufus Rastus,* and critical accounts suggest that it was a variety entertainment focusing especially on Hogan's comedic talents. A Boston performance just prior to the New York opening elicited an insightful review that commented on the qualities distinguishing Hogan from hundreds of blackface minstrels:

> Mr. Hogan has made a place for himself as an exponent of genuine, rich, spontaneous Negro humor, and needs no surroundings to add to his fame. What Harrigan was as a New York East Side type, Mr. Hogan is as a representative of the peculiar qualities of his race in real life. Not of the stage exaggerated, cake-walking type, but the easy-going, unctuous, rollicking, gullible human; tickled with a straw [one] minute and ready to cut your heart out the next, perhaps. His new play gives opportunities for the exercise of his talents to the full, and he does so to the great pleasure of his audience who could not get enough of him.

This assessment reflects the esteem in which Hogan was held and that caused Lester Walton to characterize him as the "Moses of the Colored Theatrical Profession."[4] He was a leader out of minstrelsy in both the nature and the quality of his act.

One Boston reviewer called the music "an especially important feature of the show," but no songs were singled out for special praise, nor do any surviving songs seem to have broken new musical ground. The numbers included a Jonah-man song, "Enough, That's Enough"; a song with a Cuban textual theme called "In the Shade of Moro Castle" (song allusions to North America's Spanish-speaking neighbors and territorial possessions were frequent in the decade following the Spanish-American War); and the quotation song "Yankee Doodle Coon." A topical song, "When Buffalo Bill and His Wild West Show First Came to Baltimore," represents a favorite type for Hogan—vigorous and excited and with a surprise word play or discreet substitution ("They didn't give a *ram* for the policeman") at the climax of the refrain (Facsimile 8.2).

As Hogan's own show, *The Oyster Man* allowed full play of his stage talents, but its reception pointed as well to his ability to attract strong people about him. Henry Creamer, Will Vodery, and the team of Miller and Lyles went on to highly successful theatrical careers. One critic termed the subordinate players of the show "well-trained" and also remarked that *The Oyster Man* "stood among the best of the all-Negro musical comedies." It proved to be Hogan's last show. He was taken ill with tuberculosis early in 1908 and succumbed in May 1909. The show could not go on without him.[5]

The Shoo-Fly Regiment

On June 3, 1907, *The Shoo-Fly Regiment*—Bob Cole and the Johnson brothers' first full-length production not written for a white company— began playing to "appreciative Eighth Avenue audiences" at New York's Grand Opera House. It closed a week later, probably to tour out of town, and reopened at the Bijou Theatre on Broadway on August 6. The program gave credit for the book to Cole, the lyrics to James Weldon Johnson, and the music to J. Rosamond Johnson, but the trio had always collaborated closely on all elements of their shows. James Weldon Johnson explains the partnership in *Along This Way:*

> My brother, Bob Cole, and I formed a partnership to produce songs and plays. I have not known of just such another combination as was ours. The three of us sometimes worked as one man. At such times it was difficult to point out specifically the part done by any one of us. But generally we worked as a pair, with the odd man as a sort of critic and advisor. Without regard to who or how many did the work, each of us received a third of the earnings. There was an almost complete absence of pride of authorship; and that made the partnership still more curious. At first, we printed the three names at the top of the sheet, but three names on little songs looked top-heavy; so we began printing only two; sometimes we printed but one. Our first firm name for the title page was "Johnson, Cole, and Johnson." After Bob and Rosamond became noted in vaudeville under the name of Cole and Johnson, we changed our title-page signature to "Cole and Johnson Brothers."

He goes on to explain the genesis of *The Shoo-Fly Regiment:* "Bob and Rosamond were still headliners on the 'big time' in vaudeville, but a new idea was working in Bob's mind. He had first let it out in occasional hints, then broached it. The idea was that he and Rosamond drop vaudeville and go out at the head of a theatrical company. His argument was that there was a chance of clearing thirty or forty thousand dollars a year with a company of their own; that, whatever happened, they could always go back into vaudeville."[6] Cole and Rosamond Johnson were to be the featured performers as well as the principal contributors of lyrics and music.

The action of the play relates the adventures, feuds, and loves of students at the Lincolnville Institute, Alabama, who volunteer to serve in the Spanish-American War. The second act follows the members of the Shoo-Fly Regiment (with their girlfriends) to the fight in the Philippines, where several military engagements take place. The Regiment is victorious in a final battle and returns triumphantly to Alabama.

Harrigan and Hart had exploited the idea of rival military groups onstage in their Mulligan Guards comedies of the 1880s, featuring black and Irish characters, and the comic military motif was prevalent in many songs of the 1890s. Titles such as "The Darkies' Dress Parade" (1894) by Ned Straight and "Ma Dandy Soldier Coon: A Humorous March Song" (1900) by Will Accooe are relatively common. A theater piece with a military theme allowed a considerable amount of stage action and the opportunity to evoke national pride through the performance of several patriotic songs. This crowd-pleasing formula did not go unnoticed by minstrel companies looking for effective finales. George M. Cohan (1878–1942) was revealed in full "Yankee Doodle Dandy" glory in his highly successful shows *Little Johnny Jones* (1904) and *George Washington, Jr.* (1906). Perhaps Cole and Johnson had some of these precedents in mind in building their show.[7]

Critics listed many songs of *The Shoo-Fly Regiment* as hits. "There's Always Something Wrong" is Bob Cole's homage to Bert Williams. Its tune contains more syncopation than most of Williams's or Hogan's songs, and its melodic construction, characteristic of Rosamond Johnson, is highly economical. All of the phrases in the chorus derive rhythmically from the first two measures (see Example 8.1).

"De Bo'd of Education" (Example 8.2) is a humorous patter song that

Example 8.1. Bob Cole and J. Rosamond Johnson, "There's Always Something Wrong" (New York: Jos. W. Stern & Co., 1907), chorus, mm. 1–4

Dere's   al - ways some-thing   wrong, yes al - ways some-thing wrong mos' all de   time

mocks the pretensions of an ignorant board of education. They laugh merrily:

> We is de Bo'd, We is de Bo'd
> De Bo'd of Education.
> We is de men dat suprenten'
> Each school examination.
> Answers dat we can't "cricticksize,"
> We let dem pass, an jes' look wise.
> We is de Bo'd, we is de Bo'd,
> De Bo'd of Education.

The chorus, with syncopations occurring only within beats, resembles typical ragtime tunes of the previous decade, such as Kerry Mills's hit "At a Georgia Camp Meeting" (1897). "On the Gay Luneta," with lyrics by Cole and music by James Reese Europe (1881–1919), presumably was sung in a Filipino location during the second act (its text begins, "When the moon was shining over Manila Bay"). A Spanish tone is provided by a habañera rhythm in the bass line of the verse. The snapping syncopation

Example 8.2. James Weldon Johnson and J. Rosamond Johnson, "De Bo'd of Education" (New York: Jos. W. Stern & Co., 1906), chorus, mm. 1–4

We is   de Bo'd,   We is   de Bo'd, De   Bo'd of   Ed - u   -   ca - tion

of the chorus melody over an ostinato bass provides an effective contrast to the verse (Facsimile 8.3). In "Floating Down the Nile," a number with no apparent relation to the plot, Rosamond Johnson cleverly paints the first verse of the text. A persistent drone bass produced by openly spaced D major and A major triads in a rolling $\frac{6}{8}$ meter, combined with a near total lack of rests in the vocal line, support the blissfully flowing description of the text:

> Sometimes I close bose of my eyes, and in ma dreams
> Go to a land, love, where we bose could be happy side by side.
> And there on a beautiful river so it seems
> In a canoe, dear, we go floating together on the tide.

Upward harmonic flotation from D major to F♯ major occurs on the phrase "we go floating," a gesture typical of Johnson but here especially appropriate to the text (Example 8.3).

Example 8.3. James Weldon Johnson and J. Rosamond Johnson, "Floating Down the Nile" (New York: Jos. W. Stern & Co., 1906), verse, mm. 9–16

The masterpiece of *The Shoo-Fly Regiment,* although it was not originally composed for the show, was "Lit'l Gal," copyrighted in 1902 (Facsimile 8.4). Rosamond Johnson had not seen fit to use it in any of the Klaw-Erlanger shows, but it was too good a song to be neglected for long. It is a gem of delicate writing, a three-section lullaby characterized by languid minor thirds placed over a well-crafted harmony in which major and minor chords are mixed with originality and suavity. Paul Laurence Dunbar wrote the dialect text. In a 1917 edition, with its title changed slightly from "Lit'l Gal" to "Li'l Gal," new tempo and expression marks are extensive, an indication that special care was devoted to its marketing. The 1917 version contains a certain self-conscious modernity: indications in French (m. 1), a modal mixture of chords (mm. 8–14), and parallel fifths à la Debussy in the accompaniment (m. 29). It was designated as being part of the "Stern Fine Art Series," probably indicating that it had already sold well and that the publisher wanted to suggest its appropriateness for the concert singer's repertory. Indeed, it sounds like nothing so much as a hybrid offspring of art song and spiritual rather than a typical musical comedy ditty. The whimsical relationship between "Li'l Gal" and "I Got Plenty o' Nothin'" shown in Example 8.4 is probably not significant, but in a general way the seeds of George and Ira Gershwin's *Porgy and Bess* (1935) can be seen in some of the phrases written thirty years earlier by J. Rosamond Johnson.

The Shoo-Fly Regiment opened late in 1906, playing mostly in Ohio and Pennsylvania. Although the out-of-town critics received the music of the show favorably, most noted the melodramatic and old-fashioned plot.

Example 8.4. Chords from J. Rosamond Johnson, "Li'l Gal," mm. 12–14, with words from Ira Gershwin, "I Got Plenty o' Nothin'"

A Boston critic wrote a comment more pertinent to the orchestra's ability than to the show itself: "The music is of the music-hall order and is pretty noisy, the bass drum and cymbals and cornet being overworked." Others found the songs "bright," "catchy," and "tuneful."[8]

The New York reaction to the show as a whole was mixed. The June performances were lauded. "The capable cast . . . resembled more nearly a choral society than a musical comedy ensemble," one writer reported, but "the music is noteworthy and especially well-orchestrated. . . . Andrew Tribble made a capital impression as a shady Sis Hopkins and was the most interesting feature of the cast. Bob Cole and J. Rosamond Johnson made their usual [positive] impression with their well known piano act. With the exception of poor enunciation and a super-abundance of noise, the rest of the cast was competent." Criticism of the August performances was stronger, however; one critic commented that "the actors did not meet the requirements of the [mostly white] audience." Another disenchanted reviewer wrote, "Everything connected with the comic opera was amateurish, and it does not call for extended criticism. If there was in it the slightest gleam of originality we failed to see it."[9] This critic grudgingly admitted to finding some worth among the musical numbers.

James Weldon Johnson recounts that the show suffered financial woes as well as critical disfavor:

> In New York, I found Bob and Rosamond back from their tour with *The Shoo-Fly Regiment*. They had started out with a company of sixty people, with some fairly good bookings and promises of more; but the bulk of it all turned out to be in one-night stands in popular-price theaters. Not yet had the fight for colored companies to play first-class houses been won. A good part of their tour had been laid out to cover small towns in the South. With a large and expensive company, it was impossible for them to make money at the prices to which they were compelled to play. Indeed, they lost money; so much that the management under which they were booked failed them and left the show to shift for itself somewhere in the far South. Bob and Rosamond used their own money to keep their company intact and bring it back to New York. A short engagement at the Bijou Theatre in New York had the result of bringing them under the more reliable management of Stair and Havlin for the coming season.[10]

James Weldon Johnson left show business in 1906 to join the foreign service and did not record the vicissitudes of *The Shoo-Fly Regiment* after this time, but the fortune of the second tour must have surpassed that of the first, because Cole and Rosamond Johnson were inspired to set out again with another show in 1908.

The Red Moon

The Red Moon was the most ambitious production that the team attempted, one of the most well-received shows on the road, and the last of the large shows in the Williams and Walker decade. No show rivaled it until J. Leubrie Hill's Darktown Follies productions of 1913.

After touring at the beginning of 1909, the show opened in New York's Majestic Theatre on May 3, only the second black company (after Williams and Walker) to play in that theater. A. L. Wilbur managed the show and the stars composed the book, lyrics, and music for all but a pair of songs in which James Reese Europe had a hand.[11]

The play relates the kidnapping, adventures, and finally the rescue of a young girl of mixed parentage, Minnehaha (Abbie Mitchell), abducted by her Indian father (Theo Pankey) from her mother's Virginia home and taken west. To the rescue are Slim Brown (Cole) and Plunk Green (Johnson), comic lawyer and bogus doctor respectively. Their antics and songs provided the centerpiece of the show.

Many musical elements are predictable in *The Red Moon*, given the basic Indian motif. Clichés of stage exoticism, drone fifths combined with pulsating eighth notes and a pentatonic melody, occur in "Big Red Shawl," for example. The show is not dominated by Indian clichés, however, and other tunes in it are charming and fresh. "Bleeding Moon" features a stately verse in moderately paced half- and quarter-notes (Facsimile 8.5). A Spanish song, perhaps inspired by the rising popularity of Latin dances at the time, was entitled "On the Road to Monterey." A habañera ostinato supports the romantic mood of the text, but several continuous phrases provide a surprising contrast by extending the four-measure melodic units (Example 8.5).

The most structurally distinctive piece in the show, entitled "Run, Brudder Possum, Run" (Facsimile 8.6), contains a verse divided into two sections, giving the tune an overall tripartite form. The middle section, beginning midverse at m. 13, is marked "Slower," and the final two

Example 8.5. Bob Cole, "On the Road to Monterey" (New York: Jos. W. Stern & Co., 1908), verse, mm. 25–31

sections feature a gradual acceleration in tempo. The tempo, phrase, and section breaks are presented in Figure 5. Each section is constructed from four-bar phrases, but the total measures increase in each successive section. The three parts contain different melodic figures; unity and bal-

Fig. 5. Structure of the Johnson brothers' "Run, Brudder Possum, Run"

$\frac{2}{4}$ meter	Intro.	Verse		Chorus
key of F	(instr.)			
(measures per section)	5	4+8	4+4+4+4	4+4+4+2+8
"Allegro Moderato"			"Slower"	
	poco a poco accel. . . . rall.			poco a poco accel. e dim.

Example 8.6. Bob Cole and James Reese Europe, "I Ain't Had No Lovin' in a Long Time" (New York: Jos. W. Stern & Co., 1908), chorus, mm. 1–4

I ain't had no lov-in' in a long time and lov-in' is a thing I___ need

Example 8.7. Noble Sissle and Eubie Blake, "If You've Never Been Vamped By a Brownskin" (New York: Witmark & Sons, 1921), chorus, mm. 1–4. Reprinted by permission.

(orig. key=E♭)

If you've nev - er been vamp'd___ by a brown

skin, You've nev - er been vamp'd___ at all

ance are preserved through the use of similar syncopated figures in the outer sections.

The naughtiest song of the show was a collaborative effort of Cole and James Reese Europe entitled "I Ain't Had No Lovin' in a Long Time" ("an' lovin' is a thing I need"). The tune of the chorus (Example 8.6) bears a family resemblance to Eubie Blake's *Shuffle Along* (1921) hit, "If You've Never Been Vamped By a Brownskin" (Example 8.7). Blake admired *The Red Moon* (he recorded "Bleeding Moon" in part of a piano medley)[12] and probably remembered "I Ain't Had No Lovin'" as an especially catchy series of intervals that could be swung gently and attached neatly to Noble Sissle's text. The text, about a girl eager for "lovin'" and a "platonically" minded boy, does not expound a typical theme. Composers of popular song seldom were as clear or imaginative in dealing with sex as were singers of folk music and blues.[13] But even in its lack of earthiness or double entendre, "I Ain't Had No Lovin'" stands apart from almost all of the other tunes in the show. The humorous similes, original rhymes, and fresh use of dialect all make this one of Cole's better pieces of verse:

> Mister Romeo Bacon is a nice young man,
> But here's where I puts him on de drying pan,

He's one o' dem gentlemen dat acts too nice,
He set up in de parlor, like a cake of ice;
He never calls me: "honey" an' he never says: "dear"
An' he never makes a noise like a cold glass of beer;
He don't give me nothing, but dat "weather" talk,
And he never even asked me for to take a walk,
Of course I'm "dickee doo,"
But I like a little lovin' too.
Chorus:
. . . You must call me by some sweet and tender name,
It takes a lot of fire to start my flame,
I ain't had no lovin' in a long time
An' lovin' is a thing I need.

It takes little imagination to hear a winning number here in the hands of a clever soubrette like Aida Overton Walker or Gertrude Saunders.

The harmonic language of J. Rosamond Johnson is consistently richer than that of his contemporaries, Will Marion Cook excepted. Gestures beyond the typical use of the tonic, dominant, and subdominant are found in many songs: the movement to a triad on the flatted-third scale degree in the third phrase of "I've Lost My Teddy Bear" (Example 8.8); a deceptive cadence in "Run, Brudder Possum, Run" (Example 8.9); and a varied series of chords to arrive at the dominant in the verse of "As Long as the World Goes Round" (Example 8.10).

Johnson's writing, emphasizing triads built on the third and sixth scale degrees, differs considerably from the major black form to emerge in

Example 8.8. Bob Cole and J. Rosamond Johnson, "I've Lost My Teddy Bear" (New York: Jos. W. Stern & Co., 1908), verse, mm. 7–9

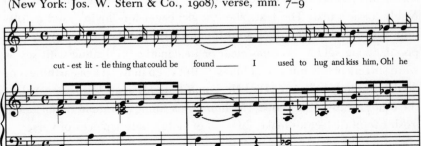

Aida Overton Walker (1908), scintillating singer and
dancer who performed with the Black Patti Troubadours company and later costarred with Williams
and Walker, Cole and Johnson, and the Smart Set.
Yale Collection of American Literature, Beinecke Rare
Book and Manuscript Library, Yale University.

print notation in the decade, the blues, which places subdominant seventh chords in a central position. It would be unfair to suggest that
Johnson was unaware of other types of black music, since his subsequent
publications of black spirituals demonstrate a great deal of interest and
knowledge, but he does draw on other genres in his show songs, particularly art songs.

Johnson had a penchant for incorporating art-song elements—arpeggi-

Example 8.9. James Weldon Johnson and J. Rosamond Johnson, "Run, Brudder Possum, Run" (New York: Rogers Bros., 1900), chorus, mm. 13–14

ated chords richly larded with sevenths and chromatic passing tones, and numerous expression and tempo markings. The appearance of such written details in light-comedy songs was quite special and reveals the unusual conscientiousness for a musical show composer of this era. Nearly all of the tunes in the show were published, reflecting a belief that the show would go over and the songs would sell.

The Red Moon played to both black and mixed audiences and on the whole had enthusiastic reviews. The *Dramatic Mirror* termed Johnson's score "often quite ambitious and pleasing to hear." Even the *New York*

Example 8.10. J. Rosamond Johnson, "As Long as the World Goes Round" (New York and Detroit: Jerome H. Remick & Co., 1909), verse, mm. 23–30

Times, which predicted a short run for the show, admitted that "several of the musical numbers were sung by the Indian and negro chorus with spirit." As late as 1934, the music publisher E. B. Marks reminisced about the show, doubtless having heard in the meantime the more celebrated shows of the 1920s, *Shuffle Along* (1921), *The Chocolate Dandies* (1924), Lew Leslie's *Blackbirds* (1928), and *Hot Chocolates* (1929), calling it "the most tuneful colored show of the century."[14]

Like *The Shoo-Fly Regiment* in its first year, *The Red Moon* also suffered from poor bookings at less than first-rate theaters. At the end of the show's tour in the spring or summer of 1910, Cole and Johnson canceled tentative plans for another new show and resolved to return to their more dependable and easily managed vaudeville career. On the abrupt conclusion of their big production efforts the *New York Age* reported, "The inability of Stair and Havlin to provide suitable booking is the primary cause of this latest and unexpected move." In October 1910 the team reappeared in vaudeville at Keith's Fifth Avenue Theatre.[15]

The Smart Set Shows of S. H. Dudley

Although he had few specific ties to the New York scene, being a Washingtonian and a traveling showman much of his life, S. H. Dudley was unquestionably an admired figure among black showpeople. Dudley's work as a comedian, a promoter, and especially as a theater manager had a broad impact.

Sherman Houston Dudley was born around 1880 in Austin, Texas. His training consisted of medicine-show singing and stump speeches. In Galveston he founded the Dudley Georgia Minstrels and later appeared with P. T. Wright's Nashville Students. He formed an act with Sam Corker, who served as business manager of Cole and Johnson's *A Trip to Coontown* and *The Shoo-Fly Regiment*, and toured the East Coast with Will Marion Cook's *Clorindy* company. He worked with star comedian Billy Kersands in *King Rastus*. In 1904 he joined Gus Hill's Smart Set company, a touring show that previously had featured Tom McIntosh and Ernest Hogan.[16]

The Smart Set, like other traveling shows, featured a play interspersed with dancing, music, comedy, and specialties. One of the early plays that featured Dudley was *The Black Politician*, "a musical comedy in three acts" written by Dudley and Steve Cassin and including "old time colored melodies and up-to-date tunes." The play's Southern locale and its horse race were familiar devices. Veteran showman Walter Crumbly told Marshall and Jean Stearns, "It was one of those Simon Legree plots where all the colored people *suffered. . . .* The show opened with everybody singing, then one scene after another, according to the story not like vaudeville acts, with a chorus line of girls and lots of comedy and dancing." One critic commented, "To say that the piece . . . is an original production would hardly be truthful, but it has been put together in an original manner. Old tunes with new words (and some of them without this change)—old scenes with innovations and improvements, and one or two hybrid specialties, are brightened much with a thick sprinkling of really funny lines."[17]

The white manager, Gus Hill, booked the show from New York. It traveled as far south as Georgia, playing mostly for white audiences. The Smart Set continued on into the next decade with S. H. Dudley as the principal comedian and produced two original shows, *Dr. Beans from Boston* (1910) and his best-known vehicle, the only one to play a Broadway house, *His Honor, the Barber.*

His Honor, the Barber came to the Majestic Theatre on May 8, 1911, having toured in the Midwest. Dudley costarred with Aida Overton Walker and other members of the Smart Set company. Edwin Handford, a white playwright, wrote the book, and James T. Brymn composed the music.

The plot involves a barber, Raspberry Snow (Dudley), who dreams of shaving the President of the United States. He goes to the White House and, doped by a navy doctor, falls asleep on the front steps. After being shooed away, he consoles himself by betting at the races and wins a large prize. The President, hearing of his success, invites him into the White House (an obvious allusion to Booker T. Washington's famous invitation from Roosevelt). About to realize his ambition at last, the hapless barber is awakened still lying outside on the steps.

As with *The Red Moon*, the *New York Times* critic felt that too much effort was expended on imitating white performers. Such statements must remain suspect unless backed up with specific evidence, since many white viewers were not satisfied with anything less than stereotypical character portrayals—what was deemed the proper way for blacks to act onstage. This particular show, however, received the same criticism from the black *New York Age* critic Lester Walton, who used virtually the same words as the *Times* reviewer. Walton also objected to the crudities of the book, noting that it was filled with guns, razors, and the slaughtering of ferocious animals. The *Times*, while calling Dudley's humor "rough," noted that the cast, including Patrick the Donkey (a live beast in blue overalls), found favor with the audience. The *Dramatic Mirror* described Brymn's music as "delightful and pleasing," and the *Times* concluded that "the choral singing is enough of a saving grace to make a visit to the Majestic worthwhile." In other words, the coon stereotypes were far from dead, and black choral singing, which had been singled out for praise time and time again, was still a key attraction.[18]

James Tim Brymn, composer, conductor, and arranger, was born in Kingston, North Carolina, in 1881 and was educated at Shaw University and the National Conservatory of Music. He came to New York around 1900 and soon published several songs showing that he had assimilated the most common varieties of popular song, waltzes, ballads, and ragtime songs. Collaborating with R. C. McPherson, he composed "Josephine, My Jo," interpolated into *The Sons of Ham* in 1900. Brymn composed at least five songs that were probably interpolated into the Smart Set shows around 1905: "Morning, Noon and Night," "O-San," "Powhatana," "Travel On," and "Darktown Grenadiers."

Brymn's syncopated melodies are leaping and propulsive tunes with sturdy ragtime bass lines. Among the best of his one hundred-odd popular songs are two that appeared in *His Honor, the Barber*, "Come After Breakfast, Bring 'Long Your Lunch, and Leave Before Supper Time" and "Porto Rico."

"Come After Breakfast," written with Chris Smith and James Burris, tells about Aunt Mandy, who welcomes all visitors as long as they don't want her food. The brief but pungent augmented chord in the third measure of the refrain (Facsimile 8.7) illustrates the harmonic variety Brymn often provides; the sonority underlines at the perfect moment the humor of Aunt Mandy's punchline after the narrative verse. "Porto Rico" immediately establishes the requisite Spanish rhythm ⁊ ♩ ♪ ♫♫♪ and a drone bass and adds two nicely balanced pairs of measures: a descending chromatic scale (mm. 1–2) and an ascending diatonic one (mm. 3–4) (Example 8.11).

His Honor, the Barber spent only two weeks in New York, but it toured for several seasons and met praise on the road as it had in New York. The San Francisco *Dramatic Record* called the book "dull" but remarked that the "musical numbers . . . rendered by a chorus of dash and go, made the audience happy."[19]

Around 1912 Dudley moved to Washington, D. C., and began to spend less time performing and more time managing. He purchased and leased several theaters in an effort to build a circuit independent of white control. He also helped to establish the Theater Owners' Booking Associa-

Example 8.11. Cecil Mack and J. T. Brymn, "Porto Rico" (New York: Gotham-Attucks Music Co., 1910), verse, mm. 1–4

tion, a circuit of Southern vaudeville houses that ultimately spread to Texas, Oklahoma, and many Northern cities.[20] He remained active as a manager and intermittently as an actor through the 1910s and 1920s. He died on February 29, 1940.

Around 1910 the brothers S. Tutt Whitney and J. Homer Tutt formed

Sherman Houston Dudley, actor, comedian, and theater owner who founded the earliest circuit of theaters to showcase black talent, the Dudley Circuit, a precursor of the Theatre Owners' Booking Association (TOBA). Billy Rose Theatre Collection, the New York Public Library at Lincoln Center, Astor, Lenox, and Tilden Foundations.

the Whitney Musical Comedy Company and toured in the Midwest and South. Later that year they began calling themselves the Southern Smart Set, continuing under that name until 1913. Both the Smart Set and the Southern Smart Set were managed by Charles E. Barton, who chose Tutt and Whitney to replace the temporarily retiring Dudley in a 1913–14 show, *The Wrong Mr. President*. The two groups became one. Tutt and Whitney toured with many shows that played periodically in New York at the Lafayette Theatre in Harlem from 1913 to 1920. James Vaughan, musical director for Williams and Walker from 1902 to 1909, joined the Southern Smart Set contingent as composer and arranger in 1915. By June 1917 the group changed its name to the Smarter Set and continued to produce shows that appeared mainly in the South.[21]

The Black Patti Troubadours Shows

From 1896 to 1910 Sissieretta Jones had appeared in the final portion of the Troubadours program in her renowned "operatic kaleidoscope," a segment more or less separate from the acts and skits that preceded it. Early skits that the Troubadours presented without her direct involvement included: "At Jolly Coon-ey Island," "A Filipino Misfit," "Dooney Dreamland," and "Prince Bungaboo." Four later productions including Jones as a character in the play were more ambitious, though little of the music for them has survived. Song titles preserved in reviews and advertisements include themes often found in other shows: love ("Love is King," Lady Angeline," "All I Want is My Honey"); nostalgia ("Mother's Chil'," "I Wish I Was in Heaven," "Goodbye, Rose"); and African motifs ("In Zululand," "My Jewel of the River Nile").[22]

A *Trip to Africa* (1910), advertised as a "three-act musical farce comedy," presented a new role for Jones. In addition to her operatic finale she played the part of a regal African princess in the skit. The story told of the rescue of a missionary in Africa from a tribe of Zulus and was written, along with the song lyrics, by her costar, John Larkins. The music was composed by Dave Peyton (ca. 1885–1955), a Chicago band director. The *Boston Transcript* said of the show, "The results to all are of the boisterous humor that colored companies carry off much better than do their white rivals. Happily, before and through the trip, the piece is well furnished with ragtime ditties and dances to match."[23]

Jones had a speaking role in the next production, *In the Jungles* (1911), costarring Julius Glenn. The story again involved a rescue in Africa, with Jones appearing in the role of "Queen Le-Ku-Li, queen of the Gumbula Tribe." The book was written by Will A. Cooke and Al F. Watts, the lyrics were provided by Rogers, and the music was written by Will Marion Cook. The show, especially the performances of Jones and Glenn, received complimentary reviews in Chicago, Cincinnati, and Louisville, and it played in New York's Grand Opera House in May 1912 to pleased audiences and critics. Sylvester Russell hailed Jones's foray into acting: "her present day experience is equal if not greater and more capable than the average white actress in musical comedy." He added that her singing, as good as ever, was "the marvel of the day." She performed such favorites as "Home, Sweet Home" and a new song, "My Jewel of the River Nile." Although he enjoyed the "quartette of the last act," Russell thought Cook's music "not quite up to his past record."[24]

The music of the next show, *Captain Jaspar* (1912), "ranged from sentimental to ragtime," proclaimed the *Freeman*,[25] but neither the reviewer nor the advertisements identified specific composers, suggesting perhaps that more than one had contributed. This was another show by Will A. Cooke in which Jones appeared as an actress and worked with Julius Glenn.

The last show of the Troubadours, *Lucky Sam from Alabam* (1914), featured Harrison Stewart as the male comedian playing opposite Jones. Steward also wrote much of the book and music for this three-act comedy. It did not include the "operatic kaleidoscope" but featured a total of twenty-two musical numbers—an opening chorus and choral finale for each act, a double quartet in the second act, a dance medley before the third-act finale, and five numbers for Sissieretta Jones. In addition to Stewart's songs, Tosti's "Goodbye!," still a sentimental favorite, was interpolated by Jones. The show received a mixed review from Lester Walton:

> In the construction of the piece Harrison Stewart has taken several vaudeville offerings in which he has been seen with success and bound them together with some semblance of a plot. Many of the musical numbers are also reminiscent to New Yorkers, having been heard in Mr. Stewart's sketches heretofore presented at the Lafayette. . . . As a librettist and composer Harrison Stewart may not win undying fame in

Lucky Sam from Alabam, but his reputation as a comedian will be greatly enhanced.[26]

The Black Patti Troubadours shows exploited the common devices of black musical theater of their day—African themes, vaudeville specialties, and ragtime songs—and were blessed with a dazzling star and several

Matilda Sissieretta Jones, the "Black Patti," renowned soprano and star of the Black Patti Troubadours company. She appeared first as a concert singer and then traveled in variety shows for over twenty years. Schomburg Center for Research in Black Culture, the New York Public Library, Astor, Lenox, and Tilden Foundations.

talented comedians. Jones's productions involved fewer people and less scenic display than did the Williams and Walker or Cole and Johnson productions, as would be expected in a touring company, but the superior singing of Sissieretta Jones drew audiences everywhere she toured, making most other trappings irrelevant. As a national traveling show, the Troubadours spent little time in New York.

It is difficult to evaluate Jones's company's contribution to musical comedy history without adequate musical information, but there is no doubt that the "Black Patti" was an important individual performer. Marshall and Jean Stearns report:

> "Negroes were proud of Black Patti," says Professor Willis Laurence James of Spelman College, who grew up in Jacksonville and remembers the excitement caused by the arrival of the Troubadours. "In a sense, she was a kind of 'racial' heroine because she was so outstanding as a singer, even by white standards, and white people came to hear her, too."

William Lichtenwanger, in a biographical sketch for *Notable American Women*, summarizes her contribution:

> It is clear that she had a commanding presence, musicality with intelligence, a natural sense of the dramatic, and poise in both singing and speaking. With her Troubadours she fought a constant battle on the side of taste and artistic integrity, not only in her singing but also in the entire production of her "operatic kaleidoscopes." Had she been white, she might have had longer and better training; she certainly would have had opportunities to achieve higher pinnacles of success. As it is, she stands as a pioneer. Despite a white public inclined to overlook her artistry and treat her as a freak, despite a Negro public too poor and uneducated to support her effectively, despite biased critics and mediocre management, Madame Jones forced the musical and theatrical worlds in the United States to accept the Negro in a new image.[27]

9

The Productions Reviewed:
A Summary of Black Shows,
1898–1911

What did the black shows look like onstage? What did audiences expect from the star performers? What were the most familiar bits of stage business tied to romantic or ragtime songs? The answers to these questions are not always clear, even for shows as famous as *In Dahomey* or *The Red Moon*. Choreography was not recorded, films were not made, performers varied their attitudes to suit different audiences, and critical accounts vary. It would be incorrect to suggest detailed affinities between such different productions as *A Trip to Coontown, The Southerners,* and *His Honor, the Barber,* yet several details can be cited to produce a composite picture, so to speak, of the shows discussed individually:

1. On entering the theater, white members of the audience took seats in the orchestra or elsewhere in the center of the auditorium; blacks were sent to the balcony or perhaps were segregated on one side of the house. In predominantly black theaters it would be the whites who were sent to the balcony if large crowds were expected. Only rarely was seating unsegregated.

2. The members of the audience probably noticed a theater orchestra of between five and fifteen members, which may or may not have been located in a pit. One writer of the early 1890s recommends "twelve capable musicians for a theatre orchestra," consisting of three violins, one viola, one cello, one flute, one clarinet, two cornets, one trombone, one percussion, and also "two horns for a musical farce or comedy." James Weldon Johnson contrasted the English practice at London's Palace Theatre in 1903 with the American routine: "When the orchestra filed in, I counted forty men, and made a quick contrast with the scant-nine-piece orchestra in the best American vaudeville theaters and with the solitary piano player in a great many of them." Minstrel show bands sometimes played behind and above the stage on which the comedians appeared. Will Marion Cook, as conductor, reportedly faced the audience and sang along with the songs.[1]

3. The show began with an overture, either a classical piece such as Thomas's Overture to *Raymond* or a new piece written by the show's composer. The orchestra also played marches, dances, operatic medleys, and new popular tunes between the acts. These selections often were listed in programs.

4. The curtain rose to a rousing chorus, followed by a comic dialogue that laid out the lines of the plot.

5. The show consisted of either two or three acts, with three or four scenes per act and one or two songs per scene.

6. If the plot was not a central feature of the entertainment, much of the material between the songs was improvised. A longtime employee of Harlem's Apollo Theater, Francis "Doll" Thomas, declared that the early shows mostly were ad libbed and done without books or formal blocking. Often scripts provided the meager information that "music and business" took place at several points in the show. However, fairly detailed scripts do exist for some shows—*In Dahomey* and *Abyssinia,* for example—and the systematic working habits of J. Rosamond Johnson suggest that nearly everything he had a hand in was planned out well in advance, if not actually written down. A surviving notebook belonging to Bob Cole shows that he carefully timed every scene and song in successive presentations of *The Red Moon.*[2]

7. The humor and aspirations of black folk were central themes of the plots. The comic stars typically were tricksters or goodhearted ne'er-do-wells. Trips to Africa were commonly included, with the conti-

nent portrayed as civilized but not necessarily hospitable to Americans. Often comments were made about social class, wealth, and the value of education. Pompous Johnsing, a character in *Jes Lak White Fo'ks,* gives a speech that contains all these topics:

> I want you all to und'stand I got a plan in regard to di gold. I got social aspirations. You know when white men gets rich dem don stay hyeah wha everybody knows 'em en knows dey ain' much. Dey go to Europe an by m by you readin' de papers en you say: "Huh! heah Mr. Williams Vanderbilt Sunflower's daughter married a duke." But I ain goin get no bargain counter duke for my daughter, hun-uh, honey. She is goin to marry a prince.
>
> She done got huh diploma from Vassar, and I has been engaged in diplomatic negotiations wid an Af'ican King. Dis will be a ma'iage of convenience. . . . I goin' to get 'mandy a family tree. Ain' nobody what is anybody keepin' house doubt a family tree. Dey er so cheap in Europe dey use 'em fer kindlin wood. . . . 3

8. Specialty entertainers (dancers, impersonators, jugglers, acrobats, and so on) appeared between the musical numbers and comic scenes.
9. Towards the end of the first act or early in the second act, the principal comedian or comedians appeared.
10. Several songs included a featured singer with the chorus joining in on the refrain. Male quartets were also a popular combination. The accompaniment to songs was probably adapted from a standard arrangement for the orchestra at hand. A stock arrangement of "My Dahomian Queen," one of the songs in *In Dahomey,* for example, calls for piano, first and second violin, viola, cello, flute, clarinet, cornet, trombone, and drums. Specific comments relative to the use of instruments in reviews are rare. Mabel Rowland, an early Bert Williams biographer, noted, "The arrangement of the orchestration for 'Nobody' was not by any means the least important feature of the song. It was a weirdly mournful tune anyway and with the featuring of the slide trombone in the orchestra many a laugh in 'Nobody' came from the plaintive sound of the trombone and from Williams' apparently desperate efforts to catch up with it." Similarly, comic bassoon interjections are heard on Williams's recording of "The Moon Shines on the Moonshine," which he sang years later for the Ziegfeld Follies. 4

11. Scenery for musical comedies usually consisted of painted flats, but more complex scenic displays were tried occasionally, such as the manmade waterfall in *Abyssinia*, the transformation scene in *In Dahomey*, and the introduction of live animals in *His Honor, the Barber*. Virtually no comments from critics appear about stage lighting in the big shows, but Tom Fletcher cited Johnson and Dean, the cakewalk team of the 1890s, as being the first to use the flicker kinetoscope, a device that apparently produced a dazzling "crowd" of images, a sort of primitive strobe-light effect.[5] It is possible that such machines were used in dance finales and specialty acts in the larger shows.

12. The show concluded with the entire company singing and dancing, usually the cakewalk. Fletcher declared flatly that "all the big colored shows featured the cakewalk" and that its popularity did not ebb until 1910.[6]

Critics, if they liked a show, invariably cited the music, the singing style, the dancing, the unique abilities of a comedian, or some combination of these elements as the distinctive and distinctively black features of the show. For the audiences, "Negro" music seems to have meant syncopated tunes or dialect songs on a nostalgic, Old South theme. Black singing style was epitomized by a loud, vigorous, and resonant chorus. An English critic of *In Dahomey* wrote, "Their remarkable sense and unanimity of rhythm and time, the fidelity of their part-singing, and the curious half-metallic, but not unpleasant, timbre of their voices afforded a new musical sensation." This description is suggestive of a modern gospel choir sound. Of the Black Patti Troubadours, the New York correspondent for the London *Era* declared, "The spirit and musical finish displayed in the choruses are exciting nightly enthusiasm."[7]

Black dancing consisted of cakewalking and the old buck-and-wing familiar from minstrel shows, but special styles of certain performers sometimes were described in detail. George Walker was famed as a high-stepping strutter, a dancer of "extraordinary agility." Bert Williams appeared in *Mr. Lode of Koal* "with . . . the excruciating dance which is half lope and glide, with dangling arms tipped with white cotton gloves, and with the smile which is the more joyful because it comes only infrequently from the funny gloom with which the comedian in lugubrious tones tells of his misfortunes. . . ."[8]

The comic geniuses of the black stage were cited for their subtle gestures and graphic facial expressions. Bob Cole's speeches contained an "invariably irresistible quietness." One writer saw "very little of the burlesque in Ernest Hogan's methods, which were for the most part suppressed and convincing." S. H. Dudley's style was called "a safe palliation of quick and limited humor rather than the art of overdoing," while Bert Williams showed "extraordinary ease in getting quiet and deliberate effects and impresses . . . as a genuine natural comedian."[9]

Perhaps the key concept in all of these plaudits is movement that was both energetic and smooth, movement with the rhythmic timing essential to good music, dancing, and comedy. Doll Thomas declared that it was the black showpeople's response to rhythm that kept their shows alive, and much evidence corroborates his first-hand observation.[10] Left at that, however, the picture is not completely drawn. "They got rhythm" is at best a vague description and at worst a racist cliché. The performers worked themselves up, but they also worked to elicit a response. The participation of the audience inspired the performers and completed the theatrical event. The performers' secret lay in communicating vitality beyond the footlights, creating and gradually intensifying an electricity that affected players and audiences alike.

3

A Lull
in the Big Shows,
New Developments
Elsewhere

10

The Rise of Straight
Drama and Vaudeville,
1910–1915

In the early years of the twentieth century American musical comedy had begun to develop a personality of its own, and the public had responded favorably. George M. Cohan, among others, breathed life and melody into breezy comic stories and melodramas. Shows such as *The Belle of New York* (1897) and *In Dahomey* (1903) had even toured successfully in Europe. However, in 1907 Franz Lehar's *The Merry Widow* appeared in New York, and a vogue for everything Viennese prevailed on the stage for several years afterward. Gerald Bordman refers to the years from 1907 to 1914 as "the American retreat" in the face of Viennese operetta: "Those writers who could not or would not write in this gay, sweeping Central European idiom met with increasing disappointment. Native musical material was still presented regularly, but it often seemed intimidated by the cavalier elegance of the Viennese school." Large black shows held the stage simultaneously with the Viennese works, and it is not clear that the Viennese presence affected their impact at all. Ragtime music (or at least popular music with syncopation) was as marketable as a Viennese waltz in

1914; in fact, in that year Irving Berlin promised a new "ragtime opera," although it never appeared. However, interest in homegrown novelties did ebb in favor of such Viennese productions as *The Dollar Princess* (1909), *The Chocolate Soldier* (1909), and *Sari* (1914).[1]

During the second decade of the twentieth century blacks were employed in vaudeville and in stock companies, and many entered the movies. Opportunities increased for the black entertainer, yet several difficulties and stumbling blocks persisted.

The cost of mounting and touring with a large show had always been substantial, but from about 1898 to 1908, with the perseverance and guidance of men like Bob Cole and George Walker, white investors had been rewarded for supporting black theatrical efforts. White support continued through the second decade of the century to a limited extent. When white businessmen sensed that the interest among white patrons had ebbed, even slightly, they attempted to put black shows on a touring circuit of so-called second-class theaters. Sometimes the designation of "first" and "second" class was informal. It may have been meant to suggest a difference between houses that hosted mainly straight plays, musical comedies, and high-class vaudeville and those that booked burlesque shows and more male-oriented variety and music hall material.

When Cole and Johnson retired from the production of big shows in 1910 and moved to vaudeville, the *New York Age* laid the problem at the feet of the booking agents and producers.[2] The failure to book shows in first-class theaters evidently spurred several leading black showmen to leave the business. Although he remained with the Smart Set touring show three years after Cole and Johnson had retired from big shows, S. H. Dudley faced a similar situation in September 1913. He declared that he did not want to offer "first class entertainment in second class theatres," in his words: "I have been with the Smart Set for ten seasons and have had only two losing seasons, so the colored show business is not a financial failure; it is simply prejudice on the part of the syndicates that are in power and control the theatrical situation in the United States."[3]

Prejudice was just one of many reasons that black shows were consigned to a second-class road circuit. Jack Poggi's study of the economic history of the American theater clearly shows a general decrease in the number of touring theatrical companies after 1908. From 1910 to 1925, "theatres available for legitimate productions" outside of large cities fell from 1,549 to 674. Poggi points to several factors in this decline, including the upswing in the popularity of the movies, the huge rise in transportation costs (up 80 percent from 1913 to 1928), and the poor quality of the productions sent out on the road. There was, on the other hand, increased interest in producing shows for New York, an interest mirrored in the growth of theater in Harlem in the early decades of this century.[4]

Bert Williams explained his move in 1910 to the all-white Ziegfeld Follies by noting that "colored show business is at a low ebb just now. . . . It was far better to have joined a large white show than to have starred in a colored show, considering conditions." Those conditions included the lack of financial sponsorship for black shows, second-class bookings, the racism of some owners and managers, and an abrupt and tragic change of leadership. The most adept organizers and financial minds among black showpeople—Ernest Hogan, Bob Cole, and George Walker, whom Lester Walton referred to as "the business brains of the colored profession"—all had left the business by 1910.[5]

The loss through illness and death of three top-flight performers and entrepreneurs in the years from 1908 to 1910 demoralized the black theatrical community and dampened any hopes for new large companies in the immediate future. By the fall of 1910 the largest remaining touring company was the Smart Set troupe, featuring S. H. Dudley, Aida Overton Walker, and the veterans of the *Red Moon* company, Andrew Tribble, Lottie Grady, and Ella Anderson. The Black Patti Troubadours began its fifteenth season; except for minstrel shows and touring "Uncle Tom's Cabin" shows, it was the only other large company on the road. In December 1911 Sylvester Russell, writing in the *Freeman*, declared, "There is not much to be said along the musical comedy line this year except to invite the present foremost stars to keep up the fight for elevation. Both the Dudley Smart Set and Black Patti companies are on probation as yet, with Julius Glenn discovered, for the great musical comedy class now deserted by Cole and Johnson."[6] The year 1911 did contain one interesting collaboration involving J. Rosamond Johnson and J. Leubrie Hill, who provided music and lyrics for an all-white cast. The show, *Hello Paris*, was the brainchild of Jesse Lasky and Henry Harris, and the production, dubbed a "one-act musical revuette," was a last-ditch attempt to sell their dinner theater, the Follies Bergere, to the public. The show was advertised as part of the first cabaret in America, and James Weldon Johnson referred to it as a "spicy revue,"[7] but the effort at French allure failed, closing after a month. The theater, located west of Broadway on Forty-sixth Street, reopened as a regular auditorium, the Fulton Theatre.

Johnson's music was typically brisk and carefully constructed. Among other numbers the show contained a "conversation song and dance" entitled "You're the Nicest Little Girl I Ever Knew" (Example 10.1). With its coy tone, conversational text, and dotted-eighth/sixteenth-note rhythm, it is reminiscent of Jerome Kern's well-known "How'd You Like to Spoon With Me" (1906). A little syncopation appeared in "Look Me Over." "Loving Moon" is a romantic song in the style of "The Pathway of Love," and a dance number without words called "The Siberian Dip" featured the quick duple time of the Russian trepak (Example 10.2).

The 1912 season was unmarked by outstanding achievements. The Black Patti Troubadours toured with *Captain Jaspar*, but no other major productions appeared. By the fall of 1913 S. H. Dudley had turned his attention to purchasing and managing theaters, in an attempt to deal with the booking problem for black shows. This undertaking, of course, limited

Example 10.1. J. Leubrie Hill and J. Rosamond Johnson, "You're the Nicest Little Girl I Ever Knew" (New York and Detroit: Jerome H. Remick & Co., 1911), chorus, mm. 1–9

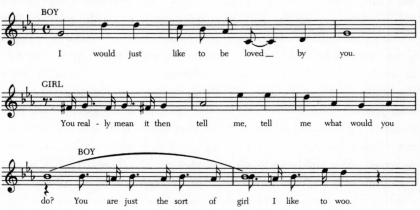

Example 10.2. J. Rosamond Johnson, "The Siberian Dip" (Detroit and New York: Jerome H. Remick & Co., 1911), mm. 5–8

his time on the stage. In 1913, for the first time in eighteen years, the Black Patti company did not go out on the road because the star was ill. Lester Walton's normally optimistic tone was absent from his outlook for the 1913–14 season. The headline for his column of September 18, 1913, read "Season Opens with Two Big Colored Shows in Storage." He followed this announcement with several forlorn paragraphs on the decline of the musical comedy since the closing of the shows of Williams and Walker, Cole and Johnson, and Hogan.[8]

If the theatrical climate was changing after 1910, one reason was that the politics of race also was changing—or at least not improving. The movement of Southern blacks to Northern cities to escape discrimination and the boll weevil scourge created larger, more active, and, to some whites, more threatening populations of blacks in the North. Segregated seating was still a part of the New York theater scene, and legalized segregation was increasing in many areas of the country; in fact, the majority of Jim Crow legislation in the South appeared in the first two decades of the twentieth century. A racial incident in the New York Theatre's roof garden, the Jardin de Paris, caused black patrons to be excluded altogether beginning in the summer of 1909. New York suffered its largest antiblack riot since the Civil War in August 1900, and if memories of it were dying by the end of the decade, a shooting spree involving black soldiers and irate townspeople in Texas in the summer of 1906, known as the Brownsville Affair, mushroomed into a national political issue by 1908 and stirred hatred among whites and blacks.[9]

In the midst of these tensions appeared the prizefighter Jack Johnson, whose heroic presence and success elated American blacks. Johnson enraged many whites by winning the heavyweight championship of the world in 1908 (the first black to reach that peak), subsequently defeating the retired champion Jim Jeffries in 1910, and becoming romantically involved with a white woman. Johnson was paid to do sparring exhibitions in vaudeville, but his defiant stance had other direct effects in the world of the theater. Lester Walton noted that antagonism toward Johnson had hurt colored show business, citing the cancellation of Black Patti Troubadours bookings in the South and the termination by the Shuberts of some appearances by Bert Williams. Apparently, managers feared for the safety of performers and their buildings before audiences apt to act out their anti-Johnson feelings.[10]

Heightened tensions and persistent patterns of discrimination in New York further solidified an already strong desire for black community involvement. Actors and playwrights were led to develop the theater in Harlem itself and to explore broader dimensions of day-to-day black experience for black audiences in Harlem. In the spring of 1913 plans were afoot for the formation of a black stock company, and in March of that year Will Marion Cook explained the plan:

> The Negro Players, a company formed for the development of Negro music and drama will begin . . . a series of productions providing . . . real pictures of Negro life both of city and plantation. The authors of the playlets will at first treat of the lighter humorous characteristics of their people until Negro actors shall have obtained a surer stage technique.
> The Negro's talent for music and dramatic expression is now unquestioned. The Negro Players hope to aid in the development and perfection of this talent.

The company, under the direction of Henry Creamer, Alex Rogers, and Will Marion Cook, produced The Traitor, "a playlet . . . full of catchy songs, pretty tableaux, bright repartee, and good singing," later that month. The show starred veteran singer Abbie Mitchell and attracted large crowds at the Lafayette Theatre, but it closed after a week, apparently because of a falling out among members of the production staff.[11]

In May a reorganized Negro Players under the guidance of Rogers and Creamer—Will Marion Cook was conspicuously absent—advertised that it would produce "playlets of real Negro life of today, yesterday and tomorrow." A newspaper announcement stressed the Players' desire for dramatic verisimilitude and noted that an orchestra of seven members would be included in its forthcoming production, *The Old Man's Boy*.[12]

The Old Man's Boy opened at the Casino Theatre in Philadelphia on May 12, 1913, coming to New York in June. The show was a play within a play. Both first and second acts featured rehearsal scenes for a musical comedy, hence making room for many musical numbers. The third act, however, was "out of the ordinary for a colored show" since it gave "an opportunity to demonstrate what Negroes can do along dramatic lines"; it originally contained no songs, but one number was added later. Despite the large amount of music in the beginning of the show and the dramatic originality of the last act, critic Lester Walton lauded *The Old Man's Boy* primarily as a "dancing show," noting that the stage movement was far superior to the singing. The acting of Alex Rogers was complimented, and the multiple contributions of Henry Creamer—his writing, acting, and stage direction—were praised. All of the musical numbers were said to be by "negro composers," but neither the newspapers nor a December 2 program identified the names of the songwriters.[13]

Despite the stated aims of the Negro Players to pursue subjects of "real Negro life," *The Traitor* and *The Old Man's Boy* evidently forsook the extravagant scenic style and large casts of such shows as *In Dahomey* and *Abyssinia* but retained the same basic comic and musical formats used by Williams and Walker and other earlier comics. A Walton critique stating that the time had come for the abandonment of the "minstrel stereotypes" onstage confirms the presence of traditional and familiar comic elements.[14]

On February 17, 1910, Lester Walton, commenting on the closing of Chicago's Pekin Theatre, asserted in the *Age* that the time was not right for the production of plays without music. However, by late 1915 New York was changing in favor of shows with less music and less blackface comedy. Anita Bush, a confident young actress who had toured with *In Dahomey*, gathered together a handful of dedicated players and produced Billie Burke's *The Girl at the Fort* at the Lincoln Theatre, West 135th Street, thus launching a new era of straight, serious drama in Harlem. A headline in the *New York Amsterdam News* announced, "New York At Last To Come Into Its Own Legitimate Drama," and the new Anita Bush

Stock Company that was described found enthusiastic audiences. Their first play, called a "drama of lofty ideals and superb sacrifices," was succeeded by a "domestic comedy-drama," *Over the Footlights*, which opened at the Lafayette Theatre on December 27. The Bush company, later known as the Lafayette Players, continued to entertain Harlem audiences until 1932.[15]

Black exploration of realistic drama as opposed to farce-comedy in the second decade of the twentieth century was in keeping with the period's spirit of racial uplift and idealism. The young singer and actor Theodore Pankey expressed the hope that the founding of black theaters would lead to the production of good, well-acted drama that would in turn "achieve a more transcendent, universal appeal and be worthy of criticism by the white press and demand the respect and appreciation of all races." The desire for approval from a wider audience should not be interpreted as an example of Tomism but rather as an expression of the optimism characteristic of the times. Such a justification for the growth of serious acting in "good" plays can also be seen as a forward look towards the assertive, antistereotypical stance of the "New Negro" generation of the 1920s.[16]

Many black entertainers also turned to vaudeville during the first decades of the twentieth century, undertaking specialties in dancing, singing, comedy, impersonation, acrobatics, and other novelties such as hoop-rolling and body contortion. With the decrease in the number of large shows around 1909, the number of vaudeville acts multiplied rapidly. In 1906 Ernest Hogan, in an article for *Variety*, estimated that more than "fifty acts employing over two hundred black people" were working in vaudeville. By early 1909 over one hundred acts employing between three hundred and four hundred people can be found listed in the theater pages of New York newspapers, and the number continued to rise throughout the decade.[17]

Performers frequently participated in both vaudeville and musical comedies, appearing one season in an independent skit booked over a vaudeville circuit and the next in a book show (show with a story line and a fully plotted script) in which they shared the spotlight with many other entertainers. Hattie McIntosh, who appeared in vaudeville with her husband Tom and was known in the 1890s as "America's most distinguished female baritone," sang and acted in *In Dahomey, Abyssinia, Bandanna Land,*

and *Mr. Lode of Koal.* Olga Burgoyne traveled to Europe with *In Dahomey* and then became an independent businesswoman and entertainer in St. Petersburg, Russia. Aida Overton Walker was a skillful solo singer and dancer featured in both big shows and vaudeville. Williams and Walker, Cole and Johnson, and Ernest Hogan used bits from their large shows in subsequent vaudeville acts or developed vaudeville acts that later became parts of larger shows; indeed, most of the early big shows were little more than a series of self-contained vaudeville skits and specialties.[18]

Several black stars had long, important, and lucrative careers in vaudeville without much contact with big shows. Joe and Sadie Britton did a husband-and-wife dancing act for many years; well-known names in comedy included the teams of Avery and Hart, the Wangdoodle Comedy

The team of Joseph Hodges and Nina Launchmere, among the handful of successful pioneers of black vaudeville. They reportedly urged Williams and Walker as unknowns to try their luck as comedians in New York. Courtesy of McGown Collection, Hargrett Rare Book and Manuscript Library, University of Georgia Libraries.

Four, and Avery and Robinson; the Kraton Family was famous for its juggling and hoop-rolling; the Sunny South Company featured a dancing and singing male quartet; Fiddler and Shelton were comedian and pianist, respectively, in the Cole and Johnson style; and Eph Thompson displayed trained elephants.[19]

The number and variety of black acts were great, yet some entertainers chose to stick with tried and true formulas by imitating famous teams such as Williams and Walker. Black vaudevillians occasionally were upbraided by both black and white critics for all being the same.[20] However, only a limited range of styles for black actors was acceptable to white critics. The undeniable strength of blacks in entertainment had created a powerful convention—the regular presence of a black act on a vaudeville bill. But at the same time, the range of what was permissible points again to a restrictive, stereotypical stance by viewers and owners. In a comment on a vaudeville act called the Four Georgia Belles, *Variety* declared:

> The American public refuses to take the colored race seriously as entertainers. It wants them with a dash of comedy and consistently refuses to accept them in any guise than the jester's motley. The Georgia Four (formerly the Creole Belles) take themselves very seriously and cling tenaciously to the sentimental songs. There is no unbending from their severity except for a solemn and decorous dance step. Even the costuming is dignified to a degree. The voices are pretty and the harmony is well-arranged, but they would do better did they make a concession in favor of popular prejudice and confine themselves more to plantation songs and native melodies. However, there is an element of novelty in the idea of a colored quartet of this nature. The public's verdict will be interesting. . . .[21]

With such strong presuppositions about what black acts should be, it must have taken truly outstanding performers to succeed in other than the standard roles. Given the widespread practice of keeping at most one black act on a vaudeville bill, the competition must have been strong. The black acts on the major circuits were among the best and were not derivative from Hogan, Cole and Johnson, and Williams and Walker. *Variety* praised one such team: "Fiddler and Shelton have set a new standard for colored acts, and the best of it is that they would be just as good an act if Bert Williams had never lived."[22]

Other original acts featured impersonations and caricatures of foreign or American immigrant groups. Cook and Stevens performed a Chinese imitation, as did Brown and Nevarro and the early Golden Gate Quartet. Carter and Bluford sang "Spanish," "Indian," and "Arab" songs, and Theodore Pankey and Anna Cook called their act "Les Filipino," appearing in publicity photos and presumably on stage in mantilla and sombrero.[23]

Like black entertainers of the nineteenth century, vaudevillians traveled abroad in large numbers from 1910 to 1914 and scored successes from Paris to Peking. Dan and Minnie Washington, after performing their cakewalk with the *In Dahomey* company in Europe, remained to tour Italy, France, Belgium, Czechoslovakia, Turkey, Syria, and Russia. The *New York Age* noted in November 1913 the "successful engagement of Hen Wise and Katie Milton at the Apollo Theatre, Shanghai, China," and a new vaudeville route between Honolulu and the Orient "opened for good colored acts who know how to conduct themselves on and off the stage."[24]

The American presence in other countries was not without impact. Lester Walton called attention to the "Argentine Largo," a Parisian dance fad that he traced to American blacks, calling it a "cakewalk played adagio." At least one writer noted that the movement toward war in Europe and the burgeoning anti-German feeling in both America and Europe augured well for blacks. He reasoned that since Germans had been prominent in the fields of music and theater, their exclusion by pro-English managers would create a gap that blacks might fill.[25] Whether anti-German prejudice worked to the advantage of black acts is an open question, but as the war intensified in Europe in the fall of 1914, many black acts overseas returned home. The *New York Age* reported that "many of the acts have been in foreign lands for over twenty years."[26]

The new film industry also offered employment for the vaudeville entertainer. Tom Fletcher describes what was perhaps a typical attitude among black entertainers towards the medium:

> When the flickers, or moving pictures, were developed along around 1900, my partner, Al Bailey, and I got leading comedy parts. The studio was on 22nd Street, between Broadway and Fourth Avenue. I was the talent scout for the colored people. There were no "types,"

just colored men, women and children. Bailey and I did parts in the pictures that today would pay no less than four figures weekly, but we didn't take it seriously. To us it was just something that would never get any place.

You never heard the words "lights," "action," "camera," "roll 'em," or "cut" which are so common today. There were no script writers, no make-up artists, just one man, everybody called him Mr. Porter, and I never took time to find out his first name, who placed you in your positions and gave you your actions, lit the scene and then turned the camera. His assistant was a fellow named Gilroy whom everyone called Gil. When we went on location it was to North Asbury Park, about the best place around New York for the purpose. The trees, gardens and farms gave just the right atmosphere.

At the end of each day Gilroy would hand me the money to pay off. I am not quite sure but I think it was three dollars a day for each of the people. Bailey and I got eight dollars each. We all considered it a lot of fun with pay. Vaudeville, private parties, music and show business kept me too busy to pay any real attention to the moving picture business.[27]

Fletcher's assumption that movies were just another fleeting novelty was at first as common among theater owners as among performers. In 1910 vaudeville performers and films were included on the same bill; a short film was just one more specialty act. The advent of the sound film industry and the rapid growth in its appeal ultimately contributed to the demise of vaudeville, but in the short run films may have encouraged theater owners unsure of the drawing power of short silent features to hire local entertainers who otherwise might have remained idle.

The complete entertainer did many things, and vaudeville was one of the most profitable and steady activities once one's reputation was made. Only a few black acts played the "big time"—theaters that featured one matinee and one evening show a day and that were owned by moguls such as B. F. Keith or Martin Beck—as opposed to "small-time" houses with more demanding schedules. Efforts like J. Leubrie Hill's formation of the Colored Vaudeville Exchange in 1912 reflected a desire to expand the access of black performers to theaters and audiences nationwide. Similarly, the efforts of S. H. Dudley and other managers to form black vaudeville theater circuits in the 1910 decade and to establish the Theatre Owners' Booking Association (TOBA) in 1920, albeit headed by a white

S. H. Dudley (1912) as a vaudeville star in blackface
makeup, with fellow entertainer and partner Lottie
Grady. His more famous partner, however, was a
"talking" mule. Billy Rose Theatre Collection, the
New York Public Library at Lincoln Center, Astor,
Lenox, and Tilden Foundations.

theater owner, helped to increase exposure. The TOBA was a business
not noted as especially charitable towards performers, but it succeeded in
providing a showcase for black entertainers that had not existed before,
especially in the South. In 1922, according to *Billboard,* vaudeville was
still flourishing in the United States, with over 360 black theaters employing some 600 acts.[28]

11
Dance and Comedy in Harlem, 1910–1915

J. Leubrie Hill and the Darktown Follies
In early February 1911 a touring company from Washington, D. C., under the direction of J. Leubrie Hill, a former member of Cole and Johnson's *Red Moon* company, presented *My Friend from Dixie* at the Amphion Theatre in Brooklyn. The performances were poorly advertised and poorly attended, but the show made a favorable impression on a few members of the audience. Lester Walton, writing in the *Age*, commented, "It cannot be classed with such productions as *Mr. Lode of Koal* and *The Red Moon*, for it is not so ambitious an offering in the manner of lavish scenic effects nor with reference to the assemblage of talented thespians. And yet *My Friend from Dixie*, book and music by J. Leubrie Hill, ensembles by Will Vodery, can be referred to in a complimentary manner."[1] In addition to other former players from *The Red Moon*, the show contained another legacy from the previous decade of black shows and minstrelsy: action and dialogue full of gunplay, watermelons, dice games, gin and razors, elements to which Walton objected. "Meet Me

When the Sun Goes Down" and the finale, "That Real Coon Rag," were the outstanding songs, and indeed the latter was a modern ragtime tune. The chorus melody is pervasively syncopated, featuring frequent groupings of three-plus-three-plus-two and three-plus-two-plus-three sixteenth-notes in duple time, with octaves in both the right and left hand of the piano accompaniment as well. The text, though retaining the words *coon* and *cooney*, lacks the old-style dialect but is full of slang and action words:

> Listen mister play that music sweet and low,
> Makes me feel so spooney kind o' looney you know,
> It's so entrancing,
> Keeps you a glancing,
> With goo-goo eyes that have a ragtime glow,
> (It's got me crazy, my!)

Making "goo-goo eyes" had been a popular song activity for years—even Bert Williams had written about it in 1900—but never before with "a ragtime glow."[2] Text references to "prancing" and "dancing," the eight-measure concluding dance in the piano-vocal score, and the song's placement as the finale of the show all suggest that it was danced as well as sung.

Despite its upbeat finale, *My Friend from Dixie* did not take New York by storm. Hill's out-of-town company was insignificant enough in its first appearance that it might even be ignored in a study of New York's music, except that it proved to be the kernel of another, more notable product. Two years later when Hill's company, now named the Darktown Follies, presented the revised version of *My Friend from Dixie*, called *My Friend from Kentucky*, all of New York sat up and took notice. In its full form—several hours in length—it was never seen on Broadway itself, and yet its dynamism was strong enough to draw white Broadway theater patrons to Harlem's Lafayette Theatre in droves, the first show to accomplish that feat.

My Friend from Kentucky tells the story of Jim Jackson Lee (Julius Glenn), who, with the help of his friend Bill Simmons (Sam Gaines), mortgages his father-in-law's Kentucky plantation and sets out to win fame, fortune, and a place in Washington, D.C. society, trying at the same time to escape from his wife, Mandy. Hill himself starred as the comically tall and fearsome Mandy, who ultimately finds her man and brings him back to their old Kentucky home. The 1913 version of the show evidently eliminated the stereotyped scenes with razors and other such props, since Walton does not refer to them. The plot also included a romantic number that, according to James Weldon Johnson, brought a serious love interest into black shows seven years before *Shuffle Along*. Even earlier *The Red Moon* had contained love songs sung by romantic leads, but, Johnson claimed, " 'Rock Me in the Cradle of Love' . . . in the Darktown Follies had been sung by the Negro tenor to the bronze soubrette in a most impassioned manner, demonstrating that the love-making taboo had been absolutely kicked out of the Negro theatre." Johnson identifies the *tenor* as the singer, but at least in the first New York performance this piece was a featured number for the soubrette, Alice Ramsey, in the role of Lillian Langtree. A review notes that she was "assisted by Will Brown and the chorus"; the souvenir program does not mention the tenor at all for this number.[3]

"Rock Me in the Cradle of Love" proved appealing. The gentle ostinato in the refrain (Example 11.1) and the pattern of accent similar to "That Real Coon Rag" in both the verse and the refrain supplied the rhythmic background for the swaying, chromatic melody, made smoother still with

Example 11.1. J. Leubrie Hill, "Rock Me in the Cradle of Love" (Detroit and New York: Jerome H. Remick & Co., 1914), chorus, mm. 1–3. Reprinted by permission.

Example 11.2. J. Leubrie Hill, "Rock Me in the Cradle of Love" (Detroit and New York: Jerome H. Remick & Co., 1914), verse, mm. 1–2. Reprinted by

accompanying lines of parallel sixths (Example 11.2). The tune was complemented by a tender text that manages to be both innocent and vaguely suggestive:

> Rock me in the cradle of love
> On your breast let me rest,
> Just as close as a perfect fitting glove.
> Call me pretty names and let me dream and wonder,
> Plant a goody kiss while I in loveland slumber,
> Rock the cradle gently, please don't shove. . . .

One particularly effective number, "Dear Old Dixie," featured the veteran vaudevillian Sam Gaines and the chorus. The verse begins with a mild rhythmic jolt (Example 11.3), but the tune becomes even more engaging in the refrain (Example 11.4), including a rhythm and several chords (mm. 1–2) reminiscent of Scott Joplin's "Solace" and a chromatic, syncopated tune that travels up and down an octave and up a seventh again within the first two phrases. This original shape and the syncopated leap to a high F propels the tune forward in an uncommonly strong

Example 11.3. Rhythm in J. Leubrie Hill, "Dear Old Dixie," beginning

Example 11.4. J. Leubrie Hill, "Dear Old Dixie" (Detroit and New York: Jerome H. Remick & Co., 1914), chorus, mm. 1–8. Reprinted by permission.

manner. Walton called "Dear Old Dixie" "cyclonic" and "the pronounced song hit of the show," suggesting that it was strong enough to be used as a finale rather than just the third number of the first act.

"That Real Coon Rag," the hit of the 1911 show, was not retained in the new version, but a tune called "The Gay Manhattan Rag," possessing a text in the same spirit as the original finale, was added:

> Listen at the ragtime music ringing
> Listen at the ragtime darkies singing
> A ragtime feeling to my soul is bringing
> With that spoony coony tune you never fag
> Don't stop the music mister
> Keep it 'cause it makes me feel like dancin'
> Can't stop my feet from prancin' . . .

My Friend from Kentucky differed from shows by Williams and Walker and Cole and Johnson in that it lacked, even in its revised version, a magnificent scenic apparatus, but the critics felt well compensated by the number of people onstage and the profusion of dance numbers. The show never lacked for action or interesting stage movement. Hill realized, as none of the directors before him had, that the novel impact of black performers lay in the special ways they could use their bodies and their voices, making the trappings of the nineteenth-century extravaganza or European operettas seem irrelevant. He therefore concentrated on the dancing. Ethel Williams, who danced with the Darktown Follies, told Marshall and Jean Stearns:

> We had some wonderful dancers, a featured dance called the Texas Tommy, and a fine cakewalk for the finale, but the most fun was the circle dance at the end of the second act. Everyone did a sort of sliding walk in rhythm with their hands on the hips of the person in front of them, and I'd be doing anything but that—I'd "Ball the Jack" on the end of the line every way you could think of—and when the curtain came down, I'd put my hand out from behind the curtain and "Ball the Jack" with my fingers.

The Stearns go on to explain, "For the Circle Dance the entire company formed an endless chain, dancing across the stage and off on one end, then around behind the curtain and back on stage at the other end—circling continuously, snapping fingers with a 'tango jiggle,' a 'moochee . . . slide,' and a 'Texas Tommy wiggle' (as the lyrics suggested) and singing . . . Hill's 'At the Ball That's All.'" The tango was becoming a fashionable social dance at this time—Ethel Williams recalled being asked to teach it to Irene Castle; the mooche involved shuffling forward with both feet, hips first; Ethel Williams described the Texas Tommy as "like the Lindy, but there were two basic steps—a kick and hop three times on each foot, and then whatever you want, turning, pulling, sliding. Your partner had to keep you from falling—I've slid into the orchestra pit more than once." In a 1912 dancing manual, the authors suggested that the outward spinning of the partner made "The Texas Tommy dancers . . . more acrobatic than eccentric."[4]

The song "At the Ball, That's All" had the same seductive liveliness as

"That Real Coon Rag." The text, which contains a rather complete description of what the dancers are supposed to do, comes from a long line of dance songs traceable at least to Ernest Hogan's "La Pas Ma La," published in 1895:

> Commence advancing, commence advancing,
> Just start aprancing, right and left aglancing,
> A moochee dancing, slide and glide entrancing, . . .

The number was popular enough to be purchased by Florenz Ziegfeld for his *Follies of 1914*.[5]

Another featured tune was the "Tango One-Step," and the next-to-last piece of the show, according to the souvenir program, was called "Three Styles of Dancing," featuring Johnnie Peters and his "Three Dancing Girls," Ethel Williams, Daisy Brown, and Edna Morton. A concluding chorus of "At the Ball, That's All" accompanied a cakewalk performed by the entire company, "the last big company to do the cakewalk as a feature in the grand finale," reports Tom Fletcher.[6]

Naturally the critical reaction to the Follies focused on the dancing, although reviewers praised many elements of the show. *Variety* declared "At the Ball, That's All" "the best put-on song ever seen in New York" and "the whole effect [of the final number] well worth the [three-hour] wait." Chapman Hilder wrote in *The Theatre Magazine*, "Mr. Hill's players owe their success to enthusiasm . . . there is a pleasant absence of that narrow-lidded, sophisticated languor so common in your average chorus. A refreshing spontaneity pervades the entire performance." The *New York World* asserted that the dancing topped "anything Broadway has ever seen." The *Dramatic Mirror* concurred on the spirited work of the full company, noting "one of the best looking male choruses it has been our pleasure to see" and lauding the presence of "fifty real colored entertainers, who entered into the music and dancing with enthusiasm and made every line radiate good nature." Carl Van Vechten, writing for the *New York Press*, gave a detailed and insightful critique:

> There are few musical entertainments on Broadway that compare with this one. . . . Remembering how gratefully white audiences attended

performances given by the Williams and Walker company, it is not beyond reason to suppose that if it were moved further downtown it would do a large business. . . . These chorus men and women *like* what they are doing and as a result they do it well. They enjoy themselves. . . . All the boys and girls are exceptionally good singers and dancers. There is a number in the first act in which the dancing of the chorus is so splendidly rhythmical, so aesthetically satisfying in its "thrill," that it is caused to be repeated for a great length of time. In fact, the repetitions of many of the numbers were so numerous that the curtain fell on the second act, with another long act still to come, shortly before 11 o'clock. . . .

. . . there are numerous examples of "business" for the chorus which are novel and which give the spectator who is used to the conventions of musical comedy something of a surprise.

There is . . . a newsboys' quartet, which is handled in such a manner that it does not obtrude itself as an interrupting musical number. The boys who are heard in it continue to "shoot" craps and polish shoes while they sing.

There are no waits in the performance. It moves on from one event to another with deft clarity, and there are few dull spots. . . .

Finally, all of the star comedians were praised, with Hill singled out as superior. *Variety* described precisely Hill's technique: "He talks very little but does some pointed pantomimic playing, besides which he has points built up to where a single word from him will bring a howl."[7]

With good comedy, tuneful songs, and dynamic dancing, one would have expected a profitable road tour for the show, but almost from the first *My Friend from Kentucky* met with financial and booking problems. Even though the actors were paid little and the show had brought in nearly $4,500 a week in New York, touring proved to be a financial disappointment. Shows traveling on the Progressive burlesque circuit, on which *My Friend from Kentucky* was booked, met stiff competition from the rival Columbia circuit shows. Audiences still turned out for it, however, especially black audiences. The *Freeman*, a leading black newspaper in the Midwest, called it "a very considerable achievement," and the show survived to tour into 1916. In June 1914 the show appeared on Broadway, but only in a condensed format, a forty-five-minute version that could not do justice to the original. The complete show returned to the Lafayette Theatre in Harlem for week-long engagements in October 1914, January

1915, and February 1916, always playing to record-breaking houses and featuring new dances, as Marshall and Jean Stearns recount:

> Two pioneering tap dancers who later became famous, Toots Davis and Eddie Rector, started as chorus boys in the show and worked up their own specialties. "When I saw the Darktown Follies in 1916, it was the talk of the town," says Ida Forsyne, "Eddie Rector was featured in his smooth military routine, and Toots Davis was doing his Over the Top and Through the Trenches—they were new steps then."[8]

Despite the vitality the Darktown Follies exuded and the flashy kinds of vernacular dance it displayed, white writers chided the company for adopting stage conventions from downtown, as if black shows should always be free of the eclecticism that pervaded the rest of the musical comedy world. The "incontestably mulatto" flavor of Afro-American culture, to use Albert Murray's provocative phrase, was still being contested when Van Vechten objected to "the actors . . . singing conventional hymns to the moon, with accompanying action which Ned Wayburn [Abe Erlanger's director] might have devised" and "a dash of tenor, a sprinkling of girls in long satin gowns [unnecessarily] added to [Hill's] otherwise entirely fresh Negro salad."[9] It may have been this mixture of black dance and choral work with white "hymns to the moon" and satin gowns that suggested to Ziegfeld that the white performers of his *Follies of 1914* could successfully learn the "At the Ball" finale. If a low-budget black production could combine both old and new styles effectively, why not his lavish extravaganzas?

The attempted white re-creation of the Darktown Follies spectacle was not satisfactory. Ethel Williams remembered, "I went down to the New York Theatre and showed the cast how to dance it. They were having trouble. None of us was hired for the show, and at that time I was supposed to be the best woman dancer in the whole country." A white manager confided to the *New York Age*, "The trouble is, after you get consent from J. Leubrie Hill to use the finish, you have a mighty hard time getting white performers who can 'ball the Jack' and do the 'Eagle Rock' as effectively as the colored performers."[10]

Van Vechten realized, as Ziegfeld did not, that it was the excitement of the chorus, and not simply the staging and choreography, that was essential. White dancers had little knowledge of, training in, or experience with black dance, nor did they enjoy the benefit of the active response from black audiences that Van Vechten had observed at the Lafayette:

> The feeling [of the chorus], of course, is communicative, and the spectators soon reach that semi-hysterical state of enjoyment which a camp meeting of the better sort is able to bring about.
> They rock back and forth with low croons; they scream with delight; they giggle intermittently; they wave their hands; they shriek, and at the pauses they pound their palms vigorously together in an attempt to get more out of the entertainers, and more always follows.

Of Ziegfeld's recreation Van Vechten concluded, "The tunes remained pretty; the *Follies* girls undoubtedly were pretty, but the rhythm was gone, the thrill was lacking, the boom was inaudible, the Congo had disappeared."[11]

Despite the success in Harlem of *My Friend from Kentucky*, the dancing style of the show was not successfully imitated by whites or, for that matter, by other black companies. Black dancers made a better living on vaudeville circuits, and no other black shows in the spirit of *My Friend from Kentucky* came to New York until *Shuffle Along* appeared in May 1921. Hill did not live to see this new era of black musicals; he died in August 1916.[12]

Darkydom

Toward the end of 1915 one more attempt was made to revive the big shows in the Williams and Walker style. A set of songs surrounding a slight but recognizable plot, featuring the special talents of a pair of comedians, was seen once again in *Darkydom*, which appeared at the Lafayette Theatre on October 23. *Darkydom* represented a passing of the torch from the old generation to the new one. The production team gathered together some of the familiar figures of the Williams and Walker days, notably Jesse Shipp as stage director, Will Marion Cook as composer and conductor (a role he shared with James Reese Europe), and Lester Walton (a former collaborator of Ernest Hogan as well as a critic) as director. It also included the comedy team of Miller and Lyles; they had appeared with Ernest Hogan, but their greatest success was yet to come in the big shows of the 1920s. Abbie Mitchell sang ballads, as she had in *The Shoo-Fly Regiment* and *The Red Moon*. Frank Walker did a Chinese impersonation probably reminiscent of George Catlin's Chinese act in *In Dahomey* and *Abyssinia*. The *Freeman* said of the cast as a whole, "Each name in the foreground carries a distinct weight—each has made a reputation in similar companies or in vaudeville."[13]

The plot tells the adventures of two hoboes (Miller and Lyles) who catch a ride on a train that also is carrying the president of the railroad line. In order to remove the offenders the engineer pulls onto a siding, an action that luckily prevents a train wreck with another engine approaching on the same track from the opposite direction. All aboard are saved, and the grateful railroad president attempts to reward the pair, but the hoboes mistake his agent for a hired detective seeking to bring them to justice for the free ride.

Both music and book, as well as the comedy of Miller and Lyles, were reviewed favorably, but the whole effort was viewed as passé, and one senses an air of nostalgia in the comments. The *Freeman* noted, "The music is tinctured with the characteristic Cook and Europe flavor, and here and there are bars that are reminiscent of other famous compositions by those gifted artists."[14] Two songs available from the show, "Mammy" and "My Lady's Lips," confirm that, while well made, Cook's music was not markedly different from his earlier pieces of this type.

Several white producers, writers, and socialites attended the opening, including F. Ray Comstock, who had underwritten *Bandanna Land* and *Mr. Lode of Koal;* critic and producer Charles Dillingham; Irving Berlin; and the chief publisher of Cole and Johnson, Joseph F. Stern. Interest in black theatricals apparently had not diminished as much as some had feared. The show's appeal was interpreted cynically by some black critics, among them R. W. Thompson: "The show is said to be built largely to attract white patronage and its bookings, it is said, will be for the most part in the white houses of the standard type." What would have been especially appealing to whites is not made clear, but Thompson obviously found the show old-fashioned if not downright patronizing in the old coon/minstrel style. John Cort, a major white independent theater owner in the West, picked up the show to tour over his circuit.[15]

Darkydom's moderate success and the great furor over the Darktown

Follies indicate that despite the lull around 1910, the world of black musical theater was still alive. But the personalities and the conventions—especially the acceptance of minstrelsy and blackface—were gradually changing. The death of Aida Overton Walker in October 1914, the final closing of the Black Patti Troubadours company in 1916, and the passing of J. Leubrie Hill in August 1916 represent the breaking of three more links with the era of Williams and Walker and Cole and Johnson. The war in Europe was soon to come to America, with black musicians entering military bands and black actors playing in minstrel and variety shows to entertain the troops in training on Long Island. Some black showmen continued along familiar paths. S. Tutt Whitney and J. Homer Tutt, for example, continued to tour their Smarter Set shows on the road, though remaining principally a Southern company. Stock companies formed by younger performers such as Billy King, Irvin C. Miller (brother of comedian Flournoy Miller), and Frank Montgomery developed large repertories of topical revues, historical plays, and musical comedies. Between 1918 and 1920 a steady stream of productions by resident stock companies or visiting "tab" (tabloid) shows (abbreviated musical comedies lasting an hour or more and carrying about a dozen players) appeared for one-week stints at the Lafayette and Lincoln Theaters in New York. The big shows of the 1920s—*Shuffle Along, The Blackbirds, Hot Chocolates,* and others—played to a public that had suffered no dearth of comedy or musical entertainment in the preceding decade.

Epilogue

The black shows produced in New York from 1898 to 1915 were similar in many respects to white shows of the same period. Several productions, not just those with black casts, featured transformation scenes, pantomimes, and interpolated songs. Ragtime music was widely used. Musical comedy producers of both races took an improvisational approach to the structure of many shows, including several bits of "business" not entirely worked out in advance of the performance. Most shows featured individual stars famous from vaudeville.

Nevertheless, the black productions had several distinctive elements—though not always the same elements in every show—that, together with the skin color of the performers, constituted them as appealing novelties. In *Clorindy*, for example, those elements were the enthusiasm of the chorus and the eccentric dancing of Ernest Hogan. (Hogan's performance of "Who Dat Say Chicken in Dis Crowd" was encored ten times on opening night.)[1] In *In Dahomey, Bandanna Land,* and *Abyssinia*, the wit and style of the stars, Williams and Walker, were the big attraction, and their dancing was also a special feature. The Darktown Follies' production of *My Friend from Kentucky* was certainly the most important dancing show of its day and was praised primarily for that reason.[2]

The energy and grace of performers in the black shows, whether dancing, singing, or acting, impressed the critics. "The first act of *In Dahomey* proceeds with a succession of choruses, songs and dances with constant movement and merriment, to a bustling finale," said one English critic. Of the same show, another writer commented, "The composer conducted with much vigor, singing most of the tunes with his band with a kind of untrammeled spontaneity that finds expression in the whole action of the piece, and more particularly in the dancing, which seems the natural expression of a racial instinct, not the obviously acquired art of the schools." A critic for the *Dramatic Mirror* noted the "vigor" and "grace" of several members of the company in *Bandanna Land*. The actors' spontaneity, enthusiasm, and graceful movement were again the keynotes for a *Boston Transcript* critic reporting on the Smart Set: "Colored companies like Mr. Dudley and his 'Smart Set' . . . have virtues that their white rivals might now wisely consider. No matter what their play may be, they sing and act it to the utmost of their powers. They seem to draw as much amusement and pleasurable excitement from what they are doing as does the audience itself."[3]

For black audiences, or black members of the audience if it were racially mixed, the shows had an additional appeal because they dealt with themes taken from life in black American society. The back-to-Africa movement was lampooned in the schemes of the would-be colonizers of *In Dahomey*. Many opportunities to poke fun at the army's treatment of blacks were provided by the military setting of *The Shoo-Fly Regiment*. The difficulties for blacks in gaining a college education were treated humorously in a song, "Colored Girl from Vassar," which appeared in both *In Dahomey* and *Jes Lak White Fo'ks;* the song was intended originally for *The Cannibal King*, an unproduced show. Based on a true story that had received considerable notice in the black press, a young lady outsmarts the educational authorities by posing as a foreigner:

> I am the first dark belle who ever went to Vassar
> I play my part so well I came from Madagascar

They thought I was a swell and the boys they did adore
And if I gave a smile they quickly asked for more
They sent bouquets galore to the elegant brunette
I've got a stock in store of their billet doux as yet
They did not know sufficient to come in from out the wet
And now they're sore, they're sore you bet.

Sometimes different parts of the shows drew varied reactions from different racial groups in the audience, to judge by one comment on a performance of *The Shoo-Fly Regiment:* "It was especially interesting to watch the audience, for the white people laughed moderately at incidents that made no impression on the Negroes, while the latter shouted glee at jokes that did not interest the white spectators."[4] The practice of embedding double meanings within coon songs apparently had spread to other elements of the black musicals as well. But if the scripts and improvisations provided enough variety or suggestion to please mixed audiences, the music was even more successful.

Black theater music, while generally conforming to conventional forms and familiar textual themes, had far more melodic syncopation than contemporary white show music; a marked amount of rhythmic vitality; and, occasionally, extraordinary harmonic inventiveness. Critics continually used the adjective *catchy* to describe the striking rhythmic quality. A Boston journalist said of *Rufus Rastus,* "the catchy refrains kept the head nodding and the toe tapping all over the theater by means of their irresistible rhythm." A critic for the *New York Dramatic News* stated that "the most tuneful and catchiest music by Rosamond Johnson will be a feature of the performance [of *The Red Moon*]." Syncopated tunes were so recognized as a part of the shows that a writer commenting on a performance of J. Rosamond Johnson referred to him as "the originator of syncopated songs."[5] That such an observation could be made—it is of course not accurate—suggests the especially important role musical shows played in disseminating the new musical style.

Syncopated or not, the music of the shows generally was praised. A New York writer found that the comparatively unsyncopated "music [of *Mr. Lode of Koal*] is really tuneful and pleasing, and the whole makes as good a score as Mr. Johnson has ever contributed to such an entertainment." Will Marion Cook's liberally syncopated, harmonically rich songs for *Bandanna Land* were hailed in similar terms: "The music is quite as good as is found in the average musical comedy—some of it is very much better." A Philadelphia critic felt that *The Red Moon* offered something for everyone: "From the 'Bleeding Moon' chorus at the opening until the 'War Dance' of the braves at the close, the [second] act is one repast for the love of music, whether it is for the jingly tunes that are readily caught up and whistled on the street or the musicianly efforts that appeal to the more critical ear."[6]

Many musicians who later left their mark on various aspects of American music got their start in these shows. Among those who wrote and played in musical comedies in the first two decades of the twentieth century are J. Tim Brymn, who later conducted American military bands in Europe; Will Vodery, who orchestrated and conducted the music of George Gershwin; and James P. Johnson and Charles "Luckey" Roberts, stellar jazz pianists of the 1930s. Actors who appeared in shows of the 1920s—*Shuffle Along, Runnin' Wild, Rang Tang, The Plantation Revue,* to name only a few—started out in the choruses of *Rufus Rastus, The Oyster Man, The Red Moon,* and the Darktown Follies.

Black critics and historians in the 1910s, 1920s, and 1930s also noted the special importance of the shows in the early years of the century and viewed them as benchmarks of quality. In September 1915 a writer in the *Freeman* complained, "Colored show business is not what it was in the palmy days of Williams and Walker, Ernest Hogan, and Cole and Johnson," and as late as 1920 the *New York Age* critic Lester Walton was comparing new shows with the big Williams and Walker hits of nearly two decades earlier. In 1936 Alain Locke characterized the period of black music and theater after 1895 as "a sudden floodtide of new life and vitality," and Maud Cuney-Hare, in her 1936 history of black music and musicians, noted a "new stage" of development achieved in the early Williams and Walker shows *The Policy Players* and *The Sons of Ham.* Cuney-Hare also saw the Cole and Johnson show *The Red Moon* as "a decided advance in the [musical] sphere" of musical comedy; this opinion was not repeated widely, perhaps because less rousing and more genteel songs such as "The Pathway of Love" appeared in that production. J. Leubrie Hill was one performer who might have disagreed with Cuney-

Hare, preferring, in his words, "the real Negro" onstage and not "African operetta" for his production of *My Friend from Kentucky* in 1913. In 1927 Theophilus Lewis, a black journalist, commented on Hill's contribution to black musical theater:

> The tendency to borrow from the colored stage openly . . .
> began . . . when J. Leubrie Hill produced his "Darktown Follies," . . .
> Hill's production marked the turning point in the relations existing
> between the white stage and the colored stage.
> Before that time the Negro theatre borrowed its materials and
> methods from the white stage. Our comedians had accepted the
> minstrel tradition without questioning its merits or authenticity . . . he
> [Hill] turned aside from Indian themes and South Sea motifs when he
> wrote the music and arranged the dances for the show, and it was the
> singing and dancing that carried it over.[7]

For assigning such a major role to Hill's show Lewis's comments bear further scrutiny. The interest of whites in borrowing song and dance material from black culture dates back long before the Darktown Follies, although, strictly speaking, until black minstrelsy there was no Afro-American *stage* to borrow from. After Emancipation, black actors assimilated and adapted white American theatrical conventions, using recognizable items from the white tradition. As distinctive black features emerged in theatrical productions of the period from 1898 to 1915 (they did not all suddenly appear in *My Friend from Kentucky*)—syncopated singing, vigorous vernacular dancing, and the reiteration of themes on black society in America—white stage folk recognized their vitality. Some white producers, such as Florenz Ziegfeld, adapted them for their own purposes in white musical shows. Ziegfeld's use of Hill's Darktown Follies finale for his own *Follies of 1914* was an unusually high-handed gesture, but it was similar in nature to the borrowing that is common among entertainers in any time and place.

The white minstrel and vaudeville dancer George Primrose was widely imitated by black dancers in the late nineteenth and early twentieth centuries. Ted Lewis, the white comic, got his most famous line, "Is everybody happy?," from black entertainer Ernest Hogan. There are many other examples of such borrowings. Performers were constantly working to perfect formulas that had long histories onstage, imitating or striving to surpass the most successful entertainers by adopting their material. The race of the performer was not always a factor, but it is impossible to ignore the barriers that racial discrimination and systematic stereotyping sometimes created for members of the profession.[8]

The turn-of-the-century ascendance of black entertainers in New York was followed by an explosion of activity in the 1920s, and thanks to recent Broadway revivals and the reemergence of personalities such as Eubie Blake, the music of some of these shows has become better known to modern audiences. But outstanding though many of the 1920s shows were, they did not arise from a void. Most drew upon well-established traditions in plot, music, and dance.

All of the *hows* and *whys* have not been and perhaps cannot be addressed for the early black musicals; there are severe limitations on reconstructing shows rarely mentioned in theater histories, whose books contain an uncomfortable amount of stereotyped racial material, and for which *mise-en-scenes* and much of the music are irretrievable. The reproduction of a show like *Rufus Rastus* for modern viewers probably would require so much in the way of exegesis and apology beforehand that it might not seem worth the effort. Nevertheless, a strong and influential musical theater was produced by a people only a generation out of slavery, bespeaking the surprising sources from which American culture has at times sprung. The history of early black musical theater also throws light on the direction taken by American popular music and musical theater in the 1920s and 1930s, an era itself deserving more serious attention from music historians and aficionados.

Appendix A
White Shows with Individual Songs
by Black Composers, 1895–1914

Date	Show Title	Song Title	Composer
1895	By the Sad Sea Waves	"La Pas Ma La"	Ernest Hogan
1896	Courted into Court	"All Coons Look Alike to Me"	Ernest Hogan
1899	A Reign of Error	"I Wonder What Is That Coon's Game"	Billy Johnson and Bob Cole
1900	The Belle of Bridgeport	"I Ain't Gwinter Work No More"	Cole and Johnson
		"Magdaline, My Southern Queen"	Cole and Johnson
		"Why Don't the Band Play?"	Cole and Johnson
		"Mabel Moore"	Will Accooe
		"My Dandy Soldier Boy"	Will Accooe
1900	Casino Girl	"Down de Lover's Lane"	Will Marion Cook
		"Bygone Days Are Best"	Will Marion Cook
		"Whatever the Hue of Your Eyes"	Will Marion Cook
		"Love Has Claimed Its Own"	Will Accooe
1900	The Little Duchess	"Maiden with the Dreamy Eyes"	Cole and Johnson
		"Strollin' Along the Beach"	Cole and Johnson
		"Sweet Saloma"	Cole and Johnson
1900	The Rogers Brothers in Central Park	"Run, Brudder Possum, Run"	Cole and Johnson

Date	Show Title	Song Title	Composer
1901	The New Yorkers	"Dat's All"	Will Marion Cook
1901	The Liberty Belles	"I'd Like to Be a Gunner in the Navy"	Will Accooe
1901	Supper Club	"When the Band Plays Ragtime"	Cole and Johnson
		"Don't Butt In"	Cole and Johnson
1901	Champagne Charlie	"My Heart's Desiah"	Cole and Johnson
1902	Sally in Our Alley	"When Its All Goin' Out and Nothin' Comin' In"	Williams and Walker
		"Under the Bamboo Tree"	Cole and Johnson
1902	Sleeping Beauty and the Beast	"Tell Me, Dusky Maiden"	Cole and Johnson
		"Come Out, Dinah, On the Green"	Cole and Johnson
		"Nobody's Lookin' But the Owl and the Moon"	Cole and Johnson
1902	The Wild Rose	"My Little Gypsy Maid"	Will Marion Cook
1902	Hall of Fame	"Angemima Green"	Cole and Johnson
1902	Huck Finn	"The Animals' Convention"	Cole and Johnson
1903	A Girl from Dixie	"When the Moon Comes Over the Hill"	Cole and Johnson
1903	Mr. Bluebeard	"When the Colored Band Comes Marching Down the Street"	Cole and Johnson

Date	Show Title	Song Title	Composer
1903	*Nancy Brown*	"Under the Bamboo Tree"	Cole and Johnson
		"The Congo Love Song"	Cole and Johnson
		"Save It for Me"	Cole and Johnson
		"The Soldier is the Idol of the Nation"	Cole and Johnson
		"The Katydid, the Cricket and the Frog"	Cole and Johnson
		"Octette to Bacchus" Bacchus"	Cole and Johnson
		"In Gay Ballyhoo"	Cole and Johnson
		"Cupid's Ramble"	Cole and Johnson
1903	*Mother Goose*	"The Evolution of Ragtime"	Cole and Johnson
1904	*An English Daisy*	"Big Indian Chief"	Cole and Johnson
		"Prepossessing Maid"	Cole and Johnson
1905	*A Little Bit of Everything*	"The Evolution of Ragtime"	Cole and Johnson
1905	*Foxy Grandpa*	"I'll Be Your Dewdrop"	R. H. Gerard and Tom Lemonier
1905	*The Rollicking Girl*	"My Cabin Door"	Grant Stewart and Tom Lemonier
1906	*Marrying Mary*	"He's a Cousin of Mine"	Chris Smith, R. C. McPherson, Silvio Hein
1910	*The Boys and Betty*	"Whoop 'er Up with a Whoop La La"	Will Marion Cook
1912	*Little Miss Fix-it*	"If You'll Be My Eve"	Cole and Johnson
1914	*The Girl from Utah*	"Ballin' the Jack"	Chris Smith

Appendix B
New York Shows by Black Composers, 1898–1915

N.Y. Opening Date	Title	Company/Star(s)	Principal Composer(s)	Theatre
1898	*A Trip to Coontown*	Bob Cole	Bob Cole	3rd Avenue
1898	*Clorindy*	Ernest Hogan	Will Marion Cook	Casino Roof
1899	*Jes Lak White Fo'ks*	Ernest Hogan	Will Marion Cook	Cherry Blossom
1899	*The Policy Players*	Williams and Walker	Williams and Walker	Star
1900	*The Sons of Ham*	Williams and Walker	Will Accooe, Tom Lemonier, J. R. Johnson, J. T. Brymn	Grand Opera House
1903	*In Dahomey*	Williams and Walker	Will Marion Cook	New York
1904	*Humpty Dumpty*	Frank Moulan, Maud Berri	Bob Cole and Johnson Bros.	New Amsterdam

N.Y. Opening
Date

N.Y. Opening Date	Title	Company/Star(s)	Principal Composer(s)	Theatre
1904	In Newport	Fay Templeton, Peter F. Dailey	Bob Cole and Johnson Bros.	Liberty
1904	The Southerners	Eddie Leonard	Will Marion Cook	New York
1906	Rufus Rastus	Ernest Hogan	Ernest Hogan	American
1906	Abyssinia	Williams and Walker	Williams and Cook	Majestic
1907	The Shoo-Fly Regiment	Cole and Johnson	Cole and Johnson	Grand Opera House, Bijou
1907	The Oyster Man	Ernest Hogan	Ernest Hogan, Will Vodery	Yorkville
1908	Bandanna Land	Williams and Walker	Will Marion Cook	Majestic
1909	The Red Moon	Cole and Johnson	Cole and Johnson	Majestic
1909	Mr. Lode of Koal	Bert Williams	Bert Williams, J. R. Johnson	Majestic
1910	A Trip to Africa	Black Patti Troubadours	Dave Peyton	?
1911	His Honor, the Barber	Smart Set/S. H. Dudley	J. T. Brymn	Majestic
1911	Hello Paris	Harry Pilcer, James J. Morton	J. R. Johnson	Follies Bergere
1911–1916	My Friend from Dixie/Kentucky	Darktown Follies	J. Leubrie Hill	Lafayette

N.Y. Opening Date	Title	Company/Star(s)	Principal Composer(s)	Theatre
1912	*Captain Jaspar*	Black Patti Troubadours	Will A. Cooke (?)	?
1912	*In the Jungles*	Black Patti Troubadours	?	Grand Opera House
1913	*His Excellency, the Mayor*	Southern Smart Set	?	Lafayette
1913	*The Traitor*	Negro Players	Will Marion Cook	Lafayette
1913	*The Old Man's Boy*	Negro Players	Henry Creamer, Alex Rogers	Lafayette
1914	*The Wrong Mr. President*	Southern Smart Set	?	Lafayette
1914	*The Mayor of New Town*	Southern Smart Set	?	Lafayette
1914	*Lucky Sam from Alabam*	Black Patti Troubadours	?	Lafayette
1915	*George Washington Bullion Abroad*	Smart Set/Tutt and Whitney	James Vaughan	Lafayette
1915	*Darkydom*	Miller and Lyles	Will Marion Cook	Lafayette
1915	*Broadway Rastus*	Irvin C. Miller	Domer C. Brown	Lafayette

Note. These dates reflect the New York openings, not necessarily the earliest date the shows were performed. In a few instances, the New York date is later (generally by one year) from the date given for a particular show in the text discussion.

Appendix C
Songs in Shows by Black Composers, 1898–1915

Abyssinia

Answers You Don't Expect to Get

Build a Nest for Birdie

The Capture of Yaraboo

The Dixie Ballet

Here It Comes Again

Holiday in the Market

I'll Keep a Warm Spot in My Heart for You

I'm a Ruler

The Island of By-and-by

It's Hard to Find a King Like Me

Jolly Jungle Boys

Let It Alone

The Lion and the Monk

Menelik's Tribute to the Queen Taitu

Ode to Menelik

Ode to the Sun

Pretty Desdemona

Rastus Johnson, U. S. A.

Sweetie Dear

Where My Forefathers Died

Bandanna Land

Any Old Place in Yankee Land Is Good Enough for Me

At Peace Wid de World

Bandanna Land

Bon Bon Buddy

Corn Song

Dinah

Down Among the Sugar Cane

Drinkin'

Ethiopia

Fas' Fas' World

I'd Rather Have Nothin'

I'm Crazy 'bout You

I'm Very Fond of Jokes

In My Old Home

It's Hard to Love Somebody

Just the Same

Kinky

Late Hours

The Man from Conjure Land

Maori

Merry Widow Waltz

Minuet

Nobody

Red, Red Rose

Saucy Little Sadie

Sheath Gown in Darktown

Somebody Lied to Me

Somewhere

Southland

'Taint Gwine to Be No Rain

Tired of Eatin' in Restaurants

Until Then

When I Was Sweet Sixteen

You to You is You

You're in the Right Church But the Wrong Pew

Broadway Rastus

Bye-and-bye

Can't Stop Lovin' You Now
Chinese Blues
Clutching Hand
Dandy Dan
Every Woman's Got a Man But Me
Good Night, My Dearie
I Was Made for You
Just to Be Near Salvation
Nell
Some Day
Texas Tommy
Whippoorwill
You Go Your Way and I'll Go Mine

Captain Jaspar
The Belle of New York
Goodbye, Rose
I Am By Myself
Lady Angeline
The Nightingale
O Golden Land
Shakey Rag
Sun-blest Are You
When Old Glory Waves

Clorindy
Dance Creole
Darktown Is Out Tonight
Hottest Coon in Dixie
Jump Back, Honey
Love in a Cottage Is Best
Who Dat Say Chicken in Dis Crowd

Darkydom
All Kinds of People Make a Town
Arcadia
Bamboula

Cairo
Chop Suey Sue
Coon Jine
Drive the Blues Away
Dreamin' Town
The Ghost Ship
Keep Off the Grass
Life
Live and Die in Dixieland
Magnolia Time
Mammy
My Gal from the South
My Lady's Lips
Naughty Moon
Rat-a-tat
Scaddle de Mooch

Dr. Beans from Boston
Bathing
Cuddle Up, Honey
Dearest Memories
Dr. Beans from Boston
Drinking
Eternity
Idle Dreams
Let's Make Love
Messenger Boy
Rain
Sunshine
West Virginia Dance
What Did I Say That For?

George Washington Bullion Abroad
Allah, Oh Allah
Back to Dixie
Body Guards of the Prince
Dear Old Southern Moon

The Deep Blue Sea
Dinner Bells
Don't Do That to Me, Dear
Gin, Gin, Gin
Help Cometh from Above
Love Me Anywhere
Manyanna
No Matter How Good They Treat You in This World
Smilin' Sam
We're Sailing, Sailing
When You Hear the Old Kentucky Blues

Hello Paris
Fascination Waltz
The Frisco Frizz
Hello Paris
Look Me Over
Loving Moon
Sentimental Tommy
The Siberian Dip
That Aeroplane Rag
You're the Nicest Little Girl I Ever Knew

His Excellency, the President
All I Ask Is to Forget You
Come Out, Sue
For Honor
Good Advice
Have Patience, Don't Worry
Just a Pickaninny All Dressed Up
The Intruder
The Love You Can't Forget
Romance Española
The Smart Set Tango
We Welcome Thee

What You Need Is Ginger Springs
When Your Country Calls to Arms

His Honor, the Barber
Caroline Brown
Come After Breakfast
Consolation Time
Corn Shucking Time
Cry Baby in Town
Golly, Ain't I Wicked
His Dream Is Over
I Like That
The Isle of Love
Let Him Dream
Merry Widow Brown
Pickaninny Days
Porto Rico
Rainbow Sue
That's Why They Call Me Shine
Watermelon Time
You Needn't Come at All

Humpty Dumpty
Chorus of Cooks
Chorus of King's Guards
Chorus of Villagers
Conspirators' Chorus
Cupid Reigns King
Down at the Bottom of the Sea
Down in Mulberry Bend
The Egg Has Fallen Down
Fairyland
I Am a King
I'm a Very Good Sailor on Land
Man, Man, Man
Mary from Tipperary
Mexico

On Lalawana's Shores
The Pussy and the Bow-wow
Sambo and Dinah
We've Got to Find the Ring
Will He Ever Smile Again?

In Dahomey
The Attucks March
Brown-Skin Baby Mine
Caboceer's Entrance and Choral
Captain Kidd
Chin Chin
Chocolate Drops
The Czar
Dat Girl of Mine
Dear Luzon
A Dream of the Philippines
Emancipation Day
Evah Darkey Is a King
For Florida
Good Evenin'
Happy Jim
I May Be Crazy, But I Ain't No Fool
I Wants To Be a Actor Lady
The Jonah Man
Leader of the Colored Aristocracy
Me and de Minstrel Band
Mollie Green
My Castle on the Nile
My Dahomian Queen
My Lady Frog
Returned
A Rich Coon's Babe
She's Dancing Sue
Society
Swing Along

That's How the Cakewalk's Done
Vassar Girl
When the Moon Shines on the
Moonshine
When Sousa Comes to Town
Why Adam Sinned

In the Jungles
Baby Rose
Home, Sweet Home
Love Is King
My Dreamland
My Jewel of the River Nile
Never Let the Same Bee Sting You
Twice
Oh, Say Wouldn't That Be a Dream
Plant a Watermelon on My Grave
Ragtime Love
Roll a Little Pill for Me

In Newport
Don't Go Too Dangerously Nigh
Hello, Ma Lulu
The House That Jack Built
How a Monocle Helps the Mind
Lindy
Mary Was a Manicure
The Newport Dip
Nobody But You
Peggy Is a New Yorker Now
The Rehearsal
Roaming Around the Town
Scandal
Spirit of the Banjo
Stockings
When I Am Chief of Police

Women
Zel, Zel

Jes Lak White Fo'ks
Colored Girl from Vassar
Evah Nigger Is a King
Love Looks Not at Estate
Spread de News
We's a Comin'

Lucky Sam from Alabam
Going No Place in Particular
Goodbye
Luckstone's Delight
Mournful Rag
No One
Pleading Eyes
Watch Your Step

The Mayor of New Town
Good Night, Marie
Here I Is and Here I Stay
Hot Tamale Moon
I Could Learn to Love a Boy Like You
Keep a Movin' Right Along
The Mayor of New Town
Mexico
Neat Ned Nuff Said
Tell Me, Rose
That Was Me
Those Songs I Love
You Babe, Only You

Mr. Lode of Koal
Believe Me
Blue Law
Bygone Days in Dixie

Can Song
Chink, Chink Chinaman
Fete of the Veiled Mugs
Harbour of Lost Dreams
Hodge Podge
In Far Off Mandalay
Lament
Mum's the Word, Mr. Moon
My Ole Man
The Start
That's a Plenty

My Friend from Dixie/Kentucky
At the Ball, That's All
Dear Old Dixie
Don't Be Too Fas'
Gay Manhattan Rag
Good Time While I Can
Happy Time
Honey Bunch
Lou, My Lou
The Man of the Hour
Molasses Candy
Night Time Is the Best Time
Rock Me in the Cradle of Love
Take Me Away to Jail
That's the Kind of Man I Want
Waiting All the Time
Waiting At the Depot
The Warmest Baby in Town
You

The Old Man's Boy
All Day Long
Brazilian Dreams
The Castle on the Isle of Coal

Dixie Land March Song

Hanging Around and Gone, Gone, Gone

Hello, Mr. Moon

I Lost My Way

International Rag

June Time

King Love 'Em All

Oh, You Devil Rag

Sweet Thoughts of Home

You'll Want My Love

You've Got to Bag It

The Oyster Man

All Hail the King

Blazazus Chorus

Contribution Box

Dogalo

Enough, That's Enough

Fish Chorus

I Just Can't Keep My Eyes Off You

Meet Me at the Barber Shop

Mermaids' Chorus

Mina

No You Didn't, Yes I Did

The Oyster Man

Roll On, Mighty Wave

Suanee River

Tomorrow

When Buffalo Bill and His Wild West Show First Came to Baltimore

The Whitewash Brigade

Within the Shade of Morro Castle

Yankee Doodle Coon

The Policy Players

A Broadway Coon

Asterbilts Welcome Home

Five Little Haytian Maids

Ghost of a Coon

Gwine to Catch a Gig Today

He's Up Against the Real Thing Now

Honolulu Bells

I Don't Like No Cheap Man

Kings of the Policy Shop

The Man in the Moon Might Tell

Medicine Man

Moonlight

Toughest in de Place

Uncle Sam

Who's Going to Make the Lucky Play

Why Don't You Get a Lady of Your Own

The Red Moon

Ada, My Sweet Potater

As Long as the World Goes Round

Big Red Shawl

Bleeding Moon

Coola Woola

Cupid Was an Indian Pickaninny

I Ain't Had No Lovin' in a Long Time

I've Lost My Teddy Bear

I Want My Chicken

Keep On Smilin'

Life Is a Game of Checkers

My Indian Maid

On the Road to Monterey

Phoebe Brown

Run, Brudder Possum, Run

Sambo

Wildfire

Rufus Rastus

Cock-a-doodle-doo

Consolation

Dixie Anna Lou
Eve Handed Adam a Lemon
The Hornet and the Bee
If Peter Was a Colored Man
I'll Love You All the Time
Is Everybody Happy?
The Isle of Repose
Lilly's Wedding Day
Mammy
Maude
The Monkey and the Bear
Moon Boy
My Mobile Mandy
On Grandma's Kitchen Floor
Watermelon
What We're Supposed to Do

The Shoo-Fly Regiment
De Bo'd of Education
Down in the Philippines
Floating Down the Nile
The Ghost of Deacon Brown
If Adam Hadn't Seen the Apple Tree
I'll Always Love Old Dixie
I Think an Awful Lot of You
Just How Much I Love You
Lemons
Lit'l Gal
The Little Choo-Choo Gee-Gee
My Sweetheart's a Soldier
The Old Flag Never Touched the
Ground
On the Gay Luneta
Run, Brudder Rabbit, Run
That Still Small Voice
There's Always Something Wrong

We've Been to Boston Town
Who Do You Love?
Won't You Be My Little Brown Bear?

The Sons of Ham
Beyond the Gates of Paradise
Blackville Strutters
Cairo
Calisthenics
Dinah
Down Where the Cotton Blossoms Grow
Fortune-Telling Coon
Good Afternoon, Mr. Jenkins
Josephine, My Jo
Leader of the Ball
Ma Ia
Miss Hannah from Savannah
My Castle on the Nile
Old Man's Song and Dance
Phrenologist Coon
The Promoters
She's Getting More Like White Folks
Every Day
Society
Sons of Ham
When the Corn is Wavin'
When the Heart Is Young
Zulu Babe

The Southerners
The Amorous Star
As the Sunflowers Turn to the Sun
Daisy Dean
Dandy Dan
Darktown Barbecue
Dreamin' Town
Good Evenin'

It's Allus de Same in Dixie
Mandy Lou
'Mongst the Magnolias
Where the Lotus Blossoms Grow

The Traitor
After All I've Been To You
Lover's Lane

A Trip to Africa
All Hail the King
All I Want Is My Honey
The Beaming Sun
Boola Boola
Good Enough for Me
I Ain't No Fool
I'm Going to Leave Today
In the Bright Moonlight
In Zululand
I Wish I Was in Heaven
A King Like Me
Mother's Chil'
O You Loving Man
Ragtime Baseball

A Trip to Coontown
Coontown Frolic
The Coontown Restaurant
For All Eternity
4-11-44
I Can Stand for Your Color, But Your
Hair Won't Do
If That's Society, Excuse Me
I Hope These Few Lines Find You Well
Ika Hula

I Must O' Been a Dreaming
In Dahomey
The Italian Man
I Wonder What Is That Coon's Game
A Jolly Old Rube
La Hoola Boola
Ma Chickens: Picking on a Chicken
Bone
Meet Me at the Gin Spring
Miss Arabella Jones
No Coons Allowed
Old Kentucky Home
Sweet Savannah
There's a Warm Spot in My Heart for
You
Trio from Attila
Two Bold, Bad Men
The Wedding of the Chinee and the
Coon
When the Chickens Go to Sleep

The Wrong Mr. President
All I Ask Is to Forget You
Come Out, Sue
Hesitation Waltz
The Intruder
Just a Pickaninny All Dressed Up
Romance Española
Smart Set Tango
Some Sweet Day
Those Days of Long Ago
Tourists Are We
Tutt's Todalo
We Welcome Thee
What You Need is Ginger Springs

Notes

List of Abbreviations Used in Notes

AMT   Bordman, Gerald. *American Musical Theatre: A Chronicle.* New York: Oxford University Press, 1978.

Age   New York *Age*

DM   New York *Dramatic Mirror*

HTC   Clipping files of the Theatre Collection of Houghton Library, Harvard University

JD   Stearns, Marshall, and Stearns, Jean. *Jazz Dance: The Story of American Vernacular Dance.* New York: Schirmer Books, 1968.

MOBA   Southern, Eileen. *The Music of Black Americans: A History.* 2d ed. New York: Norton, 1983.

NYPL   Clipping files of the Billy Rose Theatre Collection, New York Public Library at Lincoln Center

NYT   *New York Times*

Preface

1. Eileen Southern, ed., *Readings in Black American Music* (New York: Norton, 1971), pp. 217–23.

2. Ernst-Alexandre Ansermet, "Bechet and Jazz Visit Europe, 1919," in *Frontiers of Jazz*, ed. Ralph de Toledano (New York: F. Ungar, 1962), p. 116.

3. Among other sources, *see* August Meier, *Negro Thought in America 1880–1915* (Ann Arbor: University of Michigan Press, 1963).

4. Edward Berlin, in *Ragtime: A Musical and Cultural History* (Berkeley: University of California Press, 1980), p. 73, places the period in which jazz replaces ragtime as a popular music category as approximately 1917 to 1919.

5. *MOBA* pp. 116–21.

6. Jervis Anderson, *This Was Harlem: A Cultural Portrait, 1900–1950* (New York: Farrar, Straus, Giroux, 1981).

Chapter 1·Black Song and Dance in the Nineteenth Century

1. *See* Dena Epstein, *Sinful Tunes and Spirituals* (Urbana, IL: University of Illinois Press, 1977); Eileen Southern, ed., *Readings in Black American Music*, 2d ed. (New York: Norton, 1983), especially pp. 27–50, 71–148; Henry Kmen, *Music in New Orleans* (Baton Rouge: Louisiana State University Press, 1966).

2. The minstrelsy bibliography is extensive and includes: Robert Toll, *Blacking Up* (New York: Oxford University Press, 1974); Hans Nathan, *Dan Emmett and the Rise of Early Negro Minstrelsy* (Norman, OK: University of Oklahoma Press, 1962); Gary D. Engle, ed., *This Grotesque Essence: Plays from the American Minstrel Stage* (Baton Rouge: Louisiana State University Press, 1978); Carl Wittke, *Tambo and Bones* (Durham: Duke University Press, 1930); Walter Ben Hare, *The Minstrel Encyclopedia* (Boston: Walter H. Baker, 1921); Edward LeRoy Rice, *Monarchs of Minstrelsy* (New York: Kenny Pub., 1910); Constance Rourke, *American Humor: A Study of the National Character* (1931; reprint ed., Tallahassee: Florida State University Press, 1986).

3. The illiteracy rates for identifiable groups of Americans for whom reliable data are available—Army enlistees and merchant seamen, for example—often top 40 percent in the early decades of the nineteenth century. Prohibitions against slave literacy would have made any general statistic higher for blacks in the antebellum period. Lee Soltow and Edward Stevens, *The Rise of Literacy and the Common School in the United States: A Socioeconomic Analysis to 1870* (Chicago: University of Chicago Press, 1981).

4. Toll, *Blacking Up*, pp. 275–76.

5. An effective re-creation of these tunes can be found in a 1985 recording, "The Early Minstrel Show," Robert Winans, musical director (New World Records, NW 338, 1985).

6. Kathryn Reed-Maxfield, "Emmett, Foster and Their Anonymous Colleagues: The Creators of Early Minstrel Show Songs" (Paper presented at the annual meeting of the Sonneck Society, University of Pittsburgh, Pittsburgh, Pennsylvania, April 4, 1987). *See also* Robert Winans, "Minstrel Show Music: The First Decade, 1843–1852" (Paper presented at the Musical Theatre in Amer-

ica Conference, C. W. Post Center, Long Island University, Greenvale, NY, April 2, 1981).

7. Thomas Riis, "The Music and Musicians in Nineteenth-century Productions of *Uncle Tom's Cabin*," *American Music* 4, no. 3 (Fall 1986): 273–77.

8. Walter J. Ong, *Orality and Literacy* (London: Methuen, 1982). Even prior to the seminal work of Milman Parry (*L'Epithète traditionelle dans Homère*, 1928) and Albert B. Lord (*The Singer of Tales*, 1960), questions of oral culture have occupied literary scholars and anthropologists. Ong includes an extensive bibliography.

9. Toll, *Blacking Up*, pp. 245–49.

10. Edmund John Collins, "Jazz Feedback to Africa," *American Music* 5, no. 2 (Summer 1987): 176–93.

11. James Monroe Trotter, *Music and Some Highly Musical People* (1880; reprint ed., Chicago: Afro-Am Press, 1969), pp. 274–82.

12. Ralph Ellison, *Going to the Territory* (New York: Random House, 1986), p. 124.

13. Ibid., p. 284.

14. Phyllis Hartnoll, *The Oxford Companion to the Theater*, 2nd ed. (London: Oxford University Press, 1969), pp. 566–67; James V. Hatch and OMANii Abdullah, *Black Playwrights, 1823–1977* (New York: R.R. Bowker Co., 1977), pp. 29, 31; Harry Birdoff, *The World's Greatest Hit* (New York: Vanni, 1947), pp. 144–85; Thomas Riis, "The Music and Musicians in Nineteenth-century Productions of *Uncle Tom's Cabin*," *American Music* 4, no. 3 (Fall 1986): 268–86.

15. Deane L. Root, *American Popular Stage Music, 1860–1880* (Ann Arbor: UMI Research Press, 1981), pp. 59–64.

16. *MOBA*, pp. 250–51; Eileen Southern, "The Origin and Development of the Black Musical Theater: A Preliminary Report," *Black Music Research Journal* (1981): 6–7.

17. Tom Fletcher, *The Tom Fletcher Story: 100 Years of the Negro in Show Business* (1954; reprint ed., New York: Da Capo Press, 1984), p. 71; *San Francisco Pacific Appeal*, April 5, 1879, p. 2; *Cleveland Gazette*, June 5, 1886, pp. 1, 2.

18. Undated program, Wilkes-Barre, PA, NYPL, *Out of Bondage* folder.

19. Charles Hamm, *Yesterdays: Popular Song in America* (New York: Norton, 1979), pp. 265–71.

20. *St. Paul Appeal*, February 28, 1891, pp. 3, 4; ibid., May 23, 1891, pp. 1, 2. See also *MOBA*, pp. 250–51.

21. *Colored American Magazine* 4 (November 1901): 50–51.

22. Ike Simond, *Old Slack's Reminiscence and Pocket History of the Colored Profession From 1865 to 1891* (ca. 1891; reprint ed., Bowling Green, OH: Popular Press, 1974), p. 7.

23. Root, *American Stage Music*, pp. 78–79; James L. Ford, "Our National Stage," *McClure's Magazine* 32 (March 1909): 497.

24. Ibid.; *AMT*, pp. 18–23, 29–35, 99, 124, 132; Cecil Smith, *Musical Comedy in America* (New York: Theatre Arts Books, 1950), pp. 13–22.

25. Root, *American Stage Music*, p. 66; Fletcher, *100 Years*, p. 41; James Weldon Johnson, *Black Manhattan* (New York: Alfred A. Knopf, 1930), pp. 95–96. *See also* George B. Oliver, "Changing Patterns of Spectacle on the New York Stage (1850–1890)" (Ph. D. dissertation, Pennsylvania State University, 1956), p. 97.

26. Sheet music cover, "Move Up, Johnson," words and music by Bob Cole (New York: Brooks & Denton Company, 1896); Hamm, *Yesterdays*, p. 271.

27. *Haverhill Evening Gazette*, August 4, 1890, n. p.; *DM*, September 6, 1890, p. 13.

28. *AMT*, pp. 128–29.

29. Hamm, *Yesterdays*, pp. 265–71.

30. Paul Oliver, *Songsters and Saints* (Cambridge: Cambridge University Press, 1984), p. 22; Charles Dickens, *American Notes* (1842; reprint ed., New York: Fromm International Publishing Co., 1985), pp. 90–91; Stanley Crouch, "In the Interest of Illumination: The Function of Jazz Writing" (Unpublished article). The most thorough discussion of the black heritage of vernacular dance is that of *JD; see also* Oliver, *Songsters and Saints*, pp. 18–46, on dance songs.

Chapter 2·Traveling Shows

1. Monroe Lippmann, "The History of the Theatrical Syndicate in America: Its Effects Upon Theaters in America" (Ph. D. dissertation, University of Michigan, 1937), p. 20.

2. "The Theatre Syndicate," *Literary Digest* 12, no. 3 (November 16, 1895): 3; Lippmann, "Theatrical Syndicate," p. 98.

3. "The Theatrical Syndicate," *Literary Digest* 19, no. 3 (January 20, 1900): 79–80; *AMT*, p. 122.

4. Charles H. Wesley, *Negro Labor in the United States 1850–1925: A Study in American Economic History* (New York: Vanguard Press, 1927), pp. 156–91.

5. *JD*, p. 66.

6. Benjamin Brawley, *Paul Laurence Dunbar: Poet of His People* (Chapel Hill: University of North Carolina Press, 1936), pp. 85–86. *See also* Gary D. Engle, *This Grotesque Essence: Plays from the American Minstrel Stage* (Baton Rouge: Louisiana State University Press, 1978), which includes "Uncle Eph's Dream" (p. 57).

7. James Weldon Johnson, *Black Manhattan* (New York: Alfred A. Knopf, 1930), p. 96; Ann Charters, *Nobody: The Story of Bert Williams* (London: Macmillan, 1970), p. 26.

8. *DM*, June 19, 1895, p. 11.

9. Ibid., September 21, 1895, p. 9.

10. Bernard Sobel, *Burleycue: An Underground History of Burlesque Days* (New York: Ferrar and Rinehart, 1931), pp. 51–52. *See also* Robert Nisbett, "Afro-American Musical Shows of the 1890s," paper delivered at the National Endowment for the Humanities Summer Seminar for College Teachers, Harvard University, 1982.

11. John Graziano has generously shared the information from the script with me. It is in the Rare Book Division, Library of Congress, Washington, DC. "A Trip to Coney Island" may refer to Bob Cole's skit "At Jolly Coon-ey Island," although it is also possible that the latter title, used by Black Patti in the same year, was a parody.

12. *Freeman*, December 19, 1896, p. 6.

13. Ibid., August 15, 1896, n. p.; ibid., November 7, 1896, p. 6; Johnson, *Black Manhattan*, pp. 96–97.

14. The libretto is in the Rare Book Division, Library of Congress, Washington, DC.

15. *Freeman*, September 25, 1897, n. p.

16. Wilkes-Barre (PA) *Opera Glass*, April 17, 1899, NYPL; *Freeman*, December 24, 1898, p. 1.

17. *Freeman*, June 3, 1899, n. p.; Henry Sampson, *Blacks in Blackface* (Metuchen, NJ: Scarecrow Press, 1980), pp. 65–66.

18. Typescript, NYPL, Billy McClain folder.

19. It is not clear whether this *Suwanee River* show is identical to *Down on the Suwanee River*, described in *AMT*, p. 141; Tom Fletcher, *The Tom Fletcher Story: 100 Years of the Negro in Show Business* (New York: Burdge and Co., 1954), pp. 94–97.

20. *NYT*, May 26, 1895, II, p. 16.

21. Fletcher, *Tom Fletcher Story*, pp. 91–102.

22. Others include Flora Batson Bergen, Sidney Woodward, Will Marion Cook, and J. Rosamond Johnson. Sissieretta Jones is said to have studied voice in Boston and other cities with a variety of teachers, the most famous of whom is Louisa Cappiani. *See* Willia Daughtry, "Sissieretta Jones: A Study of the Negro's Contribution to Nineteenth Century American Concert and Theatrical Life" (Ph. D. dissertation, Syracuse University, 1968); William Lichtenwanger, "Sissieretta Jones," in *Notable American Women 1607–1950*, vol. 2, ed. Edward T. James (Cambridge, MA: Belknap Press of the Harvard University Press, 1971), pp. 288–90.

23. *Toronto Globe*, October 13, 1892, n. p., clipping in Sissieretta Jones file, Moorland Collection, Moorland-Spingarn Research Center, Howard University; *New York Echo*, n.d., Moorland Collection; *New York Review*, n.d., Moorland Collection; *Detroit Tribune*, n.d., Moorland Collection.

24. Lichtenwanger, "Sissieretta Jones," p. 289.

25. A letter of Will Marion Cook, dated November 23, 1934, in the Jewel Cobb papers calls Bob Cole "a genius." Sylvester Russell, critic for the *Chicago Defender,* ranked him as the "best actor" among his black contemporaries: *Freeman,* November 24, 1910, p. 5. He reportedly played many instruments, stage-managed the Black Patti show and others, and of course both wrote and performed songs.

26. Cole's sister, Carriebell Cole Plummer, wrote a biography of her brother that still exists in a draft held by Dr. Jewel Cobb (who had kindly granted me access to it). Lester Walton published an obituary of Cole in the *Age,* August 10, 1911, p. 6, which adds several details about Cole's early performing but appears to be based chiefly on information from the Cole family.

27. *Age,* August 10, 1911, p. 6; Ann Charters, *Nobody: The Story of Bert Williams* (London: Macmillan, 1970), p. 51; Johnson, *Black Manhattan,* p. 97.

28. Plummer biography, Cobb papers.

29. Plummer biography, Cobb papers. This story is corroborated by William Foster's early history of black show business, "Pioneers of the Stage," in the *1928 Edition of The Official Theatrical World of Colored Artists,* ed. Theophilus Lewis (New York: The Theatrical World Publishing Co., 1928), p. 48. *See also* Thomas Riis, "Bob Cole: His Life and His Legacy to Black Musical Theater," *Black Perspectives in Music* 13 (1985): 135–50.

Chapter 3·The Scene and the Players in New York

1. Moses King, *New York: The American Cosmopolis* (Boston: Moses King, 1893), p. 2; Theodore Dreiser, *The Color of a Great City* (New York: Boni and Liveright, 1923), p. vii; Henry James, *The American Scene* (1905; reprint ed., Bloomington: Indiana University Press, 1968), pp. 117–19, 186–87, 208.

2. Bayrd Still, *Mirror for Gotham* (New York: Washington Square Press, 1956), p. 250.

3. Ibid., p. 213.

4. Seth Scheiner, *Negro Mecca: A History of the Negro in New York City, 1865–1920* (New York: New York University Press, 1965), pp. 224–25.

5. W. E. B. DuBois, *The Black North in 1901: A Social Study* (New York: Arno Press, 1969), p. 11. This collection is a series of articles originally published in the *New York Times,* November–December 1901.

6. Ibid.; Scheiner, *Negro Mecca,* pp. 17–19; Jervis Anderson, *This Was Harlem* (New York: Farrar, Straus, Giroux, 1982), pp. 8–9.

7. Paul Laurence Dunbar, *The Sport of the Gods* (New York: Dodd, Mead and Company, 1902), pp. 77–78.

8. Still, *Mirror,* p. 217; Scheiner, *Negro Mecca,* pp. 45–61; Roi Ottley and William Weatherby, eds., *The Negro in New York* (Dobbs Ferry, NY: New York Public Library, 1967), pp. 146–47; Anderson, *This Was Harlem,* pp. 13–20, 92–98, 339–46.

9. Mary Henderson, *The City and the Theatre* (Clifton, NJ: James T. White and

Co., 1973), pp. 123–24, 168–70, 219. An excellent overview of the variety of New York theatrical life can be found in *AMT*. George C. D. Odell, *Annals of the New York Stage* (New York: Columbia University Press, 1927–1941), 15 vols., is an indispensable compendium of periodical notes. Studies of the New York stage that concentrate on specific national contributions include Hamilton Mason, *The French Theatre in New York* (New York: Columbia University Press, 1946), and Fred A. H. Leuchs, *Early German Theatre in New York* (New York: Columbia University Press, 1928).

10. Anderson, *This Was Harlem*, pp. 8–9.
11. James Weldon Johnson, *Along This Way* (New York: Viking Press, 1933), p. 171.
12. Ibid., p. 177.
13. The census figures were extracted from the *Eleventh United States Census*, vol. 3 (Washington, DC: Government Printing Office, 1897), p. 452; *Twelfth United States Census Special Reports: Occupations*, vol. 2 (Washington, DC: Government Printing Office, 1904), p. 650. "Colored," as defined by the 1890 census, means "persons of negro descent, Chinese, Japanese, and civilized Indian." The statistics for Negroes alone were separated from other "colored" in 1900.
14. Samuel Charters and Leonard Kunstadt, *Jazz: The New York Scene* (Garden City, NY: Doubleday, 1962), pp. 13–22.
15. *New York Herald*, October 29, 1895; *New York Evening Post*, October 7, 1897; *New York Daily Tribune*, January 24, 1898. *See also* Dena Epstein, "Jeannette Meyers Thurber," in *Notable American Women 1607–1950*, vol. 2, ed. Edward T. James (Cambridge, MA: Belknap Press of the Harvard University Press, 1971), pp. 458–59.
16. *MOBA*, pp. 266, 268, 282.
17. Plummer biography, Cobb papers.
18. Johnson, *Along This Way*, pp. 152–53.
19. Ibid., pp. 149–50.
20. Ibid., p. 187.
21. *JD*, pp. 120, 117–24.
22. James Weldon Johnson, *Black Manhattan* (New York: Alfred A. Knopf, 1930), p. 102.
23. *Age*, May 27, 1909.
24. Tom Fletcher, *The Tom Fletcher Story: 100 Years of the Negro in Show Business* (New York: Burdge and Co., 1954), pp. 139, 141; Paul Oliver, *Songsters and Saints* (Cambridge: Cambridge University Press, 1984), p. 49.
25. *Age*, May 27, 1909: *DM*, February 25, 1909.
26. Charters, *Nobody*, p. 50. An eight-page libretto of *Jes Lak White Fo'ks* survives at the Music Division, Library of Congress, Washington, DC.
27. *Age*, May 29, 1909, p. 6.

28. Ibid.

29. Alain Locke, *The Negro and His Music* (1936; reprint ed., New York: Arno Press, 1969), pp. 65–66.

30. Marva Griffin Carter at the University of Illinois has completed a dissertation devoted to the life and work of Cook. The Cook biographical information contained here is based largely on accounts found in general music histories, such as *MOBA*, supplemented by an unpublished autobiography in the papers of Will Marion Cook's son, Dr. Mercer Cook; an interview with Dr. Cook; and supplementary correspondence.

31. Unfortunately, the church records do not cover activities not directly sponsored by the church. The church historian could not confirm this information received from Dr. Cook.

32. Johnson, *Along This Way*, p. 172.

33. Ike Simond, *Old Slack's Reminiscence and Pocket History of the Colored Profession from 1865 to 1891* (1891; reprint ed., Bowling Green, OH: Popular Press, 1974), p. 23.

34. *Crisis* 10, no. 2 (June 1915): 63.

35. *MOBA*, p. 354. This group was first known as the New York Syncopated Orchestra and later as the American Syncopated Orchestra before its European tour.

36. We have only Witmark's side of the story in Isidore Witmark and Isaac Goldberg, *From Ragtime to Swingtime* (1939; reprint ed., New York: Da Capo Press, 1976), pp. 196–97, but it appears that Cook's own lawyer thought that he was in the wrong and that his accusation was at least abrupt.

37. Letter to Mr. William C. Graves, March 2 1919, James Weldon Johnson Memorial Collection of American Literature, Beinecke Rare Book and Manuscript Library, Yale University.

38. Duke Ellington, *Music is My Mistress* (Garden City, NY: Doubleday, 1973), pp. 95–97; Eileen Southern, *Music of Black Americans* (New York: Norton, 1971), pp. 432–33.

39. *AMT*, p. 191.

40. *Age*, January 12, 1911, p. 6; Charters, *Nobody*, p. 25.

41. *Freeman*, April 23, 1910, p. 6; *see also* Brooke Baldwin, "The Cakewalk: A Study in Stereotype and Reality," *Journal of Social History* 15 (1981): 205–18.

42. *Freeman*, January 14, 1911, p. 5.

43. Charters, *Nobody*, pp. 144–47; *AMT*, p. 354.

44. Charters, *Nobody*, pp. 69, 83.

Chapter 4·The Music in the Shows

1. Paul Oliver, *Songsters and Saints* (Cambridge: Cambridge University Press, 1984), p. 100.

2. Eugene Levy, *James Weldon Johnson: Black Leader, Black Voice* (Chicago:

University of Chicago Press, 1973), pp. 86–91; Lester Walton, "The Popularity of Ragtime," *Age*, January 13, 1910, p. 6.

3. Gossie H. Hudson and Jay Martin, eds., *The Paul Laurence Dunbar Reader* (New York: Dodd, Mead, and Co., 1975). Other biographical works on Dunbar include Linda Keck Wiggins, *The Life and Works of Paul Laurence Dunbar* (Napierville, IL, and Memphis: J. L. Nichols and Co., 1907); Benjamin Brawley, *Paul Laurence Dunbar: Poet of His People* (Chapel Hill: University of North Carolina Press, 1936); and Addison Gayle, *Oak and Ivy: A Biography of Paul Laurence Dunbar* (Garden City, NY: Doubleday, 1971).

4. James Weldon Johnson, *Along This Way* (New York: Viking Press, 1933), pp. 159, 160–61.

5. Levy, *James Weldon Johnson*, p. 89.

6. Charles Hamm, *Yesterdays* (New York and London: Norton, 1979), p. 292.

7. *NYT*, February 4, 1908, p. 7. *See also AMT*, pp. 236–37.

8. Edward Berlin, *Ragtime: A Musical and Cultural History* (Berkeley: University of California Press, 1980), pp. 82–88.

9. Brian Rust, *Complete Entertainment Discography* (New York: Arlington House, 1973), pp. 666–70. *See also Follies, Scandals, and Other Diversions: From Ziegfeld to the Shuberts* (New World Records NW 215, 1977); *Follies of 1919* (Smithsonian American Musical Theater Series 2009, 1977); and *"Nobody" and Other Songs by Bert Williams* (Folkways Records RBF 602, 1981).

10. Paul Steg, *"In Dahomey*, 1902–1905: A Score in Flux," paper presented at the National Endowment for the Humanities Summer Seminar for College Teachers, Harvard University, August 1982.

11. Hamm, *Yesterdays*, p. 321.

12. Michael R. Turner, *The Parlour Song Book: A Casquet of Vocal Gems* (New York: Viking Press, 1972), p. 233.

13. Isidore Witmark and Isaac Goldberg, *From Ragtime to Swingtime* (1939; reprint ed., New York: Da Capo Press, 1976), pp. 448–49; E. B. Marks, *They All Sang* (New York, 1934), p. 100; John Chipman, *Index to Top-Hit Tunes 1900–1950* (Boston: Bruce Humphries Publishers, 1962), pp. 158–59; Hamm, *Yesterdays*, p. 325.

14. *AMT*, p. 118.

15. I am indebted to Wayne Shirley of the Music Division, Library of Congress, Washington, D.C., for this apt observation.

16. Front cover of Robert Cole, "M'aimez Vous? (Do You Love Me?)" (New York: Joseph Stern and Co., 1910).

17. The Indian motif was so familiar that a satirical song in pseudo-Indian style about the New York political scene, entitled "Tammany," appeared in 1905 and became one of the big hits of the decade. Willie "the Lion" Smith alludes to the popularity of Indian songs in his memoirs, *Music On My Mind* (1964;

reprint ed., New York: Da Capo Press, 1978), and names several of them (p. 36).

18. This written indication appears on the printed copy of the song deposited in the James Weldon Johnson Collection, Beinecke Rare Book and Manuscript Library, Yale University.

19. *AMT*, pp. 113–15.

20. The librettos are in the Music Division, Library of Congress, Washington, DC.

21. Marks, *They All Sang*, p. 3.

22. Johnson, *Along This Way*, p. 178.

23. The individual titles of the songs are: "Voice of the Savage (Zulu Dance)," "Echoes of the Day," "Essence of the Jug," "Darkies Delight," "The Spirit of the Banjo," and "Sounds of the Time (Lindy)." *See also* Edward Berlin, "Cole and Johnson Brothers' *The Evolution of Ragtime*," *Current Musicology* 36 (1983): 21–39.

24. *AMT*, pp. 149, 165.

25. Ibid., p. 181.

26. Ibid., pp. 184, 190.

27. Ibid., p. 222; Levy, *James Weldon Johnson*, p. 86n.

Chapter 5· "Musical Interruptions and Occasional Specialties," 1898–1902

1. William Foster, "Pioneers of the Stage: Memoirs of William Foster," in *1928 Edition The Official Theatrical World of Colored Artists . . .*, ed. Theophilus Lewis (New York: The Theatrical World Publishing Co., 1928), p. 48.

2. *Age*, August 10, 1911, p. 6.

3. *DM*, April 9, 1898, HTC, *A Trip to Coontown* folder.

4. Henry Sampson, *Blacks in Blackface* (Metuchen, NJ: Scarecrow Press, 1980), p. 321.

5. *AMT*, p. 158; unidentified review, February 6, 1900, HTC, *A Trip to Coontown* folder.

6. E. J. Kahn, Jr., *The Merry Partners: The Age and Stage of Harrigan and Hart* (New York: Random House, 1955), pp. 275–76; *JD*, p. 119.

7. *AMT*, pp. 149, 160.

8. Will Marion Cook, "Clorindy, the Origin of the Cakewalk," in *Readings in Black American Music*, 2d ed., ed. Eileen Southern (New York: Norton, 1983), pp. 231–32.

9. Stephen Burge Johnson, *The Roof Gardens of Broadway Theatres, 1883–1942* (Ann Arbor: UMI Research Press, 1985), p. 54.

10. *AMT*, p. 159; James Weldon Johnson, *Along This Way* (New York: Viking Press, 1933), p. 151.

11. Sampson, *Blacks in Blackface*, pp. 78–79; Johnson, *Roof Gardens*, p. 55.

12. *NYT*, April 3, 1900, p. 9; unidentified reviews, December 19, 1899 and March 13, 1900, HTC, *The Policy Players* folder.
13. *NYT*, April 3, 1900, p. 9. A brief libretto exists in the Rare Book Division, Library of Congress, Washington, DC. *See also* Sampson, *Blacks in Blackface*, p. 311.
14. Edward Berlin, *Ragtime: A Musical and Cultural History* (Berkeley: University of California Press, 1980), pp. 97–98; Paul Oliver, *Songsters and Saints* (Cambridge: Cambridge University Press, 1984), p. 97.
15. See *MOBA*, pp. 275–77, for a general discussion of this link. The version of the spiritual quoted in Example 5.7 is found in J. Rosamond Johnson, *The Book of American Negro Spirituals* (1925; reprint ed., New York: Da Capo Press, 1977).
16. Henry Charles Lahee, *Annals of Music in America* (1922; reprint ed., Freeport, NY: Books for Libraries Press, 1970), p. 122; Leslie Orrey, ed., *The Encyclopedia of Opera* (New York: Charles Scribner's Sons, 1976), p. 167.

Chapter 6·On Broadway, 1903–1905

1. Ann Charters, *Nobody: The Story of Bert Williams* (London: Macmillan, 1970), p. 77.
2. John Graziano, "Sentimental Songs, Rags and Transformations: The Emergence of the Black Musical, 1895 to 1910," in *Musical Theatre in America: Papers and Proceedings of the Conference on the Musical Theatre in America*, ed. Glenn Loney (Westport, CT: Greenwood Press, 1984), pp. 211–32; Paul Steg, "In Dahomey, 1902–1905: A Score in Flux," paper presented at the National Endowment for the Humanities Summer Seminar for College Teachers, Harvard University, August 1982.
3. Reprinted in facsimile in *Show Songs from "The Black Crook" to "The Red Mill": Original Sheet Music for 60 Songs from 50 Shows, 1866–1906*, ed. Stanley Applebaum (New York: Dover, 1974), pp. 179–83.
4. *In Dahomey* libretto, Music Division, Library of Congress, Washington, DC; *NYT*, February 19, 1903, p. 9.
5. Unidentified London review, October 23, 1903, HTC, *In Dahomey* folder.
6. S. J. Pryor, *London Express*, reprinted in *NYT*, July 19, 1903, p. 3.
7. Unidentified review, May 18, 1903, HTC, *In Dahomey* folder; *AMT*, p. 185. *See also* Jeffrey Green, "*In Dahomey* in London," *The Black Perspective in Music* 11 (Spring 1983): 22–40.
8. Unidentified review, May 18, 1903, HTC, *In Dahomey* folder.
9. Unidentified review, HTC, *The Southerners* folder; *Boston Evening Transcript*, August 30, 1904, n.p.
10. Unidentified review, HTC, *The Southerners* folder; *New York Herald Tribune*, May 24, 1904, n.p.
11. *NYT*, May 24, 1904, p. 9.

Chapter 7·Williams and Walker Set the Pace

1. *AMT*, pp. 218–19; Ann Charters, *Nobody: The Story of Bert Williams* (London: Macmillan, 1970), p. 160; unidentified reviews, HTC, *Abyssinia* folder.
2. Brian Rust, *Complete Entertainment Discography* (New York: Arlington House, 1973), pp. 666–70. A lengthy article about Williams that discusses the hard-to-find early recordings is Jim Walsh, "Favorite Pioneer Recording Artists: Bert Williams, A Thwarted Genius," *Hobbies* 55 (September 1950): 23–25, 36. See also *Follies, Scandals, and Other Diversions: From Ziegfeld to the Shuberts* (New World Records NW 215, 1977); *Follies of 1919* (Smithsonian American Musical Theater Series 2009, 1977); and *"Nobody" and Other Songs By Bert Williams* (Folkways Records RBF 602, 1981).
3. Billy King papers, Moorland-Spingarn Research Center, Howard University.
4. *NYT*, February 21, 1906, p. 9; unidentified clippings, HTC and NYPL, *Abyssinia* folders.
5. William Foster, "Pioneers of the Stage: Memoirs of William Foster," in *1928 Edition the Official Theatrical World of Colored Artists . . .*, ed. Theophilus Lewis (New York: The Theatrical World Publishing Co., 1928), p. 45.
6. Sylvester Russell, *Freeman*, January 14, 1911, p. 5.
7. Charters, *Nobody*, p. 95.
8. *NYT*, February 4, 1908, p. 7; *DM*, n.d., HTC, *Bandanna Land* folder.
9. Reprinted in Charters, *Nobody*, pp. 98–101.
10. The score of "Nobody" appears in Charters, *Nobody*, pp. 135–37.
11. *DM*, n.d., HTC, *Bandanna Land* folder.
12. The film "Natural Born Gambler" was made in 1916 by Biograph. A copy exists in the American Film Institute collection, Library of Congress, Washington, DC.
13. *Age*, March 18, 1909, p. 6.
14. Charters, *Nobody*, p. 95.
15. Quoted in Willia Daughtry, "Sissieretta Jones: A Study of the Negro's Contribution to Nineteenth-Century American Concert and Theatrical Life" (Ph. D. dissertation, Syracuse University, 1968), p. 110.
16. Mabel Rowland, *Bert Williams: Son of Laughter* (1923; reprint ed., New York: Negro Universities Press, 1969), p. 79.

Chapter 8·"African Operettas" and Other Star Vehicles, 1906–1911

1. *DM*, February 1906 (date and page unclear), HTC, *Rufus Rastus* folder.
2. Ibid.
3. Published in 1895, "La Pas Ma La" contained dance directions, like many songs of the second decade of the twentieth century, and the catchy phrase "let your mind roll far." Many elements of the text found their way onto disc when Jim Jackson recorded "Bye, Bye, Policeman" in 1928; see Paul Oliver,

Songsters and Saints (Cambridge: Cambridge University Press, 1984), pp. 33–34, 291.

4. Unidentified review, November 19, 1907, HTC, *The Oyster Man* folder; *Age*, May 27, 1909, p. 6.
5. Unidentified review, n.d., HTC, *The Oyster Man* folder; *Age*, May 27, 1907, p. 6.
6. James Weldon Johnson, *Along This Way* (New York: Viking Press, 1933), pp. 156–57, 221.
7. On the military theme in minstrelsy *see* Robert Toll, *Blacking Up: The Minstrel Show in Nineteenth-Century America* (New York: Oxford University Press, 1974), pp. 120, 124, 249–51.
8. Unidentified reviews, HTC, *The Shoo-Fly Regiment* folder.
9. *NYT*, August 7, 1907, p. 7; unidentified reviews, HTC, *The Shoo-Fly Regiment* folder.
10. Johnson, *Along This Way*, pp. 239–40.
11. Mary Henderson, *The City and the Theatre* (Clifton, NJ: James T. White and Co., 1973), p. 246.
12. Eubie Blake, "Bleeding Moon," in *The Eighty-Six Years of Eubie Blake* (Columbia Records C2S 847, 1969).
13. On sexual metaphors in the blues *see* Lawrence Levine, *Black Culture and Black Consciousness* (New York: Oxford University Press, 1977), pp. 242–44, 280–81.
14. *DM*, May 1903, NYPL, scrapbook (Robinson Locke collection); *NYT*, May 4, 1909, p. 9; *AMT*, p. 249.
15. *Age*, July 14, 1910, p. 6.
16. Ibid., March 31, 1910, p. 6; ibid., August 20, 1914, p. 6; *Freeman*, January 15, 1910, n.p; Leigh Whipper papers, folder 125, Moorland-Spingarn Research Center, Howard University.
17. Undated clippings, HTC, Smart Set folder; *JD*, pp. 76–77.
18. *NYT*, May 9, 1911, p. 11; *Age*, September 28, 1911, p. 6; *DM*, May 10, 1911, NYPL, *His Honor, The Barber* folder.
19. San Francisco *Dramatic Record*, May 24, 1911, n.p.
20. *JD*, p. 78; Eileen Southern, *Biographical Dictionary of Afro-American and African Musicians* (Westport, CT: Greenwood Press, 1982), pp. 115–16.
21. *Freeman*, February 6, 1910, p. 6; ibid., January 6, 1912, p. 6; ibid., July 9, 1910, p. 1; ibid., July 10, 1915, p. 6; *Age*, June 14, 1917, p. 6.
22. Willia Daughtry, "Sissieretta Jones: A Study of the Negro's Contribution to Nineteenth-Century American Concert and Theatrical Life" (Ph. D. dissertation, Syracuse University, 1968), pp. 98–107.
23. *Boston Transcript*, April 18, 1911, n.p.
24. Willia Daughtry, "Sissieretta Jones," pp. 113–14; *Age*, May 16, 1911, p. 6; *Freeman*, September 30, 1911, p. 5.
25. *Freeman*, May 17, 1913, p. 5.

26. *Age*, September 24, 1914, p. 6.
27. *JD*, p. 77; William Lichtenwanger, "Sissieretta Jones," in *Notable American Women*, ed. Edward T. James (Cambridge, MA: Belknap Press of the Harvard University Press, 1971), pp. 289–90.

Chapter 9·*The Productions Reviewed: A Summary of Black Shows, 1898–1911*

1. Undated clippings, HTC, *Bandanna Land* and *In Dahomey* folders; *DM*, May 23, 1891, p. 13; James Weldon Johnson, *Along This Way* (New York: Viking Press, 1933), pp. 213–14.
2. Doll Thomas, personal interview, November 8, 1978. The Cole notebook is a small fragment in the Leigh Whipper papers, Moorland-Spingarn Research Center, Howard University.
3. *Jes Lak White Fo'ks* libretto, Music Division, Library of Congress, Washington, DC.
4. Mabel Rowland, *Bert Williams: Son of Laughter* (1923; reprint ed., New York: Negro Universities Press, 1969), p. 82; Bert Williams, "The Moon Shines on the Moonshine," in *Follies, Scandals and Other Diversions from Ziegfeld to the Shuberts* (New World Records 215, 1977).
5. Tom Fletcher, *The Tom Fletcher Story: 100 Years of the Negro in Show Business* (New York: Burdge and Co., Ltd., 1954), p. 112.
6. Ibid., p. 108.
7. Undated clipping, HTC, *In Dahomey* folder; *JD*, p. 78.
8. Unidentified clipping, February 18, 1903, HTC, *In Dahomey* folder; *DM*, November 13, 1909, p. 7.
9. Unidentified clipping, February 6, 1900, HTC, *A Trip to Coontown* folder; *DM*, February 1906 (date and page unclear), HTC, *Rufus Rastus* folder; *Freeman*, January 8, 1910, p. 6; clipping by "P.C." (otherwise unidentified), from an English paper, HTC, *In Dahomey* folder.
10. Doll Thomas, personal interview, November 8, 1978.

Chapter 10·*The Rise of Straight Drama and Vaudeville, 1910–1915*

1. *AMT*, pp. 230, 302.
2. *Age*, July 14, 1910, p. 6.
3. *Freeman*, September 20, 1913, p. 6.
4. Jack Poggi, *Theatre in America: The Impact of Economic Forces* (Ithaca: Cornell University Press, 1968), pp. 28–30, 36, 45.
5. *Age*, December 1, 1910, p. 6; ibid., August 3, 1911, p. 6.
6. *Freeman*, December 23, 1911, p. 12.
7. Music Division, Library of Congress, Whittlesey file; James Weldon Johnson, *Black Manhattan* (New York: Knopf, 1930), p. 118.

8. *Age*, September 18, 1913, p. 6. Dudley's acquisition of theaters is discussed extensively in the pages of the *Freeman* throughout this period and later in *Billboard*.

9. C. Vann Woodward, *The Strange Career of Jim Crow*, 2d ed. (London: Oxford University Press, 1966), especially pp. 93–102; *Age*, January 5, 1911, p. 6; Ann J. Lane, *The Brownsville Affair: National Crisis and Black Reaction* (Port Washington, NY: Kennikat Press, 1971).

10. *Age*, December 5, 1912, p. 6; ibid., December 26, 1912, p. 6.

11. Ibid., March 13, 1913, p. 6; ibid., March 20, 1913, p. 6.

12. Ibid., May 1, 1913, p. 6.

13. Ibid., May 15, 1913, p. 6; program in the Leigh Whipper Papers, Moorland-Spingarn Collection, Howard University.

14. *Age*, May 15, 1913, p. 6.

15. Ibid., February 17, 1910, p. 6; Sister Mary Francesca Thompson, "The Lafayette Players 1915–1932" (Ph. D. dissertation, University of Michigan, 1972), pp. 12, 28 ff.

16. *Age*, May 5, 1910, p. 6; August Meier, *Negro Thought in America* (Ann Arbor: University of Michigan Press, 1963), pp. 256–78.

17. *Variety*, December 15, 1906, p. 22. The *Age* conveniently grouped most of its theatrical news and names of currently performing groups on the same page every week, and *Variety* regularly listed new black vaudeville acts. A compilation of names from the first six months of 1909 produced a list of some 110 different groups. Some groups shared personnel; old groups disbanded, and new ones formed fairly frequently. The approximation of 300–400 individuals is conservative.

18. Leigh Whipper papers, folder 125, Moorland-Spingarn Center, Howard University; Helen A. Johnson, "Blacks in Vaudeville: Broadway and Beyond," in *American Popular Entertainment: Papers and Proceedings of the Conference on the History of American Popular Entertainment*, ed. Myron Matlaw (Westport, CT: Greenwood Press, 1977), p. 81; *NYT*, April 3, 1900, p. 9.

19. *Variety*, July 14, 1906, p. 11; ibid., July 21, 1906, 10; ibid., March 2, 1907, p. 11; ibid., August 24, 1907, p. 12; ibid., June 20, 1908, p. 13.

20. *Age*, July 22, 1909, p. 6; *Variety*, December 23, 1905, p. 8.

21. *Variety*, July 13, 1907, p. 12.

22. Ibid., December 11, 1909, p. 144 (*sic*).

23. Ibid., January 27, 1906, p. 6; ibid., December 10, 1910, p. 69.

24. *Age*, November 27, 1913, p. 6.

25. Ibid., January 19, 1911, p. 6; ibid., September 3, 1914, p. 6.

26. Ibid., October 1, 1914, p. 6.

27. Tom Fletcher, *The Tom Fletcher Story: 100 Years of the Negro in Show Business* (New York: Burdge and Co., Ltd., 1954), pp. 121–22.

28. *JD*, p. 140.

Chapter 11·*Dance and Comedy in Harlem, 1910–1915*

1. *Age*, February 16, 1911, p. 6.
2. Williams's song, published in 1900, is entitled "If You Love Your Baby, Make Them Goo Goo Eyes." John Queen published "Just Because She Made Dem Goo-Goo Eyes" in 1901. In 1909 William Jerome and Jean Schwarz came out with "That Spooney Dance."
3. James Weldon Johnson, *Black Manhattan* (New York: Alfred A. Knopf, 1930), p. 174; *Age*, December 30, 1913, p. 6. The souvenir program appeared as a back page on several musical numbers from the show, printed by Jerome Remick.
4. *JD*, pp. 125, 129.
5. Ibid., p. 129; Paul Oliver, *Songsters and Saints* (Cambridge: Cambridge University Press, 1984), pp. 29–46; *JD*, p. 125.
6. Tom Fletcher, *The Tom Fletcher Story: 100 Years of the Negro in Show Business* (New York: Burdge and Co., Ltd., 1954), p. 108.
7. *Variety*, December 12, 1913, p. 21; J. Chapman Hilder, "The Darktown Follies," *Theatre Magazine* 19 (March 1914): 135; the *New York World* is cited in *JD*, p. 129; *DM*, November 12, 1913, p. 4; B. Kellner, ed., *"Keep A-Inchin' Along": Selected Writings of Carl Van Vechten* (Westport, CT: Greenwood Press, 1979), p. 20; *Variety*, December 12, 1913, p. 21.
8. *Freeman*, April 18, 1914, p. 5; *JD*, p. 127.
9. Albert Murray, *The Omni-Americans* (New York. Outerbridge and Dienstfrey, 1970), p. 22; Kellner, *"Keep A-Inchin' Along,"* p. 24.
10. *JD*, p. 130; *Age*, January 28, 1915, p. 6.
11. Kellner, *"Keep A-Inchin' Along,"* pp. 21, 25.
12. *Age*, September 7, 1916.
13. *Freeman*, October 23, 1915, p. 4.
14. Ibid.
15. *Age*, October 28, 1915, p. 6; *Freeman*, October 30, 1915, p. 6; Monroe Lippmann, "The History of the Theatrical Syndicate: Its Effect Upon Theatres in America" (Ph. D. dissertation, University of Michigan, 1937), pp. 152–54.

Epilogue

1. Will Marion Cook, "Clorindy, the Origin of the Cakewalk," reprinted in *Readings in Black American Music*, 2d ed., ed. Eileen Southern (New York: Norton, 1983), p. 232.
2. Ibid.; *NYT*, February 4, 1908, p. 7.
3. Unidentified clippings, HTC, *In Dahomey* folder; *DM*, undated, HTC, *Bandanna Land* folder; *Boston Transcript*, November 5, 1909, HTC, *His Honor, the Barber* folder.
4. Unidentified clipping, May 27, 1907, HTC, *The Shoo-Fly Regiment* folder.

5. Unidentified clipping, January 16, 1906, HTC, *Rufus Rastus* folder; *New York Dramatic News*, May 8, 1909, NYPL, Cole and Johnson scrapbook; *Toledo Blade*, May 16, 1920, NYPL, Cole and Johnson scrapbook.

6. Unidentified clipping, November 13, 1909, HTC, *Mr. Lode of Koal* folder; *Boston Globe*, September 6, 1908, HTC, *Bandanna Land* folder; *Philadelphia Inquirer*, September 15, 1908, NYPL, Cole and Johnson scrapbook.

7. *Freeman*, September 4, 1915; *Age*, July 24, 1920, p. 6; Alain Locke, *The Negro and His Music* (1936; reprint ed., New York: Arno Press, 1969), p. 54; Maud Cuney-Hare, *Negro Musicians and Their Music* (1936; reprint ed., New York: Da Capo Press, 1974), pp. 158–59, 167; *JD*, pp. 127, 131.

8. *JD*, pp. 51–53; Helen A. Johnson, "Blacks in Vaudeville: Broadway and Beyond," in *American Popular Entertainment: Papers and Proceedings of the Conference on the History of American Popular Entertainment*, ed. Myron Matlaw (Westport, CT: Greenwood Press, 1977), pp. 77–86.

Bibliography

Books and Articles

Anderson, Jervis. *This Was Harlem: A Cultural Portrait 1900–1950*. New York: Farrar, Straus, Giroux, 1981.

Applebaum, Stanley, ed. *Show Songs from "The Black Crook" to "The Red Mill": Original Sheet Music for 60 Songs from 50 Shows, 1866–1906*. New York: Dover Publications, 1974.

Archer, Leonard C. *Black Images in the American Theatre*. Brooklyn: Pageant-Poseidon, Ltd., 1973.

Austin, William. *"Susannah," "Jeannie," and "The Old Folks at Home": The Songs of Stephen Foster from His Time to Ours*. New York: Macmillan, 1975.

Bechet, Sidney. *Treat It Gentle*. New York: Hill and Wang, 1960.

Berlin, Edward. "Cole and Johnson Brothers' *The Evolution of Ragtime*." *Current Musicology* 36 (1983): 21–39.

———. *Ragtime: A Musical and Cultural History*. Berkeley: University of California Press, 1980.

Birdoff, Harry. *The World's Greatest Hit*. New York: Vanni, 1947.

"Black Musicians and Ethiopian Minstrelsy." *The Black Perspective in Music* 3 (1975): 77–79.

Bordman, Gerald. *American Musical Comedy.* New York: Oxford University Press, 1982.
———. *American Musical Revue.* New York: Oxford University Press, 1985.
———. *American Musical Theatre: A Chronicle.* New York: Oxford University Press, 1978.
Boskin, Joseph. *Sambo: The Rise and Demise of an American Jester.* New York and Oxford: Oxford University Press, 1986.
Brawley, Benjamin. *The Negro Genius.* New York: Dodd, Mead and Co., 1937.
———. *Paul Laurence Dunbar: Poet of His People.* Chapel Hill: University of North Carolina Press, 1936.
Brown, Henry Collins. *In the Golden Nineties.* New York: Valentines Manual Inc., 1928.
Brown, Thomas Allston. *A History of the New York Stage from the First Performance in 1732 to 1901.* New York: Dodd, Mead and Co., 1903.
Bubna, Augusta da. "The Negro on the Stage." *Theatre Magazine* (March 1903): 96–98.
Burton, Jack. *The Blue Book of Broadway Musicals.* Watkins Glen, N.Y.: Century House, 1952.
Butcher, Margaret Just. *The Negro in American Culture.* 2d ed. New York: Alfred A. Knopf, 1972.
Chapman, John, and Sherwood, Garrison P., eds. *The Best Plays of 1894–1899.* New York: Dodd, Mead and Co., 1955.
Charles, Norman. "Social Values in American Popular Songs, 1890–1950." Ph.D. dissertation, University of Pennsylvania, 1958.
Charosh, Paul. "Slander in Song." *Listen* 1 (December 1963): 3–7.
Charosh, Paul, and Fremont, Robert A. *More Favorite Songs of the Nineties: Complete Original Sheet Music for 62 Songs.* New York: Dover Publications, 1975.
Charters, Ann. *Nobody: The Story of Bert Williams.* London: Macmillan, 1970.
Charters, Samuel Barclay, and Kunstadt, Leonard. *Jazz: A History of the New York Scene.* Garden City, NY: Doubleday, 1962.
Chipman, John. *Index to Top-Hit Tunes 1900–1950.* Boston: Humphries Publishers, 1962.
Clapham, John. "Antonin Dvořák." *The New Grove Dictionary of Music and Musicians.* Vol. 5. London: Macmillan, 1980.
Collins, Edmund John. "Jazz Feedback to Africa." *American Music* 5 (Summer 1987): 176–93.
Cook, Will Marion. "Clorindy, or the Origin of the Cakewalk." In *Readings In Black American Music,* edited by Eileen Southern. New York: Norton, 1971.
"The Cook Family in History." *Negro History Bulletin* 9, no. 9 (June 1946): 195–96, 213–15.

Cruse, Harold. *The Crisis of the Negro Intellectual.* New York: Morrow, 1967.

Cuney-Hare, Maud. *Negro Musicians and Their Music.* Washington, D. C.: The Associated Publishers, Inc., 1936.

Daley, John Jay. *A Song in His Heart.* Philadelphia: Winston, 1951.

Daughtry, Willia. "Sissieretta Jones: A Study of the Negro's Contribution to Nineteenth-Century American Concert and Theatrical Life." Ph.D. dissertation, Syracuse University, 1968.

Dennison, Sam. *Scandalize My Name: Black Imagery in American Popular Music.* New York: Garland Publishing Co., 1981.

De Toledano, Ralph. *Frontiers of Jazz.* 2d ed. New York: Frederick Ungar, 1962.

Dickens, Charles. *American Notes.* London: Chapman and Hall, 1842.

Dreiser, Theodore. *The Color of a Great City.* New York: Boni and Liveright, 1923.

DuBois, W. E. B. *The Black North in 1901: A Social Study.* New York: Arno Press, 1969.

Ellington, Edward Kennedy "Duke." *Music is My Mistress.* Garden City, NY: Doubleday, 1973.

Ellison, Ralph. *Going to the Territory.* New York: Random House, 1986.

Engle, Gary D., ed. *This Grotesque Essence: Plays From the American Minstrel Stage.* Baton Rouge: Louisiana State University Press, 1978.

Epstein, Dena. "Jeannette Meyers Thurber." In *Notable American Women 1607–1950,* edited by Edward T. James. Cambridge, MA: Belknap Press of the Harvard University Press, 1971.

———. *Sinful Tunes and Spirituals: Black Folk Music to the Civil War.* Urbana, IL: University of Illinois Press, 1977.

Eustis, Morton. *B'way Inc!: The Theatre as a Business.* New York: Dodd, Mead and Co., 1934.

Fletcher, Tom. *The Tom Fletcher Story: 100 Years of the Negro in Show Business.* New York: Burdge and Co., Ltd., 1954.

Floyd, Samuel A., Jr., and Reisser, Marsha J. *Black Music in the United States: An Annotated Bibliography of Selected Reference and Research Materials.* Millwood, NY, London, and Schaan, Lichtenstein: Kraus International Publications, 1983.

[Foster, William.] "Pioneers of the Stage: Memoirs of William Foster." In *1928 Edition the Official Theatrical World of Colored Artists . . . ,* edited by Theophilus Lewis. New York: The Theatrical World Publishing Co., 1928.

Franklin, John Hope. *From Slavery to Freedom.* 3d ed. New York: Alfred A. Knopf, 1967.

Frazier, Edward Franklin. *Black Bourgeoisie.* Glencoe, IL: Free Press, 1957.

———. *The Negro in the United States.* Rev. ed. New York: Macmillan, 1957.

Fremont, Robert A. *Favorite Songs of the Nineties: Complete Original Sheet Music for 89 Songs.* New York: Dover Publications, 1973.

Fuld, James J. *American Popular Music (Reference Book), 1875–1950.* Philadelphia: Musical Americana, 1955.

Gates, Henry Louis, Jr., ed. *Black Literature and Literary Theory.* New York and London: Methuen, 1984.

Gayle, Addison, Jr. *The Black Aesthetic.* Garden City, NY: Doubleday, 1971.

———. *Oak and Ivy: A Biography of Paul Laurence Dunbar.* Garden City, NY: Doubleday, 1971.

Gilbert, Douglas. *American Vaudeville: Its Life and Times.* New York and London: Whittlesey House, 1940.

Giordano, Gus. *Anthology of American Jazz Dance.* Evanston, IL: Orion Publishing House, 1975.

Goldberg, Isaac. *Tin Pan Alley: A Chronicle of the American Popular Music Racket.* New York: John Day, 1930.

Gottfried, Martin. *Broadway Musicals.* New York: Abrams, 1979.

Grau, Robert. *The Business Man in the Amusement World.* New York: Broadway Publishing Co., 1910.

Green, A., and Laurie, J. *Show Biz from Vaude to Video.* New York: Henry Holt and Co., 1951.

Green, Jeffrey. "*In Dahomey* in London." *The Black Perspective in Music* 11 (Spring 1983): 22–40.

Grimsted, David. *Melodrama Unveiled: American Theatre and Culture, 1800–1850.* Chicago: University of Chicago Press, 1968.

Haas, Robert B., ed. *William Grant Still and the Fusion of Cultures in American Music.* Los Angeles: Black Sparrow Press, 1972.

Hamm, Charles. *Yesterdays: Popular Song in America.* New York and London: Norton, 1979.

Handlin, Oscar. *Race and Nationality in American Life.* Boston: Little, Brown and Co., 1948.

Handy, W. C. *Father of the Blues.* New York: Macmillan, 1941.

———. *Negro Authors and Composers of the United States.* New York: Handy Brothers Music Co., 1938.

Hare, Walter Ben. *The Minstrel Encyclopedia.* Boston: Walter H. Baker, 1921.

Harris, Charles K. *After the Ball: Forty Years of Melody.* New York: Frank-Maurice, 1926.

Hartnoll, Phyllis. *The Oxford Companion to the Theatre.* 2d ed. London: Oxford University Press, 1957.

Hatch, James V., and Abdullah, OMANii. *Black Playwrights, 1823–1977: An Annotated Bibliography of Plays.* New York: R. R. Bowker, 1977.

Henderson, Mary. *The City and the Theatre.* Clifton, NY: James T. White and Co., 1973.

Henri, Florette. *Black Migration: Movement North 1900–1920*. New York: Anchor Press, 1975.

Hitchcock, H. Wiley. *Music in the United States: A Historical Introduction*. 3d ed. Englewood Cliffs, NJ: Prentice-Hall, 1988.

Howe, Daniel Walker, ed. *Victorian America*. Philadelphia: University of Pennsylvania Press, 1976.

Hudson, Gossie H., and Martin, Jay, eds. *The Paul Laurence Dunbar Reader*. New York: Dodd, Mead and Co., 1975.

Hughes, Langston, and Meltzer, Milton. *Black Magic: A Pictorial History of the Negro in American Entertainment*. Englewood Cliffs, NJ: Prentice-Hall, 1967.

Huneker, James. *The New Cosmopolis*. New York: Charles Scribner's Sons, 1915.

Ikonné, Chidi. *From DuBois to Van Vechten: The Early New Negro Literature, 1903–1926*. Westport, CT: Greenwood Press, 1981.

Isaacs, Edith. *The Negro in the American Theatre*. 1947. Reprint. College Park, MD: McGrath Publishing Co., 1968.

James, Henry. *The American Scene*. 1905. Reprint. Bloomington: Indiana University Press, 1968.

Johnson, Helen Armstead. "Blacks in Vaudeville: Broadway and Beyond." In *American Popular Entertainment: Papers and Proceedings of the Conference on the History of American Popular Entertainment*, edited by Myron Matlaw. Westport, CT: Greenwood Press, 1977.

Johnson, James Weldon. *Along This Way*. New York: Viking Press, 1933.

———. *The Autobiography of an Ex-colored Man*. 1912. Reprint. New York: Alfred A. Knopf, 1927.

———. *Black Manhattan*. New York: Alfred A. Knopf, 1930.

———, ed. *The Book of American Negro Spirituals*. New York: Viking Press, 1925.

———, ed. *The Second Book of Negro Spirituals*. New York: Viking Press, 1926.

Johnson, Stephen Burge. *The Roof Gardens of Broadway Theaters, 1883–1942*. Ann Arbor: UMI Research Press, 1985.

Kahn, E. J., Jr. *The Merry Partners: The Age and Stage of Harrigan and Hart*. New York: Random House, 1955.

Katz, Bernard, ed. *The Social Implications of Early Negro Music in the United States*. New York: Arno Press, 1969.

Kellner, B., ed. *"Keep A-Inchin Along": Selected Writings of Carl Van Vechten about Black Artists and Letters*. Westport, CT: Greenwood Press, 1979.

Kimball, Robert, and Bolcom, William. *Reminiscing with Sissle and Blake*. New York: Viking Press, 1973.

King, Moses. *New York: The American Cosmopolis, the Foremost City in the World*. Boston: Moses King, 1893.

Kinkle, Roger D. *The Complete Encyclopedia of Popular Music and Jazz, 1900–1950*. 4 vols. New Rochelle: Arlington House Publishers, 1974.

Kmen, Henry A. *Music in New Orleans.* Baton Rouge: Louisiana State University Press, 1966.

Lahee, Henry Charles. *Annals of Music in America.* 1922. Reprint. Freeport, NY: Books for Libraries Press, 1970.

Lane, Ann J. *The Brownsville Affair: National Crisis and Black Reaction.* Port Washington, NY: Kennikat Press, 1971.

Larson, Magali Sarfatti. *The Rise of Professionalism: A Sociological Analysis.* Berkeley: University of California Press, 1977.

Laurie, Joe. *Vaudeville from Honky-Tonks to the Palace.* New York: Henry Holt and Co., 1953.

Lax, Roger, and Smith, Frederick. *The Great Song Thesaurus.* New York: Oxford University Press, 1984.

Leavitt, Michael Bennett. *Fifty Years in Theatrical Management, 1859–1909.* New York: Broadway Publishers, 1912.

Leuchs, Fred A. H. *Early German Theatre in New York.* New York: Columbia University Press, 1928.

Levine, Lawrence. *Black Culture and Black Consciousness: Afro-American Folk Thought from Slavery to Freedom.* New York: Oxford University Press, 1977.

Levy, Eugene. *James Weldon Johnson: Black Leader, Black Voice.* Chicago: University of Chicago Press, 1973.

Levy, Lester S. *Grace Notes in American History: Popular Music from 1820 to 1900.* Norman: University of Oklahoma Press, 1967.

Lichtenwanger, William. "Matilda Sissieretta Joyner Jones." In *Notable American Women 1607–1950,* edited by Edward T. James. Cambridge, MA: Belknap Press of the Harvard University Press, 1971.

Lippmann, Monroe. "The History of the Theatrical Syndicate in America: Its Effect Upon Theaters in America." Ph.D. dissertation, The University of Michigan, 1937.

Locke, Alain. *The Negro and His Music.* 1936. Reprint. New York: Arno Press, 1969.

Loney, Glenn, ed. *Musical Theatre in America: Papers and Proceedings of the Conference in Greenvale, N.Y.* Westport, CT: Greenwood Press, 1984.

Lovell, John, Jr. *Black Song: The Forge and the Flame.* New York: Macmillan, 1972.

McLean, Albert F. *American Vaudeville as Ritual.* Lexington: University of Kentucky Press, 1965.

Mantle, Burns, and Sherwood, Garrison P., eds. *The Best Plays of 1899–1909.* New York: Dodd, Mead and Co., 1944.

———. *The Best Plays of 1909–1919.* New York: Dodd, Mead and Co., 1934.

Marcuse, Maxwell. *This Was New York: A Nostalgic Picture of Gotham in the Gaslight Era.* New York: LIM Press, 1969.

Marks, E. B. *They All Sang from Tony Pastor to Rudy Vallee.* 1934. Reprint. New York: Viking Press, 1959.

Mason, Hamilton. *The French Theatre in New York.* New York: Columbia University Press, 1946.

Mattfeld, Julius. *Variety Music Cavalcade: Musical-Historical Review, 1620–1969.* 3d ed. Englewood Cliffs, NJ: Prentice-Hall, 1971.

Meier, August. *Negro Thought in America 1880–1915.* Ann Arbor: University of Michigan Press, 1963.

Monroe, John Gilbert. "A Record of the Black Theatre in New York City." Ph.D. dissertation, University of Texas, 1980.

Moore, MacDonald Smith. *Yankee Blues.* Bloomington: Indiana University Press, 1985.

Morath, Max. "The Vocal and Theatrical Music of Bert Williams and His Associates." In *American Popular Entertainment: Papers and Proceedings of the Conference on the History of American Popular Entertainment,* edited by Myron Matlaw. Westport, CT: Greenwood Press, 1977.

Mordden, Ethan. *Broadway Babies.* New York: Oxford University Press, 1983.

Morris, Lloyd. *Incredible New York: High Life and Low Life of the Last Hundred Years.* New York: Random House, 1951.

Murray, Albert. *The Omni-Americans: New Perspectives on Black Experience and American Culture.* New York: Outerbridge and Dienstfrey, 1970.

Nathan, Hans. *Dan Emmett and the Rise of Early Negro Minstrelsy.* Norman: University of Oklahoma Press, 1962.

The New York Times Theatre Reviews 1870–1919. 6 vols. New York: Arno Press, 1976.

Odell, George. *Annals of the New York Stage.* 15 vols. New York: Columbia University Press, 1927–1949.

Oliver, Paul. *Songsters and Saints.* Cambridge: Cambridge University Press, 1984.

Ong, Walter. *Orality and Literacy: The Technologizing of the Word.* London and New York: Methuen, 1982.

Orrey, Leslie, ed. *The Encyclopedia of Opera.* New York: Charles Scribner's Sons, 1976.

Ostendorf, Berndt. "Anthropology, Modernism and Jazz." In *Ralph Ellison: Modern Critical Views,* edited by Harold Bloom. New York, New Haven, and Philadelphia: Chelsea House Publishers, 1986.

Ottley, Roi, and Weatherby, William, eds. *The Negro in New York: An Informal History.* Dobbs Ferry, NY: New York Public Library Oceana Publications, Inc., 1967.

Ovington, Mary White. *Half a Man.* New York: Longmans, Green, 1911.

———. *The Walls Came Tumbling Down.* New York: Harcourt, Brace and Co., 1947.

Patterson, Cecil Lloyd. "A Different Drum: The Image of the Negro in the Nineteenth-Century Popular Song Book." Ph.D. dissertation, University of Pennsylvania, 1961.

Patterson, Lindsay, ed. *Anthology of the American Negro in the Theatre*. New York: The Publishers Co., Inc., 1967.

Poggi, Jack. *Theatre in America: The Impact of Economic Forces 1870–1967*. Ithaca: Cornell University Press, 1968.

Raymond, Jack. *Show Music on Record from the 1890s to the 1980s*. New York: Frederick Ungar, 1982.

Reed-Maxfield, Kathryn. "Emmett, Foster and Their Anonymous Colleagues: The Creators of Early Minstrel Show Songs." Paper presented at the annual meeting of the Sonneck Society, University of Pittsburgh, Pittsburgh, April 1987.

Riis, Thomas. "The Music and Musicians in Nineteenth-century Productions of *Uncle Tom's Cabin*." *American Music* 4 (Fall 1986): 268–86.

Rice, Edward Le Roy. *Monarchs of Minstrelsy: From Daddy Rice to Date*. New York: Kenny Publishing Co., 1910.

Roach, Hildred. *Black American Music Past and Present*. Boston: Crescendo Publishing Co., 1973.

Root, Deane Leslie. "American Popular Stage Music, 1860–1880." Ph.D. dissertation, University of Illinois, 1977.

Rourke, Constance. *American Humor: A Study of the National Character*. 1931. Reprint. Tallahassee: Florida State University Press, 1986.

Rowland, Mabel. *Bert Williams: Son of Laughter*. 1923. Reprint. New York: Negro Universities Press, 1969.

Rust, Brian. *Complete Entertainment Discography*. New York: Arlington House, 1973.

———. *Jazz Records, 1897–1942*. 2 vols. Rev. 4th ed. New Rochelle: Arlington House, 1978.

Sampson, Henry T. *Blacks in Blackface: A Source Book on Early Black Musical Shows*. Metuchen, NJ: Scarecrow Press, 1980.

Schafer, William J., and Riedel, Johannes. *The Art of Ragtime*. Baton Rouge: Louisiana State University Press, 1973.

Schatz, Walter, ed. *Directory of Afro-American Resources*. New York and London: R. R. Bowker, 1970.

Scheiner, Seth. *Negro Mecca: A History of the Negro in New York City, 1865–1920*. New York: New York University Press, 1965.

Simond, Ike. *Old Slack's Reminiscence and Pocket History of the Colored Profession From 1865 to 1891*. 1891. Reprint. Bowling Green, OH: Popular Press, 1974.

Smith, Cecil. *Musical Comedy in America*. New York: Theatre Arts Books, 1950.

Smith, Harry B. *First Nights and First Editions*. Boston: Little, Brown and Co., 1931.

Smith, Willie "the Lion." *Music on My Mind*. 1964. Reprint. New York: Da Capo Press, 1978.

Sobel, Bernard. *Burleycue: An Underground History of Burlesque Days*. New York: Farrar and Rinehart, 1931.

Soltow, Lee, and Stevens, Edward. *The Rise of Literacy and the Common School in the United States: A Socio-economic Analysis to 1870*. Chicago: University of Chicago Press, 1981.

Southern, Eileen. *Biographical Dictionary of Afro-American and African Musicians*. Westport, CT: Greenwood Press, 1982.

————. *The Music of Black Americans: A History*. 2d ed. New York: Norton, 1983.

————, ed. *Readings in Black American Music*. 2d ed. New York: Norton, 1983.

Spaeth, Sigmund. *A History of Popular Song in America*. New York: Random House, 1948.

Staples, Shirley. *Male–Female Comedy Teams in American Vaudeville 1865–1932*. Ann Arbor: UMI Research Press, 1984.

Stearns, Marshall, and Stearns, Jean. *Jazz Dance: The Story of American Vernacular Dance*. New York: Schirmer Books, 1968.

Stefan-Gruenfeldt, Paul. *Antonin Dvořák*. Translated by Y. W. Vance. New York: The Greystone Press, 1941.

Still, Bayrd. *Mirror for Gotham*. New York: Washington Square Press, 1956.

"The Theatre Syndicate." *Literary Digest* 11 (November 16, 1895): 3.

Thompson, Sister Mary Francesca. "The Lafayette Players 1915–1932." Ph. D. dissertation, University of Michigan, 1972.

Thornbrough, Emma Lou. *T. Thomas Fortune: Militant Journalist*. Chicago: University of Chicago Press, 1972.

Toll, Robert. *Blacking Up: The Minstrel Show in Nineteenth-Century America*. New York: Oxford University Press, 1974.

Trotter, James Monroe. *Music and Some Highly Musical People*. 1880. Reprint. Chicago: Afro-Am Press, 1969.

Turner, Michael R. *The Parlour Song Book: A Casquet of Vocal Gems*. New York: Viking Press, 1972.

United States Census Special Reports. Washington, D. C.: Government Printing Office, 1897 and 1904.

Walsh, Jim. "Favorite Pioneer Recording Artists: Bert Williams, A Thwarted Genius." *Hobbies* 55 (September 1950): 23–25, 36.

Wesley, Charles H. *Negro Labor in the United States 1850–1925: A Study in American Economic History*. New York: Vanguard Press, 1927.

Who's Who in Colored America. New York: Who's Who in Colored America Corporation, 1927.

Wiggins, Linda Keck. *The Life and Works of Paul Laurence Dunbar*. Napierville, IL and Memphis: J. L. Nichols and Co., 1907.

Wilder, Alec. *American Popular Song: the Great Innovators, 1900–1950*. Edited by James T. Maher. New York: Oxford University Press, 1972.

Williams, Bert. "The Comic Side of Trouble." *American Magazine* 85 (January 1918): 33–35, 58–61.

Winans, Robert. "Minstrel Show Music: the First Decade, 1843–1952." Paper presented at the Musical Theatre in America conference, C. W. Post Center, Long Island University, April 24, 1981.

Winter, Marian. "Juba and American Minstrelsy." *Dance Index* 6 (1947): 28–47.

Witmark, Isadore, and Goldberg, Isaac. *From Ragtime to Swingtime*. 1939. Reprint. New York: Da Capo Press, 1976.

Wittke, Carl. *Tambo and Bones*. Durham: Duke University Press, 1930.

Woll, Allen. *Dictionary of the Black Theatre*. Westport, CT: Greenwood Press, 1983.

Woodson, Carter. *The Negro Professional Man and the Community*. Washington, D. C.: Association for the Study of Negro Life and History, 1934.

Woodward, C. Vann. *The Strange Career of Jim Crow*. 2d ed. London: Oxford University Press, 1966.

Zeidman, Irving. *The American Burlesque Show*. New York: Hawthorn Books, Inc., 1967.

Zellers, Parker. *Tony Pastor: Dean of the Vaudeville Stage*. Ypsilanti: Eastern Michigan University Press, 1971.

Periodicals

Age (New York)
Billboard
Chicago Defender
Crisis
Dramatic Mirror
Freeman (Indianapolis)
New York Times
Variety

Sheet Music Facsimiles

Facsimile 1.1. C. A. White, "Good-By, Old Cabin Home." Courtesy of Music Division, Library of Congress, Washington, D.C. Only the front cover and the final chorus are reproduced here, owing to the song's extended length.

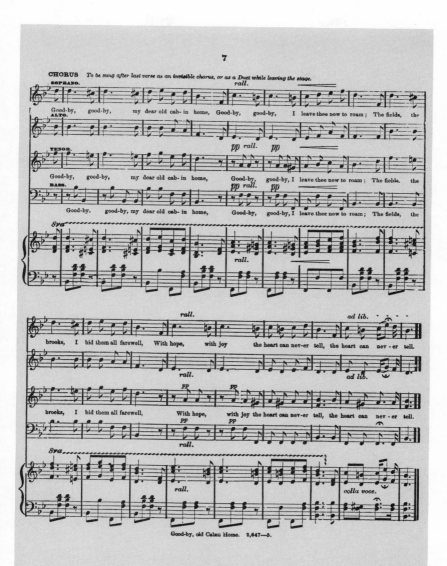

Good-by, old Cabin Home. 2,647—5.

Facsimile 1.2. Bob Cole, "Move Up, Johnson." Courtesy of Moorland-Spingarn Research Center, Howard University.

Fly, Fly, Fly.
NEGRO SONG and CHORUS.
By BOB. COLE. 40¢

Johnson's Darkie Jubilee.
NEGRO SONG and CHORUS.
By DAN. EMERSON. 50

Facsimile 5.1. Billy Johnson and Bob Cole, "No Coons Allowed." Courtesy of Moorland-Spingarn Research Center, Howard University.

No coons allowed 3.

Facsimile 5.2. Paul Laurence Dunbar and Will Marion [Cook], "Hottest Coon in Dixie." Courtesy of William L. Clements Library, the University of Michigan.

on my silk plug hat so gay, My neck - tie is a
not be - cause I've got the tin, But then I am so

beaut', _____ Put on my gloves and cane in hand, I
sweet', _____ The la - dies can - not pass me by, I've

wan - der down the way, _____ When e'er I meet some
al - ways got a girl, _____ And this is just the

mer - ry beaux, Here's what the dark - ies say. _____
pro - per cry, They give me, with a whirl.

Hottest coon in Dixie - 3 - 1367

Facsimile 5.3. R. C. McPherson and James T. Brymn, "Josephine, My Jo."
Courtesy of Hargrett Rare Book and Manuscript Library, University of Georgia
Libraries.

Facsimile 6.1. Will Marion Cook, "Swing Along!" Yale Collection of American Literature, Beinecke Rare Book and Manuscript Library, Yale University.

Facsimile 6.2. Harry B. Smith, Cecil Mack, and Will Marion Cook, "The Little Gypsy Maid." Courtesy of E. Azalia Hackley Collection of the Detroit Public Library.

The little Gypsy Maid.

Paul Lawrence Dunbar and Will Marion Cook's Negro Classic
"GOOD EVENIN:"

The little Gypsy Maid.

Will Marion Cook's Characteristic March & Two Step

"ON EMANCIPATION DAY."

Introducing Chorus of the great song.

Facsimile 6.3. Bob Cole and James Weldon Johnson, "Mexico." Courtesy of Hargrett Rare Book and Manuscript Library, University of Georgia Libraries.

4304-6

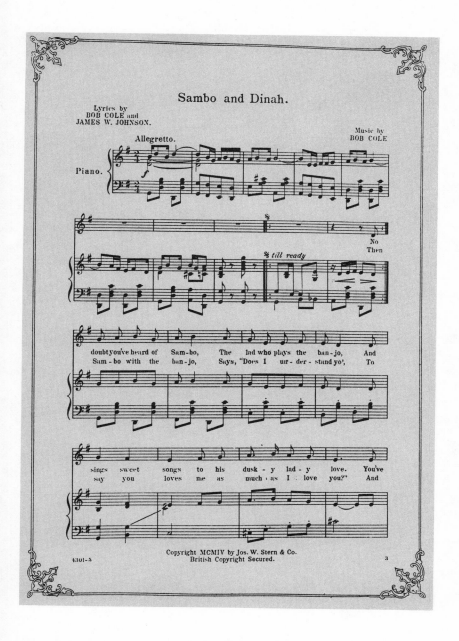

Facsimile 6.4. Bob Cole and James Weldon Johnson, "Sambo and Dinah."
Courtesy of Moorland-Spingarn Research Center, Howard University.

Facsimile 7.1. Alex Rogers and Bert A. Williams, "Let It Alone." Courtesy of Moorland-Spingarn Research Center, Howard University.

4

do, _____ Now at these times I'm go - in' to tell _____ you
say, _____ He's lay - in' in the gut - - ter you _____ can

what's the wis - est plan _____ When it comes to mix - in'
see that he's all in _____ An' on his bos - om

in wid things you don't jes' un - der - stan? _____
calm - ly gleams, a great big di - a - mond pin. _____

CHORUS.

Let it a lone, _ let it a lone, _ If it don't con - cern you,
Let it a lone, _ let it a lone, _ It _ ain't you'rn pal - ly so

mf

Let it alone.

Facsimile 7.2. Alex Rogers and Will Marion Cook, "Bon Bon Buddy."
Courtesy of Moorland-Spingarn Research Center, Howard University.

Bon Bon Buddy.

"Choc'-late drop," and "Bud-dy" seemed to stick to me some how,____ Then
there was one called "Dummy Smith" and one called Ba - by Blue,"____ And

some one add ed "Bon Bon," So here's what they call me now.____
they all used to tell me, "Bud its pret -ty soft for you."____

Chorus.

Bon - Bon Bud - dy the choc - o - late drop,____

Dat's me,____ Bon - Bon Bud - dy is

Bon Bon Buddy. 1.

Facsimile 7.3. Alex Rogers and Will Marion Cook, "Red Red Rose." Courtesy of Moorland-Spingarn Research Center, Howard University.

Red Red Rose 4 *Low Voice*

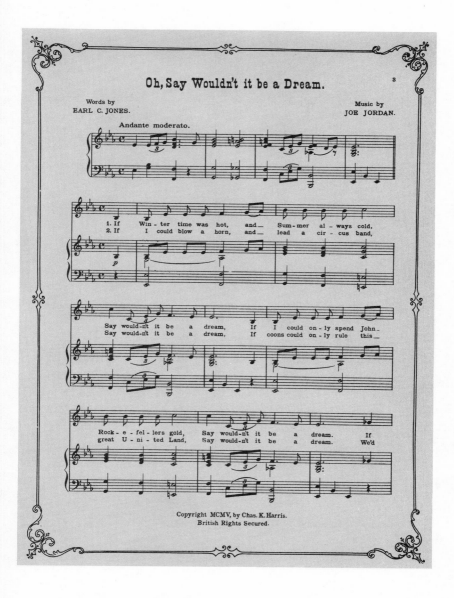

Facsimile 8.1. Earl C. Jones and Joe Jordan, "Oh, Say Wouldn't it be a Dream." Courtesy of Music Division, Library of Congress, Washington, DC.

Oh Say wouldn't &c. 2 3.

say would-n't it be a dream,   If Broad-way was a gard-en full of
say would-n't it be a dream,   The Halls of Con-gress would be full of

wat - er - mel - ons ripe,   And ter - rap - pin was cheap-er far than
coons as dark as sin,   They'd paint the White house black and christ - en

wein - er wurst or tripe;   Oh,   say would-n't it be   a
bat - tle ships with gin;   Oh,   say would-n't it be   a

dream,   Oh,   say would -n't it   be   a   dream.
dream,   Oh,   say would -n't it   be   a   dream.

Oh Say wouldn't &c. ₌ 3.

Facsimile 8.2. Henry S. Creamer, Will H. Vodery, and Ernest Hogan, "When Buffalo Bill And His Wild West Show First Came To Baltimore." Courtesy of Music Division, Library of Congress, Washington, DC.

driv - ers left their teams____ While In - di - ans scared ev - 'ry - - bod - y
when they tried to pass,____ And ev - 'ry one with sense went in, for

with their aw - ful screams.___ The A - rabs flew a - bout And raised an aw - ful
cops were ver - y scarce.___They closed up all sa - loons And ran out all the

shout,___They shot and yelled up at the moon and dared it to come out.
coons,___The cow- boy band then marched a - round and played some aw- ful tunes.___

When

Horses.

CHORUS.

Buf-f'lo Bill and his Wild West show first came to Bal-ti - more_____ The

cow- boys went a - round, And shot up the whole blame town. The

In - di - ans and A - rabs too, my! how they yelled and swore,____ They

did -n't give a ram for the po - lice-man, when they came to Bal- ti - more.____ When more.__

M.W.&SONS 8114-4

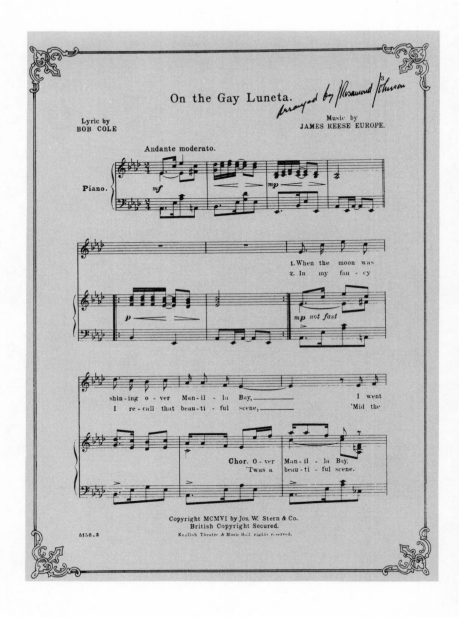

Facsimile 8.3. Bob Cole and James Reese Europe, "On the Gay Luneta." Yale Collection of American Literature, Beinecke Rare Book and Manuscript Library, Yale University.

5156-3

Facsimile 8.4. Paul Laurence Dunbar and J. Rosamond Johnson, "Lit'l Gal."
Courtesy of Music Division, Library of Congress, Washington, DC.

Facsimile 8.5. Bob Cole and J. Rosamond Johnson, "The Bleeding Moon."
Courtesy of E. Azalia Hackley Collection of the Detroit Public Library.

Facsimile 8.6. James Weldon Johnson and J. Rosamond Johnson, "Run Brudder Possum Run." Yale Collection of American Literature, Beinecke Rare Book and Manuscript Library, Yale University.

git, out de way You bet-ter run some-whar an' hide,
git out de way You bet-ter run some-whar an' hide,
git out de way You bet-ter run some-whar an' hide

Slower.

D'ole moon am sink-in' down be-hind de tree,
You sho' is cun-nin', but you git-tin' too fat,
Dey gwine to houn' you all a-long de line,

D'ole coon am think-in' whar you gwinter to flee,
D'ole dog is run-nin', right to whar you'se at,
When dey done foun' you, whas de use in sigh'n

D'ole dog am blink-in' and frisk-y az kin be,
D'ole coon is gun-nin', jes lem-me tell you dat,
Wid tat ers roun' you. sho-ly would tase fine,

Run Brudder, &c 4

Run Brudder, &c 4

Run Brudder, &c 4

Facsimile 8.7. J. T. Brymn, Chris Smith, and James Burris, "Come After Breakfast." Courtesy of Moorland-Spingarn Research Center, Howard University.

Index